BOLDER

BOLDER

Making the Most of
Our Longer Lives

CARL HONORÉ

**SIMON &
SCHUSTER**

London · New York · Sydney · Toronto · New Delhi

A CBS COMPANY

First published in Great Britain by Simon & Schuster UK Ltd, 2018
A CBS COMPANY

1 3 5 7 9 10 8 6 4 2

Simon & Schuster UK Ltd
1st Floor
222 Gray's Inn Road
London WC1X 8HB

www.simonandschuster.co.uk

Simon & Schuster Australia, Sydney
Simon & Schuster India, New Delhi

Some of the names in this book have been changed
to protect people's identity.

A CIP catalogue record for this book
is available from the British Library

Hardback ISBN: 978-1-4711-6435-4
Trade Paperback ISBN: 978-1-4711-6436-1
eBook ISBN: 978-1-4711-6437-8

Typeset in Palatino by M Rules
Printed and bound by CPI Group (UK) Ltd, Croydon, CR0 4YY

To Maurice and Danielle

Age is an issue of mind over matter.
If you don't mind, it doesn't matter.

—Mark Twain

CONTENTS

INTRODUCTION

Birthday Blues

Hope I die before I grow old.
—PETE TOWNSHEND,
'My Generation'

I have been chasing a ball with a stick for decades. Hockey is so much more than my favourite sport: it's a punishing workout, a chance to hang out with friends and a link to my Canadian roots. It is also a way to dodge the fact that I am growing older. As long as I play hockey, I can put off thinking about my age and what it means. What is there to worry about when I still feel like a teenager every time the ball touches my blade?

Then came that tournament in Gateshead, a blue-collar town in the north of England.

With the clock ticking down in the quarter-finals, my team was locked in a stalemate with opponents we had annihilated the year before. I could feel the nerves and indignation coursing through our squad. Then, in the final minute of the game, with a penalty shootout looming, I pulled off one of the hardest tricks in hockey.

To restart play, the referee drops the ball between two rival forwards. This 'face-off' is a test of strength, balance, reflexes, hand–eye co-ordination and speed of thought. The aim is to win control of the ball. Scoring straight from a face-off is rare. In that quarter-final, though, I did just that, snapping the ball into the bottom corner of the net five metres away before anyone moved. My face-off rival swore under his breath. The beaten goalkeeper whacked his stick on the ground in disgust. My team was in the semis – and I was walking on air.

After the post-whistle hugs and high fives, and with the goal still replaying in my mind, I wandered into the dressing room. There, on the other side of a mountain range of damp, smelly hockey gear, a tournament official was scrolling through the team profiles, comparing ages. The youngest player was 16. The oldest? 'Mate, it's you!' he cried, a little too gleefully. 'You're the oldest player in the whole tournament!'

I was 48 years old at the time, with greying hair and crow's feet to match. But the news still knocked the wind out of me. Scoring a highlight-reel goal to win the quarter-finals was instantly eclipsed by the damning arithmetic: there were 240 players at the tournament and all of them were younger than me. In the blink of an eye, I had gone from Goalscorer to Grandad.

As I left the dressing room and began sizing up the other players at the tournament, the questions crowded in: Do I look out of place here? Are people laughing at me? Am I the hockey equivalent of the fifty-something guy with the twenty-something girlfriend? Should I take up a more gentle pastime? Bingo, perhaps?

It comes to all of us in the end: that icy, crushing moment when you suddenly feel Old. Your birthdate, once just numbers in a passport, turns into a taunt, a memento mori, whispering proof that you're over the hill and on a one-way track to elasticated waistbands and the rocking chair. Life as you know it, as you want it to be, is over. You start worrying about what is age-appropriate. Is this outfit too young for me? This haircut, this job, this lover, this band, this sport? The trigger might be a milestone birthday, an illness or an injury, a romantic snub or a missed promotion at work. It might be the death of a loved one. For me it was being the oldest player at a hockey tournament.

Look a little closer, though, and you find a silver lining: more of us than ever before are now living long enough to be goalscoring grandads. That is because the 20th century unleashed a longevity revolution. Better nutrition, health, technology, sanitation and medical care, along with less smoking and rising incomes, are helping us live much longer. Global life expectancy at birth has more than doubled from 32 years in 1900 to 71.4 years today, with the figure now topping 80 years in the rich world. In 1963, Japan began giving a silver sake dish known as a *sakazuki* to every one of its citizens who turned 100. The tradition ended in 2015 because Japanese centenarians are now too numerous.

This is not to say that no one lived to a ripe old age in the past. Average life expectancy was so low through most of history because child mortality was so high. If you survived into adulthood in the pre-industrial era you could end up living a long time. Records suggest that up to 8 per cent of the citizens of the Roman Empire were aged over 60, and that more than 10 per cent of the population of England, France and Spain were that age in the 17th and 18th centuries. Isaac Newton died at 84. From time to time the odd superager even made headlines. England fell under the spell of a farm labourer named Thomas Parr who claimed to be 152 years old when he died in 1635. Despite claims he had confused his birthdate with that of his grandfather, the English public lapped up stories of his spartan diet ('subrancid cheese and milk in every form, coarse and hard bread and small drink, generally sour whey') and colourful love life, which included doing penance for adultery and siring a child out of wedlock as a centenarian. Such was his fame that 'Old Parr' was painted by Van Dyck and Rubens and buried in Westminster Abbey.

Though no one has come close to living as long as Parr claimed to have done, the longevity revolution is, by any yardstick, a huge leap forward, a soaring monument to human ingenuity, a cause for celebration – and yet often it doesn't feel that way. Why not? Mainly because our attitude to ageing has failed to keep pace with the demographic bounty spreading out before us. Rather than crack open the champagne to toast all those extra years of life, we more often double down on the idea that growing older is a Bad Thing. Instead of savouring our hockey heroics, we freak out about our receding hairlines.

Consider how public discourse routinely presents the surge

in longevity as a buzzkill trend to place alongside climate change and economic inequality. Media reports that the global centenarian population now tops 450,000 or that the over-65s will soon outnumber the under-fives are usually seasoned with phrases such as 'silver tsunami' and 'ticking time bomb'. The prophets of doom warn that all this long living will bring economic sclerosis, labour shortages, fiscal meltdown, plummeting stock markets, the collapse of social services, intergenerational warfare, the end of innovation. If we don't start loosening the rules on euthanasia, they warn, we will be swamped by incontinent oldsters who never shut up about how much better life was in the past.

Our own personal ageing inspires similar dread. When was the last time you met someone looking forward to hitting 40 or 50, let alone 60 or 70? True, surviving past 80 or 90 can become a point of pride, but before then the very idea of growing older usually evokes fear, angst, scorn, even revulsion. We cleave to the view that ageing is a curse, that after a certain point each birthday makes us less attractive, less productive, less happy, less energetic, less creative, less healthy, less open-minded, less loveable, less strong, less visible, less useful – less ourselves.

Everywhere, the message is the same: younger is better. Traffic signs depict older people hunched over walking sticks and the cosmetics industry markets 'anti-ageing' products as if ageing were a disease. These days it's hard to find an adult birthday card that doesn't mix good wishes with pity and persiflage. One shows a woman recoiling in B-movie horror beneath the words, 'Good God, you're 30!!'

The notion that Being Older Sucks is woven into our vernacular. Forgetting something is a 'senior moment' and 'feeling your age' means feeling sore, feeble, inferior. We undermine compliments by tacking on the words 'for your age' and call 60 the new 40 or 50 the new 30, as if reaching the age of 50 or 60 were somehow a thing to avoid rather than aspire to. Or consider how, when discussing people in later life, we routinely fall into the 'still' syndrome: we say he's *still* working, they're *still* having sex, she's *still* sharp as a tack – as if engaging with the world after a certain age were a minor miracle. The word 'old' is so toxic that actor Dame Judi Dench has banned its use in her home. 'Vintage' and 'retire' are also on her prohibited list. 'I don't want any of those old words,' she explained, shortly after her 80th birthday.

Even pro-ageing groups struggle to find the right language for the cause. Jonathan Collie, co-founder of the London-based Age of No Retirement, faces the same hurdle every time he pens a press release or gives an interview. 'The problem,' he says, 'is that the two words you need to use are "age" and "old", but as soon as you use them it switches everyone off.' Laura Carstensen, founding director of the Stanford Center on Longevity, runs into the same problem stateside. 'Over the past 40 years or so, I've tried to persuade people to use the word "old" proudly, but I have so far failed to get a single person to do so,' she says. 'In fact, even I avoid "old" for fear that the term might offend.'

Recoiling from ageing is not new. In ancient times, Greek and Roman poets and playwrights ruthlessly mocked their elders. Aristophanes portrayed them as frail, pathetic and prone to embarrassing erotic desires and Plautus pioneered the dirty-old-man trope. Aged cuckolds populate the works of medieval writers ranging from Boccaccio to Chaucer. More than two centuries ago, Samuel Johnson, creator of the first English dictionary, detected an all-too-familiar bias against ageing brains. 'There is a wicked inclination in most people to suppose an old man decayed in his intellects,' he wrote in 1783. 'If a young or middle-aged man, when leaving a company, does not remember where he laid his hat, it is nothing; but if the same inattention is discovered in an old man, people will shrug their shoulders and say, "His memory is going."'

Has anything changed since then? Yes, but not for the better. Our aversion to growing – or even just looking – older is more acute than ever. We now drop US$250 billion on anti-ageing products and services every year. Twenty-somethings are turning to Botox and hair implants before job interviews and even teenagers use cosmetic procedures to 'freshen up' their appearance.

Sometimes it feels like open season on anyone past a certain age. When academics at the Yale School of Public Health searched Facebook for groups set up to discuss older people, they found 84 of them with a combined following of 25,489 users. Every group but one traded in unflattering stereotypes. In their site Descriptions, more than a third advocated banning older people from driving, shopping and other public activities. One user proposed a final solution for seniors: 'Everyone over the age of 69 should immediately face a firing squad.'

Though few go as far as backing execution or euthanasia, elder-bashing is now the last form of discrimination that dare speak its name. After the Brexit referendum in 2016, when older citizens voted overwhelmingly for the United Kingdom to leave the European Union, some commentators suggested stripping the over-65s of the vote. In a similar vein, Mark Zuckerberg, the founder of Facebook, once told an audience at Stanford University that 'young people are just smarter'. After winning plaudits for displaying her post-cancer baldness on the red carpet at the Grammy Awards, singer Melissa Etheridge lamented the social pressure to colour her hair: 'I can be bald in front of the world but I can't be grey.'

Even academics who study ageing feel the pressure. Take Debora Price, professor of social gerontology at the University of Manchester. When we meet at a café beside the River Thames in London, she talks fluently and cogently about every aspect of ageing until one subject knocks her off kilter: hair. Price is in her early 50s and brunette thanks to regular visits to the colourist. 'I would say vehemently that I never indulge in any anti-ageing anything and yet I colour my hair and the only reason I do it, absolutely without question, is to look younger,' she says, squirming slightly. 'It's all part of the anti-ageing culture that is ubiquitous – even among gerontologists.'

I am part of the same culture. In my 20s, my default setting when contemplating anyone over 35 was a brew of disdain and horror. I remember smiling wryly when Martin Amis observed in *London Fields* that '. . . time goes about its immemorial work of making everyone look and feel like shit'. I lapped up, with hungry schadenfreude, John Updike's portrait of Rabbit sliding into the despond of middle age, with his 'thick waist and cautious stoop ... clues to weakness, a weakness verging on anonymity'. I've sung the Who's 'My Generation' and taken cruel pleasure in belting out the line, 'Hope I die before I get old.' Now that I'm knocking 50, I'm in full denial mode, deploying every trick in the book to conceal from the world – and myself – my own ageing. Year of birth withheld on Facebook? Check. Living in soft focus to avoid wearing reading glasses? Check. Keeping my hair short to mask the grey? Check. How long before I, like Nora Ephron, start feeling bad about my neck?

Sometimes my age cringe tips into the absurd. The other day I was unable to read the small print on a light bulb in a hardware store. After much squinting, I decided to ask for help. Around me were several twenty-somethings who could have read the text in a flash, but somehow I couldn't bring myself to ask them: I felt too ashamed. So instead I marched around the store until I found an older woman with glasses perched on her nose.

Such dodges seem harmless, if a little pathetic. Maybe you've done something similar. But the truth is they're not harmless at all. Small decisions like the one I made in that hardware store, like the one Price makes every time she books a session with the colourist, add up to a big problem: they are the tiny acts of betrayal and denial, the unscripted micro-aggressions, the sighs of surrender that endorse the cultural diktat that ageing is a shameful game of loss and decline.

Of course, there really are downsides to growing older. To hear time's winged chariot hurrying near can be an existential bummer of the first order. No matter how much kale you eat or how many hours of Pilates you do, your body will gradually work less well over time and your brain will lose some zip. You are also more likely to see people you love fall ill or die. Yet the biggest downside of all may be dealing with our toxic view of ageing itself. Not only does this condemn us to spend much of our lives feeling rotten about how old we are, it also narrows horizons. Just imagine all the roads untravelled, the potential untapped, all the life unlived, thanks to that little voice inside our heads whispering: 'You're too old for this.' A grim view of later life can even act as a self-fulfilling prophecy. Studies show that exposure to downbeat ideas about ageing causes older people to perform worse in memory, hearing and balance tests and to walk more slowly.

I wonder if something similar happened to me at that hockey tournament. After my status as the resident grandad was revealed, my performance dipped. Did I begin playing as I imagined an old person would? Did I start trying too hard? We'll never know. But after my team lost in the semi-finals I left the tournament with something much more valuable than a hockey trophy. I came away with a mission: To learn both how to age better *and* how to feel better about ageing.

That may not be as quixotic as it sounds. Why? Because as soon as you look past the stereotypes you realise that life after 30 is not a miserable descent into decrepitude. Far from it. Just think of your own social circle. Does everyone you know go into a terminal tailspin the day they no longer qualify for a Contiki holiday? The hell they do. If you're like me, you know loads of people thriving in their 40s, 50s, 60s and beyond. My own parents, aged 77 and 83, are having the time of their lives – travelling, cooking, exercising, socialising, studying, working when it takes their fancy.

The idea that older people are a burden with nothing to contribute is clearly absurd. History is full of folk smashing it in later life. Three centuries after Michelangelo finished painting the frescoes in the Pauline chapel at the age of 74, Giuseppe Verdi premiered his finest comic opera, *Falstaff*, at 79. Architect Frank Lloyd Wright was 91 when he finished the Guggenheim Museum in New York. Georgia O'Keeffe made notable art into her 90s and Stanley Kunitz became Poet Laureate of the United States at the age of 95. Philosophers such as Kant, Gorgias and Cato produced their finest work in old age. So, who's smarter now, Zuckerberg?

Today, the public sphere is jammed with people doing extraordinary things on the 'wrong' side of 50. Clint Eastwood won his first Academy Award for Best Director at the age of 62 and his second at 74. Mary Robinson is fighting for climate justice in her 70s. Jane Goodall travels the world in her 80s to deliver sold-out lectures on her work with chimpanzees in Tanzania. Warren Buffett is on track to celebrate his ninetieth birthday as one of the most successful investors in the world. In their 90s, Sir David Attenborough makes award-winning nature documentaries while Queen Elizabeth II attends more than 400 events a year.

We are now pushing the limits of what all of us can

achieve long after the first flush of youth. These days amateurs aged 40–49 are running the London Marathon faster than those in their 20s. After undergoing fertility treatment, an Indian woman gave birth in 2016 to a healthy baby boy at the age of 72. A year later, a D-Day veteran became the oldest person ever to skydive when he leapt 15,000 feet from a plane – at 101. At the same time, IQ levels have been rising steadily across all age groups, including the over-90s. 'The good-news story is that it's never been a better time to be an older adult,' says Esme Fuller-Thomson, director of the Institute for Life Course and Ageing at the University of Toronto. Even language itself is evolving to reflect this upbeat spirit. In the 14th century, Dante said that old age began at 46. In 2017, Japan's Geriatric Society and its Gerontological Society proposed moving the age when someone is deemed *rojin*, or old, from 65 to 75.

The push to embrace ageing as a privilege rather than a punishment is starting to feel like a movement. Everywhere, people are banding together into groups, such as Age Demands Action, which spans 60 countries, to help us make the most of our longer lives. Governments are joining the battle, too. To break down the barriers and prejudices between young and old, France's Ministry of Education encourages teachers to mount intergenerational projects throughout the school year. To foster lifelong learning, Singapore now gives money to every citizen over the age of 25 to put towards training or a university course. The World Health Organization has pledged to make 2020–2030 the first ever Decade of Healthy Ageing.

Individual crusaders are picking up the torch, too. Now in her 80s, actor Jane Fonda campaigns for making the most of what she calls the 'third act' of life. Since publishing *This Chair Rocks: A Manifesto Against Ageism* in 2016, Ashton Applewhite, a sparky American writer and activist, has spoken everywhere from TED to the United Nations. She first showed up on my radar at a time when the idea of writing about the longevity revolution filled me with doubt. I feared that a book about ageing would be bleak, boring, unsexy. That there wouldn't be enough good news about growing older to outweigh the bad. That taking on the cult of youth was a fool's errand. Seeking a shot in the arm, I arranged to drop by Applewhite's apartment in Brooklyn, New York.

On a crisp, winter morning, I find her out front taking photographs of the political graffiti on some hoardings across the street. Tomorrow she plans to join a march for women's rights. With her short, curly hair, rapid-fire delivery and take-no-prisoners humour, she reminds me of my first boss. I like her immediately. At the kitchen table inside her apartment, which is crammed with books and files, we settle down with green smoothies (this is Brooklyn, after all). One by one, she starts shooting down my doubts. 'The more you think about ageing, the more fascinating it gets,' she tells me. 'Ageing is like falling in love or motherhood: it's a difficult, complex and beautiful thing. It's how we move through life, how we interact with society and each other, and what could be more interesting than that?'

Okay, I'll buy that. But how about overcoming the aversion to ageing that seems to have been there since ancient times? What would that feel like and is it even possible? Applewhite nods her head. 'The truth is that once you get rid of the oppressive, acculturated dread attached to ageing then everything about growing older looks a whole lot better,' she says. 'It won't be easy, though.'

Not easy is not the same as impossible. One big reason for optimism is that more and more people across the world are ageing better and more boldly than ever before. They are sailing round the globe in their 40s; going back to school in their 50s; starting companies or families in their 60s; running marathons in their 70s; modelling or joining political campaigns in their 80s; falling in love in their 90s; making art as centenarians. By doing so, they are raising expectations of what we can do with our longer lives as well as demolishing the shibboleth that an ageing population must be a burden.

They are also living proof that chronological age is losing its power to define and constrain us. These days, what matters more and more is not when you were born so much as how you think, talk, look, move, exercise, dance, dress, travel and play. What will define you in the future, much more than your age, is the choices you make: the books you read, the television you watch, the music you listen to, the food you eat, the people you love, the politics you espouse and the work you do. This shift dovetails with the wider cultural move towards diversity and personal freedom. We now express sexual orientation and gender identity in ways that would have been unthinkable not so long ago. Age can be the next frontier. Based at the University of Oxford, the Future of Humanity Institute brings together leading thinkers in mathematics, philosophy and science to debate the big questions facing mankind. Its director, Nick Bostrom, thinks chronological age has had its day: 'The important thing is not how many years have passed since you were born, but where you are in your life, how you think about yourself and what you are able and willing to do.'

~

A few days after meeting Applewhite, I visit the Cho Heng Rice Vermicelli Factory in Thailand. This sprawling, 30-acre complex on the outskirts of Bangkok churns out more than $100 million worth of rice flour and noodles every year. Yet what really puts it on the map is that staff carry on working here till either death or disability steps in. The oldest employee is a maintenance manager who struts around the grounds with raffishly dyed hair and the latest iPhone strapped to his belt. He is 86 years old. Laid down by the factory's founder nearly a century ago, the policy of retaining older workers is so successful that government officials, mindful that the Thai population is ageing fast, hold up Cho Heng as a model for other companies. Towards the end of my visit, I sit down with Darunee Kramwong, a 73-year-old cleaner who has been on the payroll for four decades. She perches on the edge of a sofa in the conference room, serene and solicitous, like a schoolgirl waiting to be interviewed in the headmaster's office. With her fine features and beatific smile, she has the sort of charisma that makes *National Geographic* photographers go weak at the knees. Her voice, soft, strong and flecked with irony, makes me swoon a little.

After starting on the production line, Kramwong joined the team that cleans the factory's high-tech laboratories and still puts in six eight-hour shifts per week. Her children want her to retire but she likes working at Cho Heng too much to pay them heed. 'I'm good at my job because I know the labs really well, what to clean and what not to clean,' she says, sitting up a little taller on the sofa. 'My family want me to stay at home but I want to keep working every day because I prefer doing things, being active, seeing friends, earning money, helping people. I just love coming to the factory.'

When I ask if she feels in any way troubled or held back by her age, Kramwong looks at me with the same mixture of surprise and pity she might direct at a misshapen noodle on the assembly line. On the contrary, she says, her 73 years are a badge of honour. She feels like one of the gang at Cho Heng, and is proud that younger colleagues seek her advice on both cleaning and romance. 'They are like brothers and sisters to me,' she says. 'Sometimes they tease me and call me "Gran" but I don't mind because I am old enough to be their gran!' She laughs, and her laughter is so warm, so pure, that everyone in the room instinctively joins in. I catch myself thinking: *If this is what 73 feels like, then bring it on.*

～

Ageing is the most natural thing in the world: twelve months from now every one of us will be one year older. Barring a scientific breakthrough of Promethean proportions, that will not change. What can change is *how* we age and how we *feel* about it.

16

My aim, with this book, is to harness the Kramwong Effect. To understand and embrace ageing. To show how the longevity revolution can be a blessing rather than a burden. To work out what all of us, alone and together, can do to make growing older better for everybody.

To do so, we'll travel the world to learn from people who are putting the cult of youth in its place by living every stage of life on their own terms. We'll hit the dance floor with an eighty-something DJ in Poland, hang out with middle-aged graffiti artists in Spain and attend the first Miss Senior Universe pageant in Las Vegas. We'll meet an eighty-something gamer and brave the traffic of Bangkok with a mature bus driver. We'll visit students living in a nursing home in the Netherlands, a 70-year-old teaching tailoring tricks to young fashionistas in New York and the octogenarian behind a recycling revolution in Beirut. We'll even try on something called an 'ageing suit' to see what it feels like to have an older body.

This book is also a personal journey. By the end of it, I want to stop fretting about my age. I want to feel okay with looking in the mirror, with asking for help when I can't read the small print in a store, with playing hockey against people young enough to be my children. I want more of what Kramwong has.

In a nutshell, my goal is to stop dreading – and maybe even start looking forward to – growing older. Too much to ask? Let's find out.

CHAPTER 1

HOW AGEING GOT OLD

I grow old ... I grow old ...
I shall wear the bottoms of my
trousers rolled.

—T. S. ELIOT,
'The Love Song of
J. Alfred Prufrock'

Shoreditch is the sort of place Mark Zuckerberg had in mind when he sang the praises of younger brains, a place that can make anyone north of 35 feel a little superannuated. In recent years, this corner of east London has blossomed into a miniature Silicon Valley. The narrow streets are thronged with tech companies and startups along with the usual camp followers: cocktail bars, sushi joints, cafés serving cold-brew coffee. Young people from all over the world glide past on scooters and fixies. In between hackathons and beta tests, they blow off steam and plot world domination over gluten-free pretzels and craft beer. All eyes are on the same prize: launching, or at least owning stock in, the next unicorn.

I am in Shoreditch tonight to watch that entrepreneurial energy unleashed on the business of ageing. The occasion is a pitch-off that promises to 'accelerate innovation to improve the lives of older adults around the world'. Ten startups will present business plans to an audience of entrepreneurs, investors and policy wonks. Judges will then pick one winner to progress to the European final. Two questions are already burning a hole in my notebook: What do the young turks of Shoreditch understand by the phrase 'older adult'? And how do they propose to improve their lives?

The venue is Campus London, Google's hub for entrepreneurs. When I arrive, a young man in a tight waistcoat is pacing up and down outside like a nervous sentry, barking into a smartphone about a meeting with venture capitalists. 'They totally love the idea of doing something with old people,' he shouts. So far, so Shoreditch.

Inside, the lobby is festooned with gadgets from my youth that are now antiques – an original iMac, a transistor radio, a cathode ray television set, a Super 8 film projector. One wall bears a slogan straight from the startup playbook: 'Bigger. Brighter. Bolder. Braver.' People are already gathered round a table, nibbling nachos and burrata. It's a young crowd. I approach a bearded twenty-something to ask what brings him to an event on ageing. 'I'm a serial entrepreneur so I'm always looking for the next big thing,' he tells me. 'And ageing is hot right now.'

His mercenary tone makes me wince, but then I remember

this is a pitching event. On the upside, the room is packed with clever, can-do folk who are thinking hard about ageing and how to improve our experience of it – what's not to like?

I sit down to listen to the pitches. First up is a gadget that measures your risk of having a fall and fracturing a hip. Then comes an app to reduce social isolation among older adults by simplifying messaging and photo sharing. Next is a fresh-faced, fast-talking entrepreneur who explains that the best way to tackle abuse, depression and malnutrition among older people is to digitise the supply of home carers. After that we are shown an 'omnidirectional' wheelchair that goes up and down as well as forwards, backwards and sideways. The eventual winning pitch is for an aggregator site selling products to help with dementia.

Every one of these ideas can help make the world a better place, and the zeal of the entrepreneurs is infectious. Even as they hail the potential for profit, most talk of being inspired by the plight of someone close to them. The winner spent years caring for his dementia-ravaged mother. As applause sweeps the room, I find myself joining in the messianic swell.

Yet I also feel slightly deflated. Why? Because every product, every pitch, every business plan starts from the same premise: being 'older' means being lonely, frail, forgetful, immobile, sad or vulnerable – or all of the above. What about the growing legions of happy, healthy people taking later life by the scruff of the neck? Nothing on show here feels relevant to someone like Darunee Kramwong. Or to me, for that matter. Surrounded by the *jeunesse dorée* of Shoreditch, and with my own 50th birthday tiptoeing into view, I qualify as an 'older adult' – yet many years could pass before I need anything unveiled here tonight. Why has no one taken to the stage with a tool to help someone like me build an app? Or to show someone like Kramwong how to pitch a startup in Shoreditch?

After the event, as I join the queue for Ubers outside, it occurs to me that tonight's pitching line-up illustrates where we go wrong with ageing. When asked to imagine what it means to be 'older', we default to the worst-case scenario. Think about it for a moment. What does ageing conjure in your mind? If you're like me, or the well-meaning innovators of Shoreditch, what swims into view is mostly grim: decline, decrepitude, digital ineptness, dementia, death. It's the pitiable, repugnant Dorian Gray portrait festering in the attic. The nursing-home resident dribbling through another game of bingo. Granny struggling to recognise a relation or find her way home. Grandad unable to climb the stairs or wipe his own bottom.

To make the most of our longer lives we have to break out of this worst-case-scenario mode of thinking. And, to do that, we must first understand where our aversion to ageing comes from and how it became so ingrained.

∼

Let's start by naming the problem. In 1969, Robert N. Butler, an American gerontologist, coined the term 'ageism' to describe the 'systematic stereotyping of and discrimination against people because they are old'. Later the definition widened to include the denigration of ageing itself. Though age stereotyping is usually cruel (the old are forgetful, sad, weak, cranky, unattractive, boring), it can sometimes be kind (the old are wise) or even directed at the young (millennials are snowflakes). But the net effect is always the same: to stuff everyone with the same birth year into the same box and make all of us feel bad about growing older.

Ageism has a USP that sets it apart from other forms of discrimination such as racism or sexism: it comes with a hefty side order of self-loathing. A white supremacist will never be black. A male chauvinist pig is unlikely to morph into a woman. But all of us are growing older. To indulge in ageism is therefore to denigrate and deny your future self. As Bernardino of Siena, a Franciscan missionary, put it back in the early 14th century: 'Everyone wishes to reach old age, but nobody wishes to be old.'

So, what are the roots of ageism? The obvious place to start is with the D-word. Benjamin Franklin said death and taxes are the only certainties in life, and not even the cleverest accountant can help you evade both. Every day, around 150,000 souls shuffle off this mortal coil. And just as certain as death is our desire to avoid it. Evolution has endowed us with an all-trumping, never-surrender instinct for survival. Think of Ernest Shackleton crossing the freezing, storm-tossed seas of Antarctica in a lifeboat. Or the survivors of that Andean plane crash feeding on the corpses of fellow passengers to stay alive.

Even those who believe in an afterlife are seldom in a rush to reach it, which is why the yearning for immortality stretches across time and cultures. The *Epic of Gilgamesh*, one of the oldest surviving works in literature, features a

Sumerian king seeking to live forever. Later, pretty much every alchemist in medieval Europe was locked in a race to crack the recipe for eternal life and several emperors in China's Tang dynasty perished after downing elixirs of youth laced with mercury or lead.

If anything, the appetite for cheating death has sharpened in the modern world. Immortality of the virtual kind is already upon us now that companies such as Forever Identity and Eternime are turning clients into digital avatars and holograms that will live on after they breathe their last breath. In the offline world, billions of dollars are flowing into the race to stop ageing in its tracks. One of the many theories now being explored is that we can rejuvenate the old with blood transfusions from the young. The movement to 'cure' death even has its own poster boy, a biomedical gerontologist named Aubrey de Grey, who, armed with an Old Testament beard and a PowerPoint presentation, travels the world telling audiences that the first human being to live to a thousand may already be alive.

Yet putting an end to death is still more sci-fi than sci-fact. Despite our lengthening lives, we remain programmed, at our cellular core, to die. Researchers at the University of Arizona have used mathematical models to show that stopping the ageing process altogether in complex, multicellular organisms such as human beings is a pipe dream. 'Ageing is mathematically inevitable – like, seriously inevitable,' says Joanna Masel, a professor of ecology and evolutionary biology and senior author in the study. 'There's logically, theoretically, mathematically no way out.'

The fact that death, the destroyer of worlds, awaits us all turns ageing into the enemy. How can it not? Every year, every month, every week, every day, every minute moves us closer to the end that nobody wants to reach. Even the tiniest sign of ageing – a wrinkle, a grey hair, a creaky joint – is another reminder that the Grim Reaper is coming for us, that the time we have left to do all the things we want to do is running out.

The fear of death is probably more acute today. Not only has secularisation taken away the solace of the afterlife, but we have messed up the whole business of dying. In much of the world, death has been medicalised and institutional-ised. When we approach the end, the default setting is to do everything possible – whatever the cost in money, pain, dis-tress and loss of dignity – to keep us alive. 'We imagine that we can wait until the doctors tell us there is nothing more they can do. But rarely is there nothing more doctors can do,' writes surgeon Atul Gawande in his book, *Being Mortal*. 'They can give toxic drugs of unknown efficacy, operate to try to remove part of the tumour, put in a feeding tube if a person can't eat: there's always something.' This can turn our final days, weeks or even months into a hell worthy of Hieronymus Bosch, leaving us to die hooked up to machines and surrounded by medical staff. We have all seen this sce-nario played out in TV dramas or in our own lives – and it sends a chill down the spine. The take-home: 'If ageing leads to this, count me out.'

Even without the shadow of death, ageing gives itself a poor press by changing us in unwelcome ways. It starts gently, with diminished stamina, strength and libido, weaker eyesight and hearing and a dip in short-term memory. In our dotage, things can turn really ugly. Shakespeare, as usual, put it best. In the 'seven ages of man' speech in *As You Like It*, he describes the final chapter before death as a 'second childishness and mere oblivion, sans teeth, sans eyes, sans taste, sans everything'. No wonder ageing is excised from every paradise or utopia ever imagined.

Of course, not everyone experiences Shakespearean levels of suffering at the end of life. Teeth are better nowadays, and many of us remain in fine fettle until the day we keel over. Others merely endure a brief period 'sans everything'. The trouble is that none of us knows for sure how our own final act will unfold – and the temptation is to imagine the worst, especially now that modern medicine has devised a million ways to keep us alive long after we might prefer to be six feet under. 'There may be more angst about growing older now because it's pretty certain it's going to happen: you have to be unlucky not to live into your 70s and beyond,' says Pat Thane, an expert in the history of ageing at King's College London. 'The problem is you don't know what state you'll be in when you get there.'

That uncertainty is compounded by our reluctance to think hard about our future selves. I can remember pretty clearly what I was like at 40, 30 or 20, and any gaps in my memory can be filled by looking at videos and photographs, rereading my own writing from the time or consulting people who knew me back then. I feel a strong kinship with the younger me. By contrast, my future self is a blank slate.

My life could veer off in a million different directions, so building a portrait of myself at 60 or 70, never mind 80 or 90, feels like the cognitive equivalent of trying to understand *Infinite Jest*. The task is made that much harder by human hardwiring. Our hunter-gatherer ancestors had no reason to ponder or plan for the future because they lived in the moment, focusing on whatever had to be done to survive another day. 'We have been oriented from an evolutionary perspective to pay attention to right now and the present has a powerful pull on us,' says Hal Hershfield, a psychologist at UCLA's Anderson School of Management. 'We are just not designed to think about the long-term future and that creates a fundamental emotional disconnect with our older selves.'

That disconnection fuels ageism in two ways. First, it allows our darkest prejudices about ageing to flourish unchallenged. Second, it makes it easier to stuff older people into a box marked 'Other'.

But if we struggle to imagine our futures, let alone see much good in them, perhaps there's hope for our ageing selves to be found in the past.

~

Conventional wisdom tells us the past was a golden time for ageing, that growing older was less of a burden to our ancestors because the old were held in high esteem. Was that ever true? And, if so, what does it tell us about the drivers of ageism today?

Certainly there could be upsides to ageing in the past. Elders earned kudos by performing key roles in traditional societies: gathering food; teaching the young to make weapons, tools, baskets and clothes; caring for grandchildren; serving as political and spiritual leaders and advisers. Their knowledge of history, song and medicine made them the Google of the pre-literate era. As one African proverb goes, 'When an old man dies, a library burns down.'

Many of the great civilisations enshrined deference to age in law. The old sit at the top of the Confucian hierarchy and children could be punished for mistreating their elderly parents in Ancient Greece. In both the Mayan and Inca empires, the young were expected to pay absolute obedience to their elders. Just as older men always spoke first in the public councils of Athens, Sparta and Rome, Puritan meeting houses in colonial America reserved the most honoured places for the oldest members of the congregation. Even the architects of the French Revolution, so disdainful of tradition, tried to make respect for age a patriotic duty. They created a new national holiday, the Fête de la Vieillesse, when towns paid homage to their older citizens by decorating their homes, parading them through the streets and singing secular hymns proclaiming their virtue. One sung in Toulouse in 1797 went thus:

> *But learn that to this honourable age*
> *The sage arrives only through peace*
> *That alone provides a durable health*
> *The wicked never grow old.*

Indeed, some saw reaching a very old age as proof of strength, discipline and virtue. Exaggerating your age upwards, as

Old Parr likely did, was therefore not uncommon. In 1647, Thomas Fuller, an English clergymen and scholar, warned that 'many old men ... set the clock of their age too fast when once past seventy, and growing 10 years in a twelvemonth, are presently fourscore; yea, within a year or two after, climb up to a hundred.'

As well as kudos, age could also confer real clout. You had to be at least 50 to act as a jury member in Ancient Greece. Cicero, a Roman politician in the first century BC, rhapsodised about 'the crowning glory of old age ... its power, authority and influence'. During the Renaissance, Venice elected its savviest male elder to the powerful office of doge. Through much of history, and across cultures, fathers wielded power over their offspring by controlling the family land until death. In 17th- and 18th-century Europe, young men tried to grab a piece of that kudos and clout by dressing up to look older. They wore powdered wigs and clothes tailored to give the impression of narrow, rounded shoulders, thicker waists and hips, and even a slightly stooped spine.

Another advantage in the past: you were far less likely to be written off because of your chronological age. Records were so scant, and numeracy so rare, that most of our ancestors never had more than a sketchy idea of how old they were. It was not until 1900 that the US government added a section for date of birth to its census forms. Angsty references to turning 30, 40 and 50 are rare in the historical records because the numbers themselves held less intrinsic meaning or power. The idea of coming down with a case of the 'birthday blues' would have seemed risible to a peasant in medieval Europe or a bureaucrat in the Qin dynasty because being a certain age on paper did not expose you to a torrent of prejudices. Instead, what defined you was milestones – work, marriage, parenthood, bereavement, inheritance – that could happen at almost any age.

Compare that to today, when not knowing how old you are is taken as a sign of cognitive impairment and chronological age determines so much about your life: what ads appear in your social media; how much you pay for insurance; when you can buy cigarettes and alcohol, have sex, study, vote, join the army, earn the minimum wage, retire, draw a pension, enter a retirement community. Nowadays, when asked our age, many of us squirm a little before answering because inside our heads we're calculating what assumptions others will make, what biases will kick in, once the number is said aloud. Will they think I'm too young or too old? That I lack experience or energy? That I'm ageing well or badly? No wonder the first answer that comes up when you type the phrase 'I lie about my ... ' into Google Search is 'age'. Or that Tinder can charge extra to conceal how old you are. Or that California passed legislation giving film industry employees the right to have their birthdate expunged from their profiles in online movie databases. 'Without such clear age barriers, people in the past were judged much more on how they looked and appeared and behaved,' says Thane. 'We are more age-conscious and that probably makes ageing harder.'

Even so, historians roll their eyes when asked if the past was a golden era for growing older. It was not. For a start, the absence of modern medicine made disease, decrepitude and death harder to bear. Nor did ageing always guarantee kudos and clout. When their elders became a burden, traditional societies often killed them off with baroque cruelty. The Hopi abandoned them in special huts; the Samoans and Paraguay's Aché Indians buried them alive; the Bactrian people of Central Asia fed them to dogs; the Turco-Mongols favoured suffocation; the ancient Sardinians tossed their elders off cliffs; the Ojibwa of Lake Winnipeg and the Massagetae and Padaei peoples of Asia went in for ritual sacrifice. In northern Siberia, a man too old to hunt was expected to commit suicide by walking off into the snow.

What's more, any benefits that did accrue through ageing in the past were unevenly distributed, with elite men the chief beneficiaries. Ageing was seldom a blessing for women or the poor. Alongside history's public shows of respect ran a current of scorn and rejection of older people. Artists, playwrights and philosophers often portrayed them as frail, pompous, ugly, greedy, small-minded, malicious and inappropriately libidinous. Even as they enjoyed the best church pews, elders in colonial America were the target of ageist scorn. Increase Mather, a Puritan minister, lamented that 'to treat Aged Persons with disrespectful and disdainful language only because of their age is a very criminal offence in the sight of God, yet how common it is to call this or the other person Old Such An One, in a way of contempt on the account of their age'. Early Christians feared that God himself had an ageist streak. Psalm 71 contains a poignant plea: 'Do not cast me away when I am old; do not forsake me when my strength is gone.' Thane echoes the consensus among historians when she says:

'It's just nonsense that in the past people were respected for being old.'

~

The forging of the modern world has made ageing even less appealing. Before the 16th century, people did not believe in progress. The prevailing view across most cultures was that the world was either stagnant or in decline. If there was a better future to look forward to it was in the afterlife. All that changed, however, when the Scientific Revolution gave us the power to reshape the world, turning the idea of progress into an article of faith and a cultural lodestar. Once the belief took hold that the human condition could be improved, ageing – not to mention death – started to look like the ultimate party-pooper: it meant missing out on the better future promised right here on Earth.

The move from agrarian to industrial societies also took some of the shine off later life. Fathers lost clout as new jobs emerged that allowed their children to prosper on their own terms. The spread of literacy put knowledge once curated by older folk into everyone's hands. Fast-changing technology made new expertise more coveted than experience and hand-me-down skills. Language itself reflected age's falling stock. Many words used to describe older men in a neutral or flattering way – from fogey and greybeard to superannuated and codger – assumed a pejorative meaning in the late 18th and early 19th century. Once a badge of honour for the soldiers in Napoleon's army, the phrase 'old guard' came to mean reactionary and corrupt.

As average life expectancy began rising so too did unease about the greying population. To deal with the swelling ranks of those who were, in the words of one US union leader, 'too old to work, too young to die', modern states began setting up national pension schemes towards the end of the 19th century, which proved a mixed blessing. The upside was that millions were saved from poverty in their later years. The downside was that it locked us into a life cycle with three stages – education, paid work, pensioned leisure – that embedded the notion that somewhere in our 60s we instantly morph from makers into takers. In a culture that measures personal worth by how much you add to GDP, that final stage, even when rebranded as the 'golden years', came to look a lot like freeloading. By 1967, the Beatles were wondering: 'Will you still need me, will you still feed me, when I'm sixty-four?'

The '60s youthquake further eroded the appeal of ageing. Mankind has always admired the vigour, fertility and beauty of the young – Greco-Roman mythology is a paean to fertile bodies – but being young was seldom a goal in itself. That changed when youth culture, riding the post-war baby boom, conquered the world with its clothes, music, art, lingo and attitude. Suddenly, for the first time in history, youth was cool, coveted, aspirational, which put a big, fat target on the forehead of anyone looking a little long in the tooth. Throughout *A Hard Day's Night*, the Beatles movie released in 1964, the mop-topped quartet poke merciless fun at an aged character. 'Poor thing,' they trill. 'He can't help being old.' Five years later, Butler coined the term 'ageism'.

The fierce individualism of our times gives ageism an extra fillip. A hard truth is that growing older often means depending more on others. That might be something trivial like relying on a younger pair of eyes to read the small print in a hardware store. Or it could mean needing help to bathe, use the toilet or pay the bills. Either way, dependence plays poorly in a culture that prizes productive self-reliance.

Modern consumerism does further harm. It reinforces the mantra that younger is better by fetishising the new over the old. It also casts ageing as a problem that can be fixed if only you invest enough time, money and energy. The message coming from all sides is cruel and clear: growing older is for losers who don't try hard enough.

～

For a case study in how modernisation fuels ageism, look no further than East Asia. Many countries in the region, notably Japan, Korea, Vietnam, Singapore and China, have a long tradition of filial piety and respect for elders that is rooted in Confucianism. The theory is that reciprocity – you take care of me when I'm young and I'll take care of you when you're old – reduces anxiety about ageing. In the 1930s, Lin Yutang, the influential Chinese essayist, argued that people in the East looked forward to growing old while Westerners feared it. Even today, in many Asian countries older people still enjoy an elevated status – at least on paper. The Japanese use the honorific suffix '–san' to signal veneration of the old, and celebrate a national holiday called Respect for the Aged Day, complete with gift-giving, toasts and feasts. Japan's media routinely features older folk performing impressive physical feats or passing on their skills in everything from kabuki to shoe making. Koreans make a huge fuss over a person's 60th birthday. In the Chinese world, children have for centuries learned respect for their elders by reading classic folktales known as *The 24 Exemplary Stories of Filial Piety*. In one, a child strides into a swarm of mosquitos to save his mother and father. Another features a boy strangling a tiger to rescue his dad.

How deep the reverence for age ever went in East Asia is open to debate, but it has clearly waned. Pundits across the region now echo their Western peers by casting the greying population as a problem. The local pop culture, with its Manga-like starlets and fresh-faced boy bands, its Uniqlo, Pokémon and Gangnam Style, has become ferociously youth-centric, helping to fuel a boom in cosmetic surgery. East Asian headhunters report that older jobseekers are quietly removing birthdates from their CVs. During a diplomatic spat in 2017, the foreign ministry of North Korea played the ageist card by branding US President Donald Trump a *'neukdari'*, a common derogatory term for an old person. Even politicians eager to carry on serving are now under pressure to step down for being too aged. When Yasuhiro Nakasone, a former prime minister of Japan, was obliged to fall on his sword in 2003 at the age of 85, he penned a passive-aggressive haiku to transmit his dismay: 'Everything is human theatre/ The autumnal sun is now setting.'

The Confucian contract between the generations is also fraying as more and more Asians choose to park their elderly parents in nursing homes rather than share a roof with them. The Japanese now complain of *'kaigo-jigoku'*, or 'care-giving hell', and say that young men aspire to two things in life: owning a car and not living with Grandma. Alarmed by this shift, China has taken steps to shore up the status of its older citizens. In 2012, Beijing bureaucrats published a modern version of the traditional manual for filial piety. 'Teach your mother and father how to use the internet,' it suggests. 'Visit them as often as possible during the holidays.' To help with the latter, China passed a law compelling adults to visit their ageing parents and forcing companies to give their workers the time off to do so.

Yutang's assertion that the East was once less ageist than the West should give us hope. Why? Because it reminds us that attitudes to ageing are not fixed in stone. Human beings may be hardwired to admire young bodies and recoil from anything that portends death, but beyond that, how we feel about growing older is shaped by culture – and that means it can be reshaped.

The tectonic plates are already starting to shift. All that entrepreneurial energy I witnessed in Shoreditch shows that the move is on to change our approach to ageing, to make the most of later life rather than recoil from it.

If we have become more ageist over the last century then we can become less so in the coming one.

CHAPTER 2

MOVE: *IN CORPORE SANO*

*Our body is a machine for living. It is
organised for that, it is its nature.*

—LEO TOLSTOY

Designing a car for the elderly driver used to be a tricky
business. Young engineers had no idea what it felt like to
fasten a seat belt with stiff joints. Or get out from behind
the steering wheel with poor balance. Reading a dashboard
with failing eyesight was not part of their life experience. Nor
was twiddling dials with arthritic fingers or a diminished
sense of touch.

All that changed back in the early 2000s when Nissan, a
Japanese carmaker, invented a suit that simulates the physical limits imposed by ageing. Wearing one adds about 30
years, which can be a major-league eye-opener. Knowing
what it actually felt like to inhabit an older body made it a
lot easier for the young engineers at Nissan to design cars

for older drivers. Today, 'ageing suits' are deployed across the auto industry and beyond. Architects, for instance, use them to design retirement homes.

Now it's my turn. One of my main worries about ageing is that my body will betray me, that the aches and stiffness I feel at the end of my fifth decade are a harbinger of apocalyptic decline to come, that the day when I have to hang up my hockey stick will arrive much sooner than I would like. It is a fear that echoes through the ages, reinforced by bleak dispatches from people deep in their dotage. More than 4,500 years ago an elderly Egyptian scribe wrote: 'Feebleness has arrived ... The heart sleeps wearily every day. The eyes are weak, the ears are deaf, the strength is disappearing because of weariness of heart and the mouth is silent and cannot speak ... The bone suffers old age ... All taste is gone. What old age does to men is evil in every respect.' The novelist Philip Roth hit the same note with chilling concision: 'Old age isn't a battle; old age is a massacre.'

To confront my fear of ageing, perhaps even to vanquish it, I need to experience first-hand what it's like to have an older body – and the only way to do that is to try on an ageing suit. The nearest one to my home is kept on the campus of South Bank University, an orange pile of glass and concrete not far from London's Globe theatre, where Shakespeare's 'seven ages of man' speech was performed 400 years ago. The suit is used to foster empathy among doctors, carers and nurses and as a research tool.

Sheelagh Mealing, a former nurse with a Yorkshire accent and a no-nonsense attitude, is the official keeper of the suit.

Despite a recent hip replacement, she walks briskly, as if still doing rounds on the ward. Sitting in her cramped office, I'm itching to put on the suit, but she insists on first running through a health check. The questions come thick and fast: Am I on any medication? Do I have a heart condition? Any respiratory trouble? Musculoskeletal complaints? How is my general fitness? 'We need to be sure you can cope with the strain the suit will place on you,' she says. The strain? Is having an older body really so gruelling that you need to sign a health waiver first? My heart sinks a little.

Once the paperwork is out of the way, Mealing opens up a large case lying on the floor. It turns out the suit is not a single garment at all but rather a series of parts that look like the body armour used in contact sports or bomb disposal. Everything – the padding, gloves, braces, weights, vest, neck-immobiliser, boots – is black and held in place with buckles and Velcro straps. It takes a good 10 minutes to put it all on.

Fully suited-up, and looking like a poor man's Robocop, I rise to my feet. Though I feel heavier and a little unsteady, my first reaction is 24-carat hubris: *What's all the fuss about*? I think to myself. *This isn't so bad. Roth is obviously a drama queen.* But Mealing is just getting started. To impair my hearing, she asks me to push foam plugs into my ears and place headphones over the outside. Then it's time to choose a pair of modified glasses to degrade my eyesight. Mealing invites me to pick a disease from a printed menu that includes everything from cataracts to retinitis pigmentosa to macular degeneration. It's like ordering a coffee in Starbucks. I opt for glaucoma. Once the glasses are on, my vision darkens considerably apart from a small, milky circle in the middle. It's like peering through a filthy porthole.

Now it's time to go for a stroll. Mealing leads me out of her office into the hallway and towards the lift. Once I'm properly on the move, the combined effect of the suit's various handicaps really kicks in. I feel clumsy, weak, lumbering, off-balance, vulnerable, even a little scared. To make up for my poor vision and hearing I jerk my head from side to side, like a jack-in-the-box, seeking out any visual or aural clue that might penetrate the fog. I reach out with every step to touch the wall, a fire extinguisher, Mealing's arm, anything that will give me a little support.

Downstairs in the lobby, things take a turn for the worse at the revolving door. I usually find these too slow and often cause them to stop by bumping into the pane of glass in front of me. But this time the roles are reversed. To the artificially aged me, the door seems to be spinning like a merry-go-round in top gear.

'Is this the normal speed?' I ask Mealing.

'Yes,' she replies. 'You've just slowed down more than you realise.'

Eventually I summon the courage to step into the door, but then it stops because the pane of glass bumps into me – from behind. Sensing other people waiting to come through, I feel a flash of irritation and shame.

Out in the street it's the same. Everyone seems to be moving so fast, haring suddenly into view or overtaking me like Olympic race walkers. I fail to reach the other side of a pedestrian crossing before the green man vanishes. After about 15 minutes, my legs are tired, my breathing heavy. Halfway up a flight of stairs I notice sweat trickling down my back. 'You're staggering and dragging your feet quite a bit now,' Mealing says. 'And you're looking less steady.'

As we enter the home stretch, a young woman emerges from a door on my right. I can tell from her body language that she plans to cross my path but I decide to exercise my right of way by speeding up a little. Only I fail to speed up enough, slightly losing my balance in the process, and we end up nearly bumping into each other. I feel like an idiot.

My spirits are at rock bottom as I remove the suit back in Mealing's office. Being older felt worse than I'd imagined. A thousand times worse. 'It's quite shocking, isn't it, realising you're not in control of your body anymore?' says Mealing. You can say that again. I walk home in an existential funk, a question tinkling in the back of my mind like an irksome wind chime: How can we embrace ageing when it really is a massacre?

Or is it?

Not long after trying on the ageing suit, I take a train across the Channel to northern France. My destination is Roubaix, a small city that made its name as a textile powerhouse in the 19th century. Those glory days are long gone now. Barges no longer carry wool or finished garments along the old canal. The mills and weaving sheds stand silent and the shops are jammed with clothes made in Asia. Unemployment is rife and nearly half the local households live below the poverty line. Not long ago, Roubaix was dubbed the 'poorest city in

France'. The only thing that brings the world here nowadays is the state-of-the-art velodrome.

When I arrive, a European cycling championship is in full swing. Cars and caravans from across the continent are parked outside the velodrome. Inside, two cyclists are pelting round the pinewood track in a blur of fauvist Lycra, clocks tracking their times to the nearest 1,000th of a second. The holding pen in the middle offers up a familiar tableau. Cyclists, men and women, wander among a forest of feather-weight bikes costing more than most people earn in a month. They watch races, cheering on friends and teammates. They eat bananas and sip water. They relax with massage and meditation. Some warm up by pedalling on the spot using bike rollers that emit a bee-like hum. One rider is Skyping with family back in Italy. Every so often a national anthem warbles over the Tannoy as a trio of medal winners takes to the podium. The chit-chat is all about race times, training routines, the latest gear.

I am here to get over the trauma of wearing that ageing suit. Why? Because some of the cyclists whizzing round this velodrome are 30 years older than I am.

～

The human body has always been capable of doing sterling service long after its prime. In the middle of the third century, in the Roman province of Mauritania, which is now Algeria, a man was buried at the age of 50. The inscription on his tomb-stone states that he 'died in the flower of youth'. Many of the Silver Shields, the elite military corps that served Alexander the Great in the fourth century, were over 60. They attacked first in battle, carried out special missions and undertook forced marches across the desert. Hildegard of Bingen founded an abbey in the Rhine Valley in 1165 when she was 67 and managed its resident nuns till her death at the age of 81. Gaston Phébus, the 11th Count of Foix, died at the age of 60 on his way home from a bear hunt in 1391. A year later, John Hawkwood, an English *condottiere*, took part in a jousting tournament in Bologna at the age of 72.

Michelangelo was in his mid-60s when he pulled off one of the most gruelling feats in the history of art: painting the *Last Judgement* onto the altar wall of the Sistine Chapel. Starting in 1536, he spent four years working on rickety scaffolding up to 20 metres off the ground. At one point he fell and injured himself so badly he was out for weeks. A fellow painter, Giorgio Vasari, was blown away by his resilience: 'He executed the frescoes in great discomfort, having to work with his face looking upwards, which impaired his sight so badly that he could not read or look at drawings save with his head turned backwards; and this lasted for several months afterwards ... I am astonished that Michelangelo bore all that discomfort so well.' Nor did the *Last Judgement* finish him off: he went on to produce a formidable body of work until his death at the age of 88.

Today, science is making it easier for all of us to channel Michelangelo's staying power. Driven by better nutrition and training and a savvier approach to rest and recovery, elite athletes are leading the way. At the 2008 Olympics, American swimmer Dara Torres won three silver medals in the pool at the age of 41, setting a world record in her medley relay split along the way. At the 2016 Games, a 41-year-old Uzbek named Oksana Chusovitina competed in the women's gymnastics, a sport traditionally dominated by teenagers. Earlier that same year, Jaromír Jágr, a Czech ice hockey player, skated in the NHL All-Star game aged 43. Tennis ace Roger Federer enjoyed a remarkable renaissance in his mid-30s, armed with a backhand that looked even better than in his prime. After winning the Australian Open in 2018, his third Grand Slam victory in a calendar year, he became, at the age of 36, the oldest player ever to reach the top of his sport's rankings. 'I don't think age is an issue, per se,' he said.

Where the stars go, the rest of us follow. These days YouTube is packed with clips of human bodies performing remarkable feats in later life. Recent examples include: A 101-year-old woman abseiling down a 94-metre tower. Another skydiving at the age of 82. A man who started lifting weights aged 87 pumping iron competitively 10 years later. A 67-year-old winning *National Geographic*'s People's Choice Adventurer of the Year award for finishing the longest transatlantic open-water kayaking expedition in history. The world's oldest yoga teacher is 98.

Pretty much every athletic endeavour you can think of, from track and field, swimming and cycling to skiing, tennis and hockey, now comes in a 'Masters' version for amateurs aged 30 to over 100. And though some may titter at the idea of septuagenarian skiers and centenarian sprinters (never mind fifty-something hockey players), sport in later life is a serious business. Staged every four years, the World Masters

Games – think Olympics for the over-30s – now draws more competitors than any sporting event in the world. Nor are older athletes just turning up to take part: they are in it to win it. Performance is improving by leaps and bounds at every age level, meaning that the average 35-year-old, 55-year-old and 75-year-old is getting faster, stronger and more agile every year. 'We are just at the start of an entire movement that is going to redefine what older people are capable of,' says Joe Baker, a professor at the School of Kinesiology and Health Science at Canada's York University.

～

That chimes with my experience at the Masters championship in Roubaix. The first thing you notice at the velodrome is that it is almost impossible to guess the age of a cyclist on the track. In the holding pen you see grey hair, wrinkles, incipient moobs and the odd pot belly. Yet once the cyclists don their helmets, goggles and Lycra, and start pedalling, they all look pretty much the same. The only thing that sets the octogenarian apart from the thirty-something is speed of travel – younger still means faster in Masters sports – but since everyone races within age categories that gap is seldom on display.

What really catches the eye in Roubaix, however, is that some of the cyclists are actually improving year on year. It's one thing for an entire age cohort to perform better than a decade ago; it's another for individual athletes to carry on getting faster as they grow older. Yet that is exactly what is happening here.

Not long after I arrive at the velodrome, Steve Cronshaw rolls up to the starting line for a solo time trial that will determine his seeding in the sprint event. He barrels round the track, legs pumping like a cartoon character. He covers the 200 metres in 11.3 seconds, a new world record for the 60–64 age group. The time is also a personal best. In other words, Cronshaw, a retired engineer from England, is now riding faster at 60 than he did at 40.

Other cyclists here tell similar stories. A 66-year-old now covers both 10 miles and 25 miles faster than 20 years ago. Fresh from setting a new personal best over 500 metres, Carolien van Herrikhuyzen, a 41-year-old from the Netherlands, is expecting to shave more seconds off her times over the coming decade. 'I am so much quicker than I was 10 years ago,' she says. 'And knowing my body and seeing what older athletes are doing, I know I can get even faster.' You find the same bullishness even at the most advanced ages. In 2012, Robert Marchand, a retired French firefighter, set a world record for the over-100s by cycling 14.2 miles in one hour. Two years later, at the age of 102, he set a new record by riding 16.7 miles in the same time. As Cronshaw puts it: 'We're throwing away the rule book of ageing.'

What does all this mean for ordinary mortals with zero desire to put in the hard graft needed to chase world records in cycling? Quite a lot, actually. Even if you have no interest in competitive sport, even if the only physical activity you aspire to in later life is going for a walk or playing with the grandchildren, people like van Herrikhuyzen and Cronshaw are worthy of your attention. As well as helping create a world where sport is an acceptable pastime at any age, they are living proof that later life can be so much more than a Rothian massacre.

~

The human body usually reaches its physical peak around the age of 30. Then, for reasons that remain a mystery, it embarks on a steady decline. Hair whitens and skin weathers. We lose height, bone density, strength and stamina. Joints stiffen, sight and hearing diminish and arteries clog. After the age of 30, we become more susceptible to disease, with our risk of death doubling every seven years. Menopause, which usually starts after the age of 40, puts an end to female fertility and can cause months or more of physical and emotional distress. Along the way, both sexes experience a deceleration in their movements, memory and metabolism. Or, as comic John Wagner once quipped: 'Everything slows down with age, except the time it takes cake and ice cream to reach your hips.'

Total nightmare, right? Wrong. The good news is that not all the news is bad – far from it. Ageing actually makes us more robust in some ways. A few of the nastier diseases – diabetes, leukaemia, breast cancer – pack less punch in later life. Headaches and migraines become less common as we age, and allergies, such as hay fever, can fade away. Ageing also cuts your chances of coming down with a common cold thanks to all the immunity you build up over the years.

Age-related decline also kicks in more slowly than we imagine. Motor control and hand-eye co-ordination, for example, can hold up into our 70s and beyond. Putting on an ageing suit is traumatic because it inflicts every conceivable impairment at the same time – and not many people are that unlucky in real life. Most of us will only suffer from some of the suit's handicaps, and those will strike gradually enough to give us time to adjust. The best part is that ageing is a surprisingly moveable feast. Part of how our bodies change over the years is fixed by genetics, and thus (for the time being, at least) beyond our control. But much of it comes down to lifestyle – how you eat, work, exercise, sleep, socialise and relax; your relationship with drugs, alcohol and smoking; where you live. That gives all of us, athletes and sportsphobes alike, plenty of levers to pull to lead longer, healthier lives.

Advice on how to keep the body fit into later life goes way back. Galen, a celebrated physician during the Roman Empire, prescribed, among other things, horse-riding, ball-throwing, eating plums and travelling on ships. Though modern advice is based more on hard science, some of it is too gruesome to contemplate – and I'm not talking about living on a diet of wheatgrass and spirulina. One example: research suggests that the surest way for a man to add 14 years to his life is to become a eunuch. Er, no thanks.

Thankfully, modern scientists agree on a more palatable recipe for keeping you *in corpore sano*: Stay physically active. Eat a healthy diet. Drink alcohol in moderation and don't smoke. Form strong social bonds. Have a purpose in life that gets you up in the morning. Be less materialistic. Laugh a lot.

Of all the items on that list, exercise seems the closest to a magic bullet. Hippocrates declared it to be man's best medicine back in 400BC. 'It is what we were made to do,' says Nick Cavill, a public health researcher at the University of Bristol. 'Everyone probably knows the basic point, but often we overlook it in our busy modern lives. We are hunter-gatherers. We were designed to be physically active all day long.'

When it comes to the human body, the moral of the story is use it or lose it. Though grip strength tends to peak in our mid-30s and then fall off quickly thereafter, assembly line workers who do lots of gripping keep their strength well into their 60s. The same goes for playing the piano. Professional pianists maintain their finger-tapping speed into later life even though the rest of us start losing ours after the age of 30.

A similar lesson comes from the so-called 'Blue Zones'. Sprinkled around the world, these longevity hotspots are full of very old people in very good nick. Some are now places of pilgrimage for experts and quacks seeking the elixir of youth. Years ago I visited a Blue Zone called Vilcabamba, a village nestled in a lush valley in southern Ecuador. There were no gyms or velodromes yet physical activity was woven into the daily routine. Vilcabambans walked everywhere and most did some form of manual labour. It was not uncommon to see locals carrying sacks of grain or steering livestock towards fields tilled by their great-grandchildren. Halfway through an interview, when my Dictaphone fell to the ground, a woman in her 90s bent down to pick it up with the elasticity of a teenaged gymnast.

Thankfully, though, you do not have to move to a Blue Zone for your body to age better. Nor do you have to take up

CrossFit or hire a personal trainer. Even small adjustments in daily life can help: Taking the stairs rather than the lift. Getting up from the sofa to change TV channels instead of using the remote. Hopping off the bus one stop early or parking further from your destination so as to walk more. By the same token, the exercise targets set by the experts are not especially daunting. Most recommend 150 minutes of moderate aerobic activity, 75 minutes of vigorous exercise, or a blend of the two, every week, plus some resistance training. That works out to a modest 15–25 minutes per day. Moderate aerobic exercise can be a brisk walk or a bike ride, while jogging counts as vigorous exercise. Resistance training can mean lifting weights or simply carrying the shopping bags or digging in the garden. Wheelchair users can get their fix by doing sitting exercise routines or playing chair-based versions of sports ranging from badminton to basketball.

However you choose to break a sweat, your body will be grateful. Studies show that regular exercise can guard against strokes, cancer, diabetes, heart disease, falls and hip fractures. It can stabilise weight and blood pressure and reduce the chance of dying early. When British researchers studied a group of male and female amateur cyclists between the ages of 55 and 79 who had exercised regularly throughout their adult lives they were astonished to find how little their bodies had declined over time. They had lost neither strength nor muscle mass nor (in the case of the men) testosterone, and they were free of middle-aged spread. Most surprising of all, the older cyclists had immune systems that were as robust as those seen in twenty-somethings.

If you're reading this and thinking it's too late to start exercising, then think again. Even if you've been a couch potato till now, you can still enjoy an exercise dividend. One study in Norway found that men who started getting fit in their 40s and 50s cut their risk of stroke to the same level as those who had always worked out. Nor do you have to feel guilty every time a friend posts a triathlon photo on Facebook, because exercise is subject to the law of diminishing returns. In other words, more is more but only up to a certain point. As Cavill puts it: 'A marathon runner or a triathlete is not doing much better for their health than somebody who is reasonably active.' Bottom line: With sensible upkeep and the right attitude, most of us can go on doing amazing things with our bodies.

That message is sinking in. From Hong Kong to Houston to Hamburg, people are keeping more active by running, hiking, cycling, rowing or just racking up 10,000 steps a day. The over-50s now make up more than 40 per cent of adventure travellers in the US. In the UK, the fastest-growing travel group are the 65–74-year-olds – and they favour action-packed holidays. Many are smashing ageist stereotypes to get their exercise fix. The fastest-growing age group taking up martial arts such as taekwondo, karate and aikido is the over-50s. In Cosmo City, a hardscrabble township on the outskirts of Johannesburg, South Africa, women over 60 are flocking to boxing classes.

The exercise boom partly explains why the average over-65-year-old is now in better shape than ever before. And why much of the bad stuff we associate with growing older – blindness, deafness, strokes, heart disease – is now striking later in life. In the EU, *healthy* life expectancy after the age of 50 is rising more quickly than life expectancy itself, which suggests we are stretching the good years while shrinking the bad bit that often comes before death. According to the Institute for Health Metrics and Evaluation at the University of Washington, a British boy born in 2015 can look forward to six more years of life than one born in 1990 – and five of those years will be healthy. A similar trend is visible in the United States, where disability-free life expectancy is rising among over-65s. 'The new data coming out in the last five years is fabulous,' says Esme Fuller-Thomson, the Canadian ageing specialist we met earlier. 'Everything's getting better and it's taking all of us in the field by surprise.'

~

Not everyone, however, has climbed aboard the exercise bandwagon. Physical inactivity still ranks among the top 10 causes of disability and disease in many countries. Being a lazybones is thought to kill as many Britons as smoking. Across the world, rising obesity rates in every age group threaten to undo the gains of the longevity revolution.

To make the most of our longer lives, we need to spread the exercise revolution more widely, and to do so we must make a host of changes. That includes building more physical activity into the school curriculum, making exercise a central plank in medical treatment and redesigning cities to encourage – or even oblige – people to walk and cycle more.

Japan is leading the way in new ideas for keeping active in later life. At Sendagaya University, which caters for students over the age of 60, physical exercise is stitched into the schedule between lectures. In a similar vein, Japanese architects are designing homes with sloped, bumpy floors that make walking into more of a workout.

We also need to find the right way to promote fitness. While super-fit older people deal a welcome blow to the stereotype that ageing must make us frail and feeble, studies suggest they can also be a turn-off to lesser mortals. Sean Horton, an associate professor of kinesiology at the University of Windsor in Canada, has attended many Masters sports competitions as both a competitor and a researcher. He warns against holding them up as the new ageing ideal. 'Masters athletes can be excellent role models for young people but they may actually backfire with their own age group,' he says. 'They are seen as so outrageous and extreme in their accomplishments that other older people will look at them and think, *I've got no chance, I'll never be able to do that* and be put off trying any form of exercise or sport.' His solution: share stories of people of all ages being active at a range of levels.

∼

When it comes to getting more mileage out of our ageing bodies, there is more good news: our brains can pick up some of the slack. How? By wielding our remaining physical prowess more shrewdly. Elite athletes have always worked this trick. Professional golfers drive the ball less far as they age but make up for it with greater accuracy. Late in his career, when he no longer had the superhuman spring in his legs that turned him into a basketball legend, Michael Jordan replaced the gravity-defying leap immortalised in those Nike ads with a fade-away jump shot. The payoff: more years as a point-scoring machine at the top of his sport.

When a player carries on thriving past his physical prime in soccer, commentators often say: 'The first yard is inside his head.' That means he uses his superior understanding of the game, of its contours and currents, to keep his edge over younger rivals who are stronger and faster. Researchers have spotted the same phenomenon among goalkeepers in several sports. Even as ageing slows their reflexes and movement, they carry on performing well by improving their reading of the game and the movement of shooters. Older brains even learn to recognise and exploit the sounds made by teammates and rivals. 'Up until a very late period in your life you are able to compensate for many things you lose through ageing by your brain's ability to rewire itself to do things more efficiently and faster,' says Baker, the kinesiologist.

Of course, this mind-over-matter trick only works for so long. Eventually the body fades to a point where no amount of cognitive compensation can bridge the gap. Don't bet on Federer winning tennis Grand Slams at 45 or Jágr playing in the NHL All-Star game at 50.

Most of us, however, are not elite athletes desperate for one more season in the big leagues. We just want to carry on doing our favourite activity – be that hiking, hula-hooping or hockey – for as long as possible. Again, the expert advice is reassuring: keep going as long as your body can take it but adjust your expectations along the way. One solution is to join one of the 'walking' leagues that are springing up to offer a gentler version of sports such as netball, soccer and basketball. I am not yet ready to give up running hockey but my style of play is already evolving. I no longer have the speed, strength and stamina I did 20 years ago, but my hand–eye co-ordination is as good as ever and my reading of the game is better. Though I now score fewer goals, I rack up more assists by exploiting the running power of my younger teammates. Most important, I look forward to hockey night.

The Masters world has a nifty trick for managing expectations of what the body can achieve in later life: its athletes move up an age group every five years. Each time they enter a new cohort they are suddenly the hot rookie again, the ringer coming off the bench. In a funny way, this makes ageing seem like a bonus. A friend's mother took up competitive swimming in her 60s. Shortly after her 88th birthday, she announced that she could hardly wait to turn 90. Why? 'So I can start thrashing people in the pool again!'

Adjusting expectations works beyond the world of sports, too. To carry on performing into his 80s, pianist Vladimir Horowitz found a way to play within the limits imposed by his ageing body. He started by dropping the most taxing pieces from his repertoire. Then he rejigged the order of the remaining works, playing the slower ones first to accentuate the higher tempo of those later in the programme.

There is something we can all learn from Masters athletes and musicians like Horowitz. Rather than pining for what our bodies were able to do in the past, we should make the most of what they can do right now. But we must also accept that eventually they will wear out, which means learning to see frailty and vulnerability as a part of life rather than as a mark of failure.

∼

Whatever our age, we can all take heart from the push to make the world a more welcoming place for older bodies. Retailers everywhere are redesigning their stores to make them suitable for the ageing customer. In the United States, Sherwin Williams, a paint supplier, has added more seating and lighting and cut back on the use of small print in displays, while CVS, a large pharmacy chain, has installed slip-proof carpeting and lowered its shelving. In Tokyo, a flagship branch of the Aeon supermarket chain now boasts a health clinic and exercise area where older shoppers can play ping-pong, take part in aerobics classes or walk an indoor track that circles the store, monitoring their heart rate as they go. To help fading eyes like mine read the text on the packaging for its cat litter, Arm & Hammer has sharpened the colour contrast and made the font size 20 per cent bigger. Diamond Foods has added indentations and grooves to make the canisters for its Emerald snacks easier to grip with weaker hands.

More companies are likely to follow suit for two reasons. First, there are more older consumers in the world every year. Second, design that works for aged bodies usually goes down well with everyone else. Ford discovered this when it created the Focus. With the help of ageing suits, the company built a roomier car with a dashboard that was easy to read and controls that were easy to reach. And guess what? Younger consumers loved it too, making the Focus a best-seller across all ages.

At the same time, the startups we saw in Shoreditch are just the tip of a ballooning iceberg of innovation that will favour older bodies. Big data promises to revolutionise medicine by vastly improving our ability to detect, prevent and treat the diseases of ageing. Smart gadgets, such as wearables that track physical activity and monitor vital signs, are already helping us take control of our health in ways that would have seemed like science fiction not so long ago.

Technology will increasingly lend succour when our bodies start to wane. Robots are improving all the time and every year we inch closer to a world of driverless cars. In 2017, scientists made history when a man paralysed from the neck down moved his hand with the power of thought. A computer deciphered the signals picked up by electrical implants in his brain and sent them to sensors inserted in the muscles of his forearm. For the first time in eight years the man was able to drink a cup of coffee and eat mashed potato with a fork without any help.

Or witness the rise of 'powered clothing'. While an ageing suit hampers your muscles by increasing the load on them, the Aura Powered Suit promises to do exactly the opposite. Made from light, stretchy material, the prototype garment looks like high-end yoga wear – until you notice the small, hexagonal pods on the legs, hips, torso and back. They contain sensors that read your movements and then use electricity to activate bands woven into the fabric of the suit. These act like 'electric muscles', boosting the strength of the real muscles underneath. The idea is not to turn you into Iron Man (or Woman), but to make it easier to sit down, get up, walk, climb stairs or simply stay upright. Plus you can wear it under normal clothes. I can easily imagine donning a power suit when my body needs an extra fillip later in life, especially if someone invents a version for playing hockey.

~

Though there is no powered clothing hidden beneath the Lycra at the velodrome in Roubaix, all the cyclists here are infectiously optimistic about what their bodies will be achieving in the future. To reach that hopeful state, many first had to overcome their own ageism. When he joined the world of Masters cycling, Cronshaw held an uncharitable view of older bodies. All that aged flesh in Lycra made his skin crawl. 'When I got on the bike in my early 40s I thought, *Look at those old farts still at it in their 60s*,' he says, wincing slightly at the memory. Nearly two decades later, though, he is now a proud member of the MAMIL (Middle-Aged Men In Lycra) club. 'How many more years have I got? Don't know, but I'm loving it,' he says. 'I understand now that the ageing process isn't nearly as bad as you think it's going to be.'

After spending the weekend with Cronshaw and the rest of the Roubaix riders, I am starting to feel the same. If they can carry on being fit into later life, and doing their favourite sport without looking or feeling out of place, then so can the rest of us. My existential crisis at that hockey tournament in Gateshead now seems a little silly. Even the memory of the ageing suit is starting to fade.

My mood is slightly punctured, though, when I leave the velodrome. The walk takes me through neighbourhoods where drug trafficking and petty crime are common. No one I approach in the street has heard of Masters sports or is even aware that Lycra-clad seventy-somethings are racing round a track nearby. The locals are clearly living less healthy lives than the athletes in the velodrome.

Along the way, I fall into conversation with Daniel Bertrand, who recently lost his job as a security guard. The only exercise he now gets is strolling to and from the shops or visiting his daughter two streets away. He walks with a slight stoop and a shuffling gait. His teeth look uncomfortable and his face is spider-webbed with veins broken by a lifetime of drinking. When he asks me to guess his age, I low-ball by 10 years to avoid giving offence, but it turns out my estimate is right on the money: he looks at least sixty but is actually fifty, the same age as me.

Bertrand is a reminder that longevity has always been unevenly distributed, with the haves standing a better chance of ageing well than the have-nots. That is because wealth makes growing older easier. It buys better food, shelter and medical care, as well as more options for exercise and less punishing work. It can also insulate us from substance abuse, environmental harm and the kind of stressful events – homelessness, violent crime, bankruptcy – that appear to speed up ageing.

The only way to share the fruits of the longevity revolution more evenly is to narrow the gap between rich and poor. That is how people like Bertrand will have the same shot at ageing well as all those Masters cyclists spending the weekend in his neighbourhood.

In the meantime, I leave Roubaix with three rock-solid reasons to feel better about my own ageing body. Number one: growing older is not nearly as bad as most of us fear it will be. Number two: we can change our behaviour to age better than ever before. Number three: the world is evolving in ways that will make life easier for people with older bodies.

Now I want to know if those same reasons apply to other aspects of ageing.

CHAPTER 3

CREATE: OLD DOGS, NEW TRICKS

Imagination has no age.

—WALT DISNEY

The same daunting task awaits Stanley McMurtry every time he turns up for work at the *Daily Mail* in London. With no help from the rest of the newsroom, he must create a topical cartoon sharp enough to command prime real estate in one of the bestselling newspapers in Britain – and he must to do so within a few hours. No time for writer's block, meditative strolls or sleeping on an idea. All his creative cylinders must be firing from the moment he sits down at his desk and starts sifting through the day's headlines. Talk about the terror of the blank page!

Yet McMurtry, whose pen name is Mac, is not daunted. He simply rolls up his sleeves and gets down to the serious business of creating the laugh *du jour*. Through the morning, his mind wanders over the big news stories of the day, teasing out scenarios and subplots, toying with snippets of dialogue, testing jokes – and then comes up with a killer cartoon before the afternoon deadline. He has been pulling off the same trick longer than anyone else on Fleet Street.

As well as being the doyen of British cartoonists, Mac is also my neighbour. When he moved into our street in his late 60s, my ageist assumption was that he must be in the twilight of his career – and already resting on his laurels. How wrong I was: In 2017, shortly before his 81st birthday, he won the UK's Cartoonist of the Year award for the seventh time, with the judges calling him 'just superb' and hailing his 'beautifully drawn, clever cartoons that excelled in a supreme field'.

Not long after that triumph, we sit down in my living room to chat about ageing. Mac is like most of his cartoons: gentle, acute, amusing. He speaks softly and carries a big wit. He also has a romantic streak: one of his trademarks is to conceal the profile of his late wife, Liz, in every cartoon. Even before settling onto the sofa he tells me: 'I don't feel any different mentally from when I was in my 20s.'

Does that mean he is just as good a cartoonist today? I ask.

Better, comes the reply.

'When I look back on my early stuff it seems to me that a lot of it was badly drawn, the perspective wasn't quite right, my characters were derivative of other people's work or the ideas just weren't very clever or creative,' he says. 'I wasn't sure of myself so I sweated over everything and you tighten up because you're worried.'

Over time, though, he found his footing and forged his own style. 'My standards have gone up and I feel like I'm doing my best work now in my 80s,' he says. 'My cartoons are looser but also more assured and they have more point to them – I feel very creative.'

Those last four words stop me in my tracks. One of my main fears about growing older is losing my creative edge. Coming up with fresh ways of seeing the world is the engine behind my writing, speaking and broadcasting. These days, you find the word 'creative' sprinkled like stardust across CVs and job descriptions because it can be an asset in any line of work. I recently saw an ad seeking 'creativity ninjas' to work in a coffee shop. With the advance of artificial intelligence, creative thinking could turn out to be the ace up humanity's sleeve, our USP, the one thing we can still do better than machines. Finding new ways to do things or express yourself also makes life richer beyond the workplace, which is why dance, music, storytelling and art are found across all cultures.

That Mac is at the top of his creative game at the age of 81 should therefore make my day, but somehow, and despite that Cartoonist of the Year award, I find it hard to believe. My gut tells me he must be deluded, or a freak of nature. After all, conventional wisdom holds that creativity belongs to the young. Remember the Zuckerberg Doctrine, or the words of Vinod Khosla, a billionaire co-founder of Sun Microsystems: 'People under 35 are the people who make change happen. People over 45 basically die in terms of new ideas.'

History offers bags of evidence to bolster that view. Who came up with the first windsurfing board? A 12-year-old English schoolboy. Horatio Adams invented bubblegum at the age of 13 and Louis Braille was 15 when he devised his reading system for the blind. Blaise Pascal built the first mechanical calculator at 19. Alexander Graham Bell patented his telephone shortly after his 29th birthday – not far off the average age of employees at the top tech companies in Silicon Valley.

Mathematicians are famous for peaking young. Évariste Galois paved the way for modern algebra and Niels Abel invented group theory while they were teenagers. In 1940, a British math whizz named G. H. Hardy wrote off anyone hoping to make similar breakthroughs in later life. 'No mathematician,' he declared, 'should ever allow himself to forget that mathematics ... is a young man's game.' Albert Einstein, who unleashed the theory of relativity in his mid-20s, made a similar claim for the sciences: 'A person who has not made his great contribution to science before the age of 30 will never do so.'

You could build a similar case in the arts, where Mac and I ply our trade. Mary Shelley published *Frankenstein* at 20. J. K. Rowling was the same age, and sitting on a delayed train from Manchester to London, when the idea for her *Harry Potter* series came to her. Picasso was in his 20s when he lobbed the grenade of Cubism into the art world. Plenty of composers, from Schubert and Schumann to Mozart and Mendelssohn, have written sublime music before turning 30. In the 16th century, Michel de Montaigne, the French philosopher who more or less invented the essay as a literary genre, claimed that the 30th birthday marked the beginning of creative decline: 'I am verily persuaded, that since that age both my spirit and my body, have more decreased than increased, more recoiled than advanced.'

In a million different ways, pop culture reinforces and romanticises the idea that creativity belongs to youth. Media outlets constantly publish lists of People To Watch Under 30 – as if Montaigne were right. Movies about real and fictional prodigies – from *Billy Elliot*, *Searching for Bobby Fischer* and *Little Man Tate* to *Good Will Hunting*, *Amadeus* and *Shine* – are a Hollywood staple. John Nash, the mathematician who helped pioneer game theory in his early 20s, was immortalised in the Oscar-winning film *A Beautiful Mind*. Ideas conferences also love to feature young people giving TED-style talks about their creative home runs. After inventing a technique for the early detection of pancreatic cancer in 2012, 15-year-old Jack Andraka became a fixture on the speaking circuit.

Of course, the early years can be a time of immense creativity, and the young should be fêted for their eureka moments. But does that mean the capacity to be original withers with age? The more we learn about the brain, the more the answer to that question is a resounding No. In other words, Mac is not a freak of nature and novelist Maya Angelou was on to something when she observed: 'You can't use up creativity. The more you use, the more you have.'

Like our bodies, our brains change as we grow older. They start shrinking after the age of 20, losing about 2 per cent of their weight and volume every decade thereafter. Blood vessels wither, curbing the supply of oxygen. We keep most of our brain cells throughout life but they get smaller and have fewer contacts between them. In our 40s, the myelin sheath – the lipid coating that helps nerve axons move messages round the brain – begins to break down.

These changes take a cognitive toll. Like an ageing computer, our brains lose processing speed. We start solving maths problems and absorbing new information more slowly. We take longer to retrieve certain memories, leading to more of those tip-of-the-tongue moments when a word or name remains tantalisingly out of reach. Our focus also slips, making it harder to block out distractions and switch between demanding tasks.

None of this, however, kills our creativity. On the contrary, science is now showing that the human brain is remarkably good at making up for – and even building on – the changes wrought by ageing. Magnetic resonance imaging (fMRI) scans have revealed that in middle age we start using more regions of the brain when tackling a hard problem. Over time, that builds the rich integration that can fuel creative thinking – especially when paired with experience and knowledge.

The natural deceleration that comes with ageing may also deliver a creativity boost. When we stop rushing, the mind switches into a more creative gear that psychologists call 'slow thinking'. 'Creativity usually requires an incubation period,' says Teresa Amabile, professor and director of research at the Harvard Business School. 'People need time to soak in a problem and let the ideas bubble up.' The slight loss of focus brought on by ageing may also be a secret weapon in the struggle to create. Why? Because a more distractible mind can pick up information that at first seems irrelevant yet later proves to be the key to a creative breakthrough.

It helps that one of the most enduring stereotypes about ageing – that we become 'set in our ways' – is actually wrong. On one hand, research suggests that middle-aged people are more likely than are younger ones to cling to sacred cows and the status quo. But once we enter our 60s we loosen up again and find it easier to change attitudes in response to fresh information – a first step towards making creative leaps. In the 1970s, Stephen Hawking threw his weight behind one of the most famous theories in the history of cosmology: that nothing can escape from a black hole. Three decades later, when faced with new insights into quantum mechanics and general relativity, he changed his mind, accepting that black holes can release information about the matter they gobble up. As well as eating a large slice of humble pie in public, Hawking, who was 62 at the time, paid out on a high-profile bet with a rival scientist.

Another surprising theory is that ageing alters the structure of the brain in ways that boost creativity. The breakdown of the myelin sheath loosens up the neural architecture and allows ideas to flow around with greater ease. 'You have fewer brakes on your frontal inhibitors, and you're able to put things together in more novel and useful ways,' says Rex Jung, professor of neurosurgery at the University of New Mexico. 'When you see an increase in people's creative undertakings in retirement, it may not be just because they're retired and have more time on their hands; it may be because the brain organisation is different.' That might explain why elders have traditionally dominated folk art across all ethnic and racial groups. Why Sophocles wrote one of his greatest

plays, *Oedipus Rex*, when he was 71. Why legendary paint-
ers – Matisse, Rembrandt, Titian – and composers – Wagner,
Beethoven, Bach – have done triumphantly creative work
in later life. Why Louise Bourgeois, a French-American
artist, came up with her iconic giant spider in her 80s – and
then carried on working successfully until her death at the
age of 98.

You find the same later-life creativity in the more prosaic
world of work. Despite the Zuckerberg bias, inventors tend
to peak in their late 40s and then carry on being productive
through the second half of their careers. In the United States,
for instance, the average age for filing a patent application is
47, with the most lucrative ones often coming from those over
55. Momofuku Ando invented the instant noodle in his late
40s, Benjamin Franklin was 74 when he invented bifocals and
Thomas Edison filed patents until his death at the age of 84.

Thanks to ageism, the creative surge in later life often
comes as a complete surprise. When he was young, Sigmund
Freud wrote off the over-50s as intellectually inflexible – and
then went on to write some of his most influential work after
the age of 65. Even while griping about his faculties declining
after his 30th birthday, Montaigne published his pioneering
oeuvre, *Les Essais*, at the age of 47.

All of this runs so counter to the prevailing stereotypes
about ageing that it is worth restating in bald terms: Not
only can creativity hold up into later life, but neuroscience
tells us that growing older can rewire the brain in ways that
might make us even more creative. Mac is no outlier and
Zuckerberg is flat-out wrong.

Music to my middle-aged ears, to be sure, but the headline here is not Older People Are Just Smarter. It's that human beings can be creative at any age because there are different kinds of creativity. David Galenson, an economist at the University of Chicago, argues that innovators come in two basic flavours. 'Conceptuals' make sudden breakthroughs when still seeing their discipline with fresh eyes, which usually happens at a young age. 'Experimentalists' rely on trial and error, as well as experience and accumulated knowledge, and therefore tend to produce their most original work later in life. Both types can exist within the same discipline. Among Nobel Prize-winning economists, the conceptuals peak nearly two decades before the experimentalists. Though Orson Welles was 25 when he made *Citizen Kane*, Alfred Hitchcock banged out his three most popular movies – *Psycho*, *Vertigo* and *North by Northwest* – between the ages of 59 and 61. While Robert Frost penned 92 per cent of his most reprinted poems after his 40th birthday, Sylvia Plath shook the poetry world in her 20s. Picasso's early works sell for more than his later stuff, yet the opposite is true for Cézanne.

We need both conceptual and experimental innovators, yet the world is changing in ways that favour the latter. Many disciplines have matured to the point where future breakthroughs will be made by mastering multiple domains and building upon work done by others. In other words, they will depend on two things that only ageing can confer: time and experience. Already Nobel winners are hitting their creative peak later and later, with physics laureates tending to make their big discoveries around the age of 50.

John Goodenough is a role model not only for late bloomers but for the idea that you never have to stop blooming. In 1946, when he turned up as a 23-year-old to study physics at the University of Chicago, a professor told him he was already too old to make a mark in the field. Ageist nonsense, of course. Three decades later, aged 57, Goodenough helped invent the lithium-ion rechargeable battery. And he wasn't done there. In 2017, not long after his 94th birthday, the team he leads at the University of Texas in Austin announced that it had built a new battery that is much safer, more durable and faster-charging.

By the same token, more and more people are making a mockery of the canard that mathematics belongs to youth. In 2013, Zhang Yitang solved one of the discipline's most vexing problems by proving that the gap between successive prime numbers remains finite, no matter how high you count. He was 50 at the time. Marina Ratner was the same age when she made headlines by linking number theory with the physics of the motion of objects. After her death in 2017, a leading mathematician described her as 'one of the main examples to counter the myth that mathematics is a young person's game'.

That myth is also coming under fire in the arts. Opened in 2009, the Carter Burden Gallery in New York only exhibits and sells works by artists over the age of 60. 'Older adults do not stop being who they are because they hit a particular age,' says Marlena Vaccaro, the gallery's director. 'Professional artists never stop doing what we do, and in many cases we get better at it as we go along.' In Britain, the prestigious Turner Prize rewards original work by visual artists. For years you had to be under 50 to qualify but in 2017 the age limit was scrapped. Why? Because, in the words of chair Alex Farquharson, 'artists can experience a breakthrough in their work at any age'.

At any age: three little words to lift the spirits, whether you're struggling to make a mark early in your career or worrying that time is running out in later life. The truth is that it is never too late to create. Guess how old the 2017 winner of the Turner Prize was? Sixty-three. A year later, at the age of 89, James Ivory became the oldest Oscar winner ever when he took home the statuette for best adapted screenplay for *Call Me by Your Name*.

～

Whatever you create, the recipe for keeping your brain fighting fit is the same. Eating a healthy diet, sleeping enough and avoiding too much stress are a good start. But it also pays to apply the use-it-or-lose-it rule. Like the body, the brain is a muscle and therefore thrives on exercise. Socialising is one way to keep those neurons firing. Another is to go out of your way to perform tasks that are cognitively taxing, that force you to solve problems, grapple with complexity and learn new things. Sadly, popular 'brain games' such as sudoku are too easy to have much effect. You have to push yourself to the point where it becomes so uncomfortable that you want to stop – and then push some more. Think of it as the cognitive equivalent of doing burpees: no pain, no gain.

Consider the black-cab drivers in London. To earn a taxi licence in the British capital, you have to memorise a byzantine maze of 25,000 streets spread across more than 300 square kilometres. You also need to know where 100,000 landmarks sit on the map. The goal is to be able to calculate, as soon as a passenger climbs aboard and without using GPS, the best possible route between any two points in the city. To pull off this remarkable feat, known as The Knowledge, candidates spend three or four years roaming London on mopeds, memorising every nook and cranny – doing cognitive burpees, in other words. They then sit a series of fearsome exams that only 50 per cent pass.

In a landmark experiment, scientists used fMRI scans to monitor the brains of people studying for The Knowledge. The findings were crystal clear: all that heavy memorising causes the hippocampus, the memory centre in the brain, to grow plumper. And the cognitive payoff lasts long into later life: many black-cab drivers are in their 70s and one famously hung up his keys at the age of 92.

Similar benefits have been spotted in people performing feats of learning far less gruelling than The Knowledge. In one experiment, Denise Park, director of research at the Center for Vital Longevity at the University of Texas at Dallas, invited a group of over-60s to spend 16 and a half hours a week learning digital photography from scratch. After three months, 76 per cent of them scored higher on memory tests. Brain scans also showed a strengthening of the neural circuitry linked to attention and concentration – with the effects lasting more than a year after the photographic course ended.

That the brain remains malleable in later life is good

news for our creativity. Many conceptual innovators run out of puff not because of ageing itself but because they quit doing their cognitive burpees. They rest on the laurels bestowed by their early brilliance. They stop experimenting and taking risks. They become captives of the status quo. Because this narrowing of horizons is not an inevitable side effect of ageing, you can take steps to avoid it. How? By adopting an experimental mindset, which means pushing yourself to seek out fresh challenges and try new things, especially those that hurt like burpees. By treating ageing as a process of opening, rather than closing, doors.

George Saunders is a case in point. After a long career writing short stories and journalism, he published his first novel in his late 50s – and not just any old novel. Narrated by 162 ghosts, *Lincoln in the Bardo* is a strikingly original work that won the 2017 Booker Prize. If Saunders carries on doing his cognitive burpees, who knows what fresh literary ground he might break in his 70s or beyond?

Seeking out novelty can even keep us relevant in fields that venerate youth. Though Steve Jobs did the conceptual thing by co-founding Apple at the age of 21, he remained a restless thinker, always toying with new ideas. In his 50s, long after Zuckerberg would have written him off, he spearheaded a second creative revolution by launching the iPhone and iPad. Or look at popular music. Many pop stars blaze across the sky like supernovas when young and then spend the rest of their lives milking the same schtick ad infinitum. Mick Jagger, I'm looking at you. Others, however, carry on pushing the creative envelope till the very end. Leonard Cohen, B. B. King and Johnny Cash fit that bill, but pop's patron saint of late-life innovators has to be David Bowie. He went on taking risks, testing new sounds and styles, tugging at the limits of his own understanding and talent, searching for fresh ways to probe the world and himself. Not everything he did was wonderful, but his creative light burned just as brightly as he was dying of cancer in his late 60s as it had when he was beguiling the world with alter egos such as Ziggy Stardust and the Thin White Duke in his 20s. His first musical, *Lazarus*, premiered just a month before his death in 2016. His final album, *Blackstar*, was a masterful swan song that mixed jazz, funk, electronica and art rock in new and surprising ways. One critic hailed it as 'the latest move in a boundlessly unpredictable career'. Mac, who is more than a decade older than Bowie was when he died, channels that same spirit. 'Even after all these years I'm still always after that one nugget, that new twist,' he says.

～

To carry on creating into later life you need to keep on learning – and here again science has more good news for us. Yes, the brain is at its most plastic in the first two decades of life. New connections form, and existing ones strengthen or weaken, more easily, which is why children soak up knowledge like sponges. But that does not mean we fall off a learning cliff at the age of 20 – or 40, 60 or 80. Quite the opposite. The chief obstacle to learning in later life is *not* the ageing brain; it is the ageist stereotypes that erode our confidence and put us off trying new things in the first place.

The old adage that 'you can't teach an old dog new tricks' is not even true of dogs. Vocabulary, general knowledge and expertise go on expanding into old age. What's more, in fields that are familiar to us we can pick up new tricks even faster in later life. In a survey by Buck Consultants, two-thirds of employers reported that older workers learn new tasks more quickly than do younger ones. And even if learning in unfamiliar domains takes us a little longer, we can still do it – often with greater discipline, self-reflection and analysis than we would muster in our youth. Just look at the roll call of people mastering new skills on the 'wrong side' of 30: Andrea Bocelli started singing opera at the age of 34 and Julia Child was nearly 40 when she learned to cook. Vera Wang reinvented herself as a fashion designer in her 40s. Marie Curie learned to swim in her 50s, Tolstoy to ride a bicycle in his 60s. Jens Skou, a Nobel laureate in chemistry, mastered computer programming in his 70s. When asked by a pupil at the age of 91 why he kept on practising, cellist Pablo Casals replied: 'Because I am making progress.'

One of my favourite examples of late-life learning is Mary Ho. In her early 60s, she decided to pursue her life-long dream of playing the guitar. Unable to read music, she practised chords and notes until her fingers bled. Eventually she mastered both the acoustic and electric guitar. Today, Ho is known as Grandma Mary in her native Singapore, where she plays charity gigs and has released an album of Latin music. Her videos have racked up more than a million views on YouTube. Dolled up in a bright red-and-turquoise dress, Ho shredded her electric guitar to raucous cheers at

Singapore's National Day Parade in 2017. She was 81 years old at the time.

Of course, not everyone in later life can – or would even want to – channel Jimi Hendrix on stage. But Ho's go-for-it spirit is a beacon for all of us. She is a reminder that learning is much more than just a tool for passing exams or landing a job in our younger years. If we are going to age boldly and make the most of the longevity revolution, learning must be a way of life at every age. Novelty keeps us healthy, engaged and fulfilled. Mastering new knowledge and skills is also the best way to remain useful in today's fast-changing workplace. 'Anyone who stops learning is old, whether 20 or 80,' said Henry Ford. 'Anyone who keeps learning stays young.'

Thankfully, the world is warming to lifelong learning. Singapore set a fine example in 2016 by giving every one of its citizens over the age of 25 the sum of S$500 to spend on training, mentoring, university study or online courses. The Web is now a vast educational smorgasbord where people of all ages take courses in everything from management and marketing to game design and data science. A third of all working college students in the US are now aged 30–54.

This is welcome progress, but deeper changes are needed. We need to rewrite the rules of the workplace to allow for learning sabbaticals throughout our careers. Universities must make it easier to dip into and out of the ivory tower at every stage of life. A revolution in childhood education is also long overdue: we need more schools where taking intellectual risks is the norm, failure is welcomed as a stepping stone to deeper understanding and learning is taught as a skill in itself. We also need to do much more to promote physical fitness.

~

A belief that keeping the body in shape is good for the mind goes back to the dawn of medicine. The phrase *mens sana in corpore sano* comes from Ancient Rome. Today, scientists hail working out as a 'miracle pill' not just for the body but also for the brain. As an article on the Harvard Medical School blog put it: 'Aerobic exercise is the key for your head, just as it is for your heart.'

That is why staying active is woven into the routines of so many creative people. Steve Jobs was an avid walker. Bowie stayed in shape by boxing. A keen sportsman in his youth, Mac takes a brisk walk round the park every day and regularly plays golf. Ho breaks sweat at a daily dance class.

No one is sure why exercising is so good for the brain. One theory is it delivers an energy-and-oxygen boost by increasing the flow of blood. Another is that it fires up the body's metabolism, which in turn fuels neural growth. What is clear from many studies is that regular aerobic exercise can help keep us cognitively fit. For example, working out has been shown to stimulate the growth of white and grey matter in the frontal and temporal lobes and plump up the hippocampus by creating new brain cells – just like studying for The Knowledge. 'It is very impressive how much the functioning of our brain is impacted by physical exercise,' says Ursula Staudinger, founding director of the Robert N. Butler Columbia Aging Center in New York.

How much exercise is needed to enjoy this cognitive dividend? Once again, you don't have to take up extreme sports or run marathons. Experts recommend about 45 minutes of moderate exercise – cycling, swimming, jogging or even just an energetic walk – at least three times a week seems to do the trick. That is not far off the recipe for keeping the body fit, which means you can kill two birds with one stone. And, though the younger you start the better, it is never too late to reap the rewards: even people who take up exercise in their 60s, 70s and 80s notice improvements in cognitive function after three months and lasting neural changes after six.

Exercise may even help with what might be the most worrying cognitive cloud hanging over the longevity revolution: dementia. Today, around 50 million people suffer from the condition, with that number expected to hit 75 million by 2030. Dementia is now the leading cause of death among women in England, Wales and Australia and may affect 70 per cent of people in the world's care homes. Not only is there no cure but we do not even know why it strikes in the first place. Nevertheless, the picture is not as apocalyptic as the headlines proclaim. While more likely to strike in later life, dementia is not – repeat, it is *not* – an inevitable part of ageing. Around 17 per cent of people over the age of 80 have it, but that means the other 83 per cent do not. What's more, the latest data suggests the average age at which dementia strikes is rising and the percentage of the population affected at every age is falling. Experts put this down to more of us following the best-guess advice on how to keep our brains in good working order: eating more healthily, smoking and drinking less, exercising body and mind. With money and manpower now pouring into the study of dementia, longitudinal studies already underway could yield personalised prevention and treatment plans within a decade. As director of the Centre for Dementia Prevention at the University of Edinburgh, Craig Ritchie is on the cutting edge of research into the disease. He believes we are on our way to figuring out how to prevent dementia through drugs and lifestyle changes. 'In 10 or 15 years we'll be able to say "this is your risk and you can do this, this and this to reduce it – or maybe even eliminate it altogether," he says. 'I'm hugely optimistic about the future.'

The race to defeat dementia might even help unlock the secrets of creativity. Some people find that coming down with the disease makes them much more creative. No one knows why this happens, but one theory is that shutting down certain parts of the brain causes others to flow and fire more freely. That is not, of course, a reason to try to get dementia, but it is a reminder that the brain is a remarkably pliable and resilient organ with plenty of creative juice.

If we treat that organ right, most of us can look forward to creating, innovating and learning throughout our longer lives. We could also spark a revolution in the workplace.

CHAPTER 4

WORK: OLD HANDS ON DECK

*Exert your talents, and distinguish
yourself, and don't think of retiring
from the world until the world will be
sorry that you retire.*

—SAMUEL JOHNSON

Velma Bascome could be a knitting granny from central casting. She is 70 years old. She is also an avid knitter. But that is where the stereotype runs out of road. Bascome is the star employee at WOOLN, a company that designs, makes and sells high-end knitwear in New York City. She knits hats, blankets and snoods in cashmere, merino and alpaca that sell for hundreds of dollars online.

When we meet in a café across the street from the company headquarters in Manhattan, Bascome is hard at work on a new herringbone blanket. Dressed in jeans and a blue-and-white-striped T-shirt, she looks like one of those edgy influencers on

Instagram. Even though it's a chilly January day, her bare feet are clad in sandals, a lifelong riposte to the strict sock policy at the religious school of her youth. An iPad loaded with designs, patterns and photos of her work rests on the table.

I settle into my chair to watch Bascome in action. Her small, nimble hands dance in a blur above the pink wool, chrome needles clicking like mahjong tiles. To master the stitch, she is working up a swatch to show her boss. After a few minutes of knitting, she stops and fixes the material with a beady stare, face frozen in concentration. She counts the stitches twice. 'I can see a few mistakes in this one but I can't figure out why the row is out,' she says. 'It'll come.'

Having grown up in a family of knitters, I know a master when I see one, and it turns out Bascome has real pedigree. She started out working for yarn companies in New York City in the 1970s and discovered an uncanny knack for writing knitting instructions for garments just by looking at them. 'I was like a musician writing down music by ear,' she says. She later earned a science degree at university and taught biology and physics in high school, but has always knitted and crocheted for fun. These days, when not teaching needlework classes at a local college, she knits her own designs, either on her bed at home or out and about in New York. 'It's never work to me because when I pick up needles I just relax,' she says. 'At home I have a pile of yarn and projects on one side of my bed so that I can knit, sleep and wake up with a solution to a problem. I knit 24/7 and I love it because it's so creative.' There it is again: creativity walking with us into later life.

When I ask Bascome about the pros and cons of ageing, she shrugs as if the question never crosses her mind. 'I've never worried about getting older and I've never lied about my age,' she says. 'If you're doing what makes you happy then age doesn't really mean much.'

Once the swatch is ready we take it across the street for inspection. The WOOLN headquarters is a long, whitewashed room piled high with balls of wool, design books, patterns, offcuts and garments awaiting dispatch. It doubles as the home and studio of Bascome's boss, Faustine Badrichani. A dozen or so of her paintings are leaned up against the walls, adding to the air of bohemian endeavour. The two women greet each other warmly and then get down to work.

Badrichani inspects the pink swatch, tugging gently at the material, holding it up to the light, pressing it against her cheek. 'Good, good, it's getting there,' she says, her tone firm, businesslike. Bascome promises to work out why the stitches are not scanning properly. 'Great, I know you will,' says Badrichani, smiling. 'You always do.'

After she leaves, Badrichani tells me that WOOLN stumbled on Bascome by accident. To give their firm a social purpose, she and her partner originally set out to hire knitters from low-income immigrant communities. When that plan foundered on a coral reef of paperwork, they turned to seniors. WOOLN makes a marketing virtue of the nine sixty- and seventy-somethings now on its payroll, dubbing them 'kick-ass grandmas', posting amusing profiles on its website and attaching a name tag signed by the knitter to every garment. Knowing their fashion pieces are the handiwork of older women plays well with the firm's young, hip customers. But WOOLN is not in the tokenism business. Its older knitters are just as skilled and creative as younger rivals. Stir in their experience and they can teach the thirty-something designers a trick or two. A little while ago, Bascome came up with a tidier way to finish off the edges of garments that is now being used across the company's range.

As I try on a sumptuous alpaca snood, I ask Badrichani what she has learned from the success of WOOLN. 'That's easy,' she says. 'If you can do the job then it doesn't really matter how old you are.'

That notion held sway in the past – and not just for knitters. Greek and Roman grunts were expected to quit the army at the age of 60 but examples of birthdays triggering automatic retirement are rare in the historical records. In the pre-modern world, age as a number counted for little in the workplace. What mattered was how well you did your job. Tanners, blacksmiths, servants, weavers, farmers, physicians, butchers, bakers and candlestick makers – everyone who had to work carried on doing so until death or dotage intervened. Experience was a prize asset. In 1393, Guillaume de Harcigny was summoned, at the age of 92, to help Charles VI of France recover from a coma induced by a bout of insanity. Between 1400 and 1600, the average age of a Venetian doge was 72.

How different things are now. The idea that younger is better at work took hold during the Industrial Revolution. The modern world, with its assembly lines and ever-changing technology, rewarded and exalted the speed and vigour of youth. By 1913, a US commentator detected rampant ageism in the workplace: 'In the search for increased efficiency ... gray hair has come to be recognised as an unforgivable witness of industrial imbecility, and experience, the invariable companion of advancing years, instead of being valued as common sense would require it to be, has become a handicap so great as to make the employment of its possessor, in the performance of tasks and duties for which his life work has fitted him, practically impossible.' By 1965, 60 per cent of US companies had a ban on hiring anyone over 45.

Today, even though most countries have officially outlawed it, age discrimination remains endemic in the workplace. Many employers still prefer to hire young – and find ways to do so without triggering lawsuits. In one US study, researchers applied for lower-skilled jobs with 40,000 fake CVs. The profiles were more or less identical apart from the ages, which ranged from late 20s to late 60s. Guess who got the most callbacks? The 29–31-year-olds received 19 per cent more than the 49–51-year-olds and 35 per cent more than the 64–66-year-olds. The same study found that older female applicants for sales jobs had a 36 per cent lower callback rate than younger rivals. For administrative work, the figure was 47 per cent. Other research has shown that each extra year of age cuts the chances for either sex of landing a job interview by 4–7 per cent.

Ageism is sometimes baked right into the software used to hunt for jobs online. Investigators at the office of the Attorney General of Illinois recently found employment websites with drop-down menus where the dates for attending school or university did not go back far enough to admit anyone over the age of 70, 60 or even, in some cases, 50. An investigation by ProPublica and the *New York Times* revealed that many leading companies use Facebook and Google to make sure their help-wanted ads are only seen by younger candidates.

Even when older applicants do get a foot in the door they often receive a euphemistic brush-off. They are deemed 'overqualified', or 'too big for this role', or told they have 'too much experience' or 'will get bored quickly'. All of which are code for 'we want someone younger than you'.

Ageing on the job can also be pretty disheartening. Companies use a range of tricks to nudge mature staff towards the exit ramp, from withholding promotions to shunting them into less appealing work. One European study found that older employees are more likely to be isolated and excluded from team projects, and less likely to be given training, put into contact with technology or invited to tackle novel problems. Even those showing zero sign of flagging can feel the noose of ageism tightening round their neck. Mac spent more than 30 years working for the *Daily Mail* on a contract that could only be annulled if one or other party gave three years' notice. On his 65th birthday, the newspaper slashed that period to six weeks. 'In case you lose your marbles, they told me,' he says, wryly. Perhaps Mac was lucky to be offered a contract at all, given that a study commissioned by the UK government identified an unspoken consensus in the British corporate world that men cease to be worthy of career progression in their mid-50s, women a decade earlier.

This is folly on an epic scale. Putting people out to pasture based on their birthdate makes no sense at all – and not just because we are staying fit and healthy longer than ever before. The world has changed. Ageism made sense during the Industrial Revolution because factory work was harder to perform with an older body. In the modern workplace, however, brawn counts for less and less. What matters is cognitive horsepower – and the human brain can carry on delivering that deep into later life.

We have already seen that learning and creativity can hold firm, or even improve, as we age. Unless we fall ill, the same is true for the rest of our cognitive palette. Call it wisdom, call it higher-order reasoning, call it whatever you like – older adults tend to be better at seeing the big picture, embracing compromise, weighing multiple points of view and accepting that knowledge can only take you so far. When tackling problems in a familiar field, older brains are quicker to spot the patterns and details that open the door to finding a solution. When companies set up suggestion boxes, older staff usually generate more and better ideas than do their younger colleagues – and the best proposals tend to come from the over-55s. After sifting through piles of studies, researchers at Harvard University concluded that four key skills do not ripen fully until around the age of 50: arithmetic, vocabulary, general knowledge and a grasp of how the world works.

There is more good news. Research shows that ageing tends to enhance our emotional intelligence. We get better at reading people. We pick up more information about them – background, temperament, desires, ulterior motives – on the first meeting. Our richer vocabulary helps us speak, write and communicate better and our capacity to co-operate and negotiate improves. We also get better at putting ourselves in other people's shoes, finding compromises and resolving conflicts. Studies have shown that when various generations are asked to reply to letters sent to professional agony aunts, older respondents, especially the over-60s, tend to come up with the best advice. Other research suggests that ageing even makes our sense of humour more agreeable: we come to prefer jokes that unite people rather than those made at the expense of others. It also makes us less prone to wild swings of emotion and better able to cope with negative feelings such as anger, fear and envy. In other words, we find it easier to keep our heads while all about us are losing theirs.

That is why bus companies in Bangkok are now encouraging drivers to carry on working past the traditional retirement age of 60. Thailand's capital is an urban Thunderdome, a seething cage fight of scooters and motorcycles, backfiring jalopies, SUVs with tinted windows, antediluvian trucks and buses, bicycles, taxis, jaywalking pedestrians and tuk tuks. Speed limits and other traffic laws are flouted with impunity. On my first evening here, a bus ploughs into a food cart in Chinatown, sending woks, dumplings and boiling water crashing onto the street. A waitress at a nearby stall simply shrugs and says: 'Occupational hazard.'

The next morning, I hop on a bus a few streets away. It is one of those hot, humid days when patience and goodwill are in short supply. Wichai Boontum is at the wheel. He is 56 years old with salt-and-pepper hair, watchful eyes and a genial manner. Driving the same route for 36 years has given him a front-row seat on his passengers' lives: he has watched them grow up, fall in love, start careers, go bankrupt, have children, die. One boy with a penchant for falling asleep on the back seat is now a successful schoolteacher. At New Year, Boontum's passengers give him calendars and sweets as gifts.

As we sit waiting at a red light, the bus snorting and shuddering like a colicky dragon, I ask how his driving has evolved over the years. 'Oh, I'm much, much better now I'm older,' he says. 'My reflexes are still good, and I can handle the bus the same as always, but I'm a lot more calm and careful which is just what you need to survive in Bangkok.'

Boontum is not alone. Many of us will eventually reach a point where our vision, reflexes, strength and ability to judge speed have deteriorated so much that we become a menace on the road. That is where the stereotype of the doddery driver comes from. 'You should never drive drunk or while using a mobile phone,' goes one joke doing the rounds in Bangkok. 'It's almost as dangerous as driving sober over the age of 60.' But the stereotype is misleading and the joke is wrong. As with so many other skills in life, most of us can go on driving well past our 60th birthday because we find ways to compensate for the things that ageing takes away from us. Behind the wheel, we become more cautious, which, while irksome to more impatient road users, makes us safer: British police records show that drivers aged under 25 are twice as likely to kill a pedestrian than are those over 70. The man who drove his bus into that Chinese food cart in Bangkok was in his 20s. Boontum has not been involved in an accident for more than a decade.

Not long into our journey, he brings us to a halt at a busy junction. Continuing on his route will mean crossing three lanes of oncoming traffic. In Bangkok, such moments are often a prelude to screaming horns, screeching brakes, rude gestures and collisions. When a small gap opens in the traffic, Boontum shakes his head and says: 'One of the younger guys would probably push out and take the risk now, but not me.' Instead, he waits, right foot hovering patiently over the accelerator pedal. When another space opens in the traffic, I find myself willing him to step on it, thinking: 'Come on, you can make this!' But Boontum holds his ground. Eventually, when a sizeable gap opens up, he hits the gas and serenely crosses the three lanes. A few blocks later, when a taxi cuts him off, Boontum chuckles and gives the offender an ironic wave. 'Taxis are the worst,' he says. The same sangfroid that keeps him out of traffic scrapes also comes in handy when managing irate passengers. The other day he defused a lovers' quarrel that was threatening to turn violent. 'As I've got older I've become a lot better at dealing with people,' he says. 'Because I control my own emotions more in the heat of the moment I can keep the peace better.'

As we trundle down a main boulevard at the official speed limit, with other buses hurtling past us, I look back at Boontum's passengers to gauge their mood. Are they frustrated by the longueurs and stately pace? Or relieved not to be on a white-knuckle ride? They seem content, glancing at their phones or gazing out the window. Boontum reads my mind and supplies his own answer. 'Everyone in this city is in a hurry,' he says. 'But no one wants to die because of reckless driving.'

Boontum's lengthening career as a bus driver in Bangkok should give comfort to us all. The patience, calm and empathy that have come to him in later life are an asset in any job. Indeed, studies show that productivity improves with age in work that relies on social skills. When researchers compared the performance of staff at a Days Inn call centre they found the older ones spent longer speaking to customers on the phone. They might comment on the weather, ask about children making noise in the background or listen to vacation plans without interrupting. A waste of company time, right? Wrong. The older agents booked more reservations and brought in more revenue – thanks, the researchers suggested, to their patience and sociability.

This makes perfect sense to Barbara Jones, a consultant based in Prescott, Arizona. From her home office, she sells and services life, health and property insurance for an agency in New York. To close a deal on the phone or via email she has to listen, read between the lines, feign interest in things that bore her, establish a rapport and always use just the right tone and language. At 69, she does all of the above better than ever. 'I've always had an intuitive sense about people, but that has absolutely gotten better as I've gotten older,' she says.

Jones puts her finely tuned social antennae down to two things. First, years of practice. Second, the natural slowing-down that comes with ageing has curbed the Type-A impatience of her younger self. 'I used to be quicker to judge people and write them off,' she says. 'Now I'm more likely to explore in any conversation the real motivation for a person's actions or thinking. Instead of presuming to know what the client needs or wants, I am actively listening and repeating my understanding of what they are asking or requesting. When you take the time one on one with a client you get the sale as well as their continued trust and loyalty.'

Not long ago Jones scored a workplace win that should lift the spirits of older people everywhere. It started when the agency assigned her the client from hell. 'He wanted information but he wasn't listening to what I was telling him and he kept sending me short, abrupt emails demanding this and that,' she says. 'He was always in a hurry and on to the next thing before I could get a word in edgewise.' Jones, like Boontum, kept her cool. After taking the time to think things over, she composed an email that clearly and concisely addressed all the client's queries and misgivings. She used paragraphs and full sentences, chose her words very carefully and adopted a gentle, conciliatory tone. It worked: the client signed on the dotted line and the agency held up her email as a model for all its customer service agents.

The world is crying out for people people. Collaboration, teamwork, cross-cultural exchange, negotiation, persuasion and networking are the lifeblood of the modern workplace. Since 1980, sectors of the economy that put a premium on social skills have generated more jobs and higher wages. This trend looks likely to continue, or even accelerate, as work involving less human interaction is picked off by automation and artificial intelligence. What this means is that the world is changing in ways that favour the social smarts that come with ageing and that the longevity revolution can be a blessing rather than a burden.

Another ageist myth in need of retiring is that work ethic flags with age and that only the young are 'hungry'. When Towers Perrin, a professional services firm, surveyed 35,000 employees at midsize and large US companies, it found those aged over 50 more motivated to 'exceed expectations' than their younger colleagues. L. L. Bean, a clothing retailer, relies heavily on older workers for two reasons. One: their social acumen helps keep up the company's golden reputation for customer service. Two: their strong work ethic is a model for younger staff.

When doing work with real meaning, older people show particularly strong initiative. Mac still has the eye of the tiger. On top of his cartoon work, he is putting the finishing touches on a children's book and hatching other publishing plans for the future. 'Even though I'm 81 I still have a lot of unfulfilled ambition I'm very keen to achieve,' he says. Rather than make him yearn for piña coladas by the pool, the sight of younger cartoonists snapping at his heels spurs him to dig deeper. 'I still want to compete with them,' he says, grinning broadly. 'Every single day I go into the office I always try to do the very best I can do.' In a world where people change jobs at the drop of a hat, older workers can also represent a smart long-term investment because they are less likely to jump ship than are younger ones. Mac has been drawing cartoons at the *Mail* since 1971.

~

Now it's time to address the elephant in the room. What does the loss of processing speed that comes with ageing mean in the workplace? Is it the kiss of death? The answer is No. True, older brains take longer to retrieve certain memories, absorb information and solve maths-based problems. But while this leads to lower scores in laboratory tests, the harm done in the real world is negligible. That is because despite the macho, faster-than-thou rhetoric that suffuses many workplaces, speed isn't everything in most jobs: being right is often better than being first. By the same token, most work tasks involve multiple forms of cognition, which means the older brain can fall back on its strengths – such as greater accuracy – to make up for the speed deficit.

When given air-traffic commands in a laboratory setting, younger pilots remember them better than older ones. But in a real cockpit the old hands put those orders into action more effectively. How? By recording them with a pen and pad – and then tapping their flying experience. When economists at the Max Planck Institute for Social Law and Social Policy studied the performance of 3,800 workers over a four-year period on a Mercedes-Benz assembly line, they found that older workers kept pace with their younger colleagues by committing fewer severe errors. In a similar survey of typists aged 19–72, researchers found the older ones had slower typing speeds but still finished assignments as quickly as their younger peers. Like a veteran athlete stealing a march on younger, fleeter players by reading the angles and patterns of the game, the more seasoned typists looked further ahead in the text and thus typed more smoothly and made fewer mistakes. As that old military adage goes: Slow is smooth and smooth is fast. 'The human brain is pretty ingenious at compensating for the changes that come with ageing,' says Ursula Staudinger, founding director of the Robert N. Butler Columbia Aging Center in New York. 'And that means we can keep up our cognitive performance well into later life.'

Some even enjoy a speed boost in their twilight years. Judith Kerr is the writer and illustrator of one of my favourite children's books, *The Tiger Who Came to Tea*. I must have read it a thousand times to my children and it never lost its charm or sparkle. Now in her mid-90s Kerr is working on her 34th book. A stiff hip makes walking harder but she finds herself no less quick on her cognitive feet. 'They say you slow down as you get older, but it seems to be the opposite with me. I am getting faster,' she says. 'I also think I am getting better at it.'

When I mention this to Bascome, she nods in agreement. 'I'm a better knitter now because I know a lot more about knitting,' she says. 'I've always been fast enough to be ahead of deadlines, but now I'm even faster.'

Even in the casinos of Las Vegas, where quick wits can mean the difference between living large and losing your shirt, older brains are thriving. In 2017, John Hesp, a 64-year-old caravan salesman from England, came here to play in the world's most prestigious poker tournament, which is traditionally dominated by young players. He beat thousands of rivals, including professionals, to take fourth place and $2.6m in prize money.

By the same token, the city's casinos are home to legions of silver-haired dealers and croupiers. Aged 51, Michael

Barlow has spent 16 years working the craps tables at one of the leading resorts on the Strip. When I come across him, he is in the middle of overseeing a game. Eight gamblers are clustered round the table, smoking, cradling drinks and hollering encouragement to the young woman hurling the dice. Classic rock pounds away in the background. Each time the dice come to rest, Barlow calculates all the bets on the table, gathers up the losing chips and pays out to the winners. He also has to socialise with the players and make sure no one is cheating by moving chips after the dice have rolled. 'In craps there are a lot of things going on at once and you have to be sharp at all times,' he says.

The good news for Barlow – and the rest of us – is that experience delivers a performance boost. As long as we do not stray too far from our area of expertise, we get better both at spotting shortcuts and at picking up new tricks. After a decade and a half at the craps table, Barlow can process many bets instantly because he has seen them before. His experience also makes it easier to break down unfamiliar bets. And it helps that he does his own version of cognitive burpees by keeping records of all the bets he sees at the craps table and poring over them in his spare time. With his ample belly he looks like he'd be the last person to reach the exit if the casino caught fire, but his brain remains quick off the mark. 'If anything I'm a little faster now with the calculations than I was when I was younger,' he says. 'As long as I stay healthy, I figure I can keep doing this job for at least another 20 years. The idea that you're over the hill at 40 or 50 is ridiculous.'

Study after study comes to the same conclusion about most jobs. Peter Cappelli is a professor of management at the Wharton School at the University of Pennsylvania and an expert in human resources. While researching his book, *Managing the Older Worker,* he hunted high and low for evidence that ageing eroded our workplace performance – and found none. 'I thought the picture might be more mixed, but it isn't,' he says. 'Every aspect of job performance gets better as we age.'

~

That may explain why older people are crushing it in the startup world. When I first heard the term 'seniorpreneurs', my reaction was to sneer. After all, pop culture tells us that entrepreneurship, like learning and creativity, is for the young, experience is overrated and older people are allergic to risk. But that has always been nonsense. Startups have never been the monopoly of Huel-fuelled teens and twenty-somethings. Jimmy Wales and Jan Koum were in their mid-30s when they founded Wikipedia and WhatsApp respectively. Forty-somethings created Intel, Zynga, Craigslist and Zipcar, and fifty-somethings launched both Coca-Cola and McDonald's. Harland Sanders founded KFC in his mid-60s.

The suspicion that ageing erodes our appetite for risk goes way back. In the fourth century, John Chrysostom, a theologian in the early Christian Church, observed: 'Old age makes us pusillanimous.' But does it really? Recent research paints a more mixed picture. Some neuroscientists think the fall in dopamine levels in the ageing brain makes us less likely to gamble in pursuit of big rewards. A Taiwanese study found older bosses more likely to shy away from bold, disruptive change. On the other hand, a French study found that ageing does *not* make us more risk-averse in either the workplace or in laboratory tests. Surveys conducted in 104 countries by the Global Entrepreneurship Monitor (GEM) suggest the age group most willing to risk starting a new business are the 65–80-year-olds. Still other research has found that tolerance for risk varies from person to person but remains constant as we age.

What is clear is that ageing does not automatically turn everyone into a chicken. Christopher Columbus was in his 50s when he set off on his final journey across the Atlantic. After the meltdown of the nuclear power plant at Fukushima in 2011, hundreds of elderly Japanese volunteered to do the hazardous clean-up work. Betty Bromage, who lives in a retirement home in Cheltenham, England, showed the same spirit when she took up wing-walking on airplanes in her late 80s. Asked by a reporter about the risk, she replied: 'Well, at 88 what does it matter?'

If anything, the young are less buccaneering than we often assume. When GEM polled 18–29-year-olds who had identified a business opportunity, two in five said the fear of failure would stop them from taking the next step and starting a company. Whether this is down to mounting student debt, the fallout from the last financial crisis, meagre retirement savings or overprotective parenting is unclear. What is clear is that older people are moving in to pick up the slack. According to the Kauffman Foundation, a think tank that specialises in education and entrepreneurship, the 40s are now the 'peak age for business formation' in the United States. In Britain, the over-50s are starting companies faster than any other age group. In Korea, firms such as Hyundai are setting up programmes to help older employees make the jump to entrepreneurship. Nor are later-life entrepreneurs just going through the motions. Everywhere, they are parlaying the advantages bestowed by age – expertise, social acumen, savings, emotional evenness, connections, experience, big-picture thinking, creative verve, problem-solving nous – into thriving startups. A study of all 2.7 million new businesses launched in the United States between 2007 and 2014 reached a conclusion that should raise the spirits of everyone on the 'wrong' side of 40: 'We find no evidence to suggest that founders in their 20s are especially likely to succeed,' wrote the authors. 'Rather, all evidence points to founders being especially successful when starting businesses in middle age or beyond.' In Australia, older founders are racking up more than double the profits of their younger rivals.

One example is Jenny Holten. In 2017, at the age of 69, she shuffled onto the Australian version of *Shark Tank*, looking for a hefty investment in her bakery firm. The sharks saw an older woman with a sweet smile and a mild manner and decided she must be deluded – until they learned that her gluten-free breads retail for more than seven times their cost price. Holden walked out of the studio with an investment of A$350,000 in return for a 25 per cent stake in her company.

Even in the youth-worshipping tech world, more and more people are thumbing their noses at the idea of being 'finished at 40'. Consider Yosi Glick. While working as a software engineer for an Israeli company that built online television guides, he grew frustrated with the bluntness of video search engines. Type in a keyword like 'alien' and every movie or TV show with 'alien' in the title popped up – end of story. Glick dreamed of building a more nuanced search engine that would consider the style, mood, tone, plot and structure of the content. In other words, you would type in 'sexy action historical' or 'like *Big Bang Theory*' and be served up titles matching those descriptions.

Like many an entrepreneur with a bee in his bonnet, Glick quit his job and spent a year refining his idea and assembling a team to build the technology to bring it to life. It was a punishing slog. Everyone worked long hours and money was excruciatingly tight. Almost every week Glick flew halfway round the world in economy class to meet potential investors and partners. Eventually, though, the toil paid off. In 2011, Glick unveiled Jinni, the world's first 'taste-based search engine', which is now used by content kings ranging from Comcast and Xbox to Telus and Telefónica.

When he had his eureka moment, Glick was a long way from the startup stereotype. Rather than a twenty-something in flip-flops, he was a paunchy 49-year-old with a family of five and a fondness for dark suits. Nor did he stack the Jinni team with young guns: no employee was under 30 and the chief scientist was in his 50s. 'We were a company of old, fat people,' laughs Glick. Now 59, he is feeling the itch to dive back into the startup pool – and age is the last thing on his mind. His advice to anyone disheartened by the Zuckerberg

Doctrine: 'Being older is not a barrier to being a successful entrepreneur.'

When I ask Glick what gave him the edge against younger startup rivals, he answers with a single word: experience. All those years working for a firm that built TV guides taught him the ins and outs of his industry. He knew how video-content databases worked, their strengths and weaknesses, how earlier attempts to improve them had fared. He had the contacts and the confidence that come from knowing your stuff. 'It's not enough to wake up one morning and say, "I want to start a company,"' he says. 'I couldn't set up a company for fishing boats because I've never set foot in a fishing boat.'

Does that mean age is an advantage? I ask.

'Definitely,' says Glick. 'My theory is that there are some business problems you cannot solve unless you have the deep knowledge and experience of a domain expert – and you're more likely to have that if you are older and wiser.'

Experience never gets old. In a crisis, it is often the difference between making the right split-second decision and the wrong one. In 2009, a US Airways plane flew into a flock of Canada geese shortly after taking off from LaGuardia airport outside New York City. The collision killed both engines. With no airport within range for an emergency landing, the crew set the plane down on the Hudson River in what officials later called 'the most successful ditching in aviation history'. The pilot, Chesley Burnett Sullenberger III, was not a top gun fresh out of aviation school: he was 58 years old. In the words of the final report, the so-called 'Miracle on the Hudson' was a 'testament to experience'. Six years later, Japan raised the maximum legal age for flying commercial airlines to 67.

∽

Extending the retirement age is obviously good for people who wish or need to work longer, but what about everyone else? Is the longevity revolution bad news for younger job-seekers? Thankfully, not. The conventional wisdom that older workers steal jobs from the young is wrong. Employment is not a zero-sum game because the economy does not have a fixed number of jobs. When people – whatever their age – work, they spend their earnings and thereby create work for others. That pitching event in Shoreditch is just one example of how the growing pool of older consumers is fuelling innovation in technology, products and services. Indeed, the OECD has shown that countries where older people work more also have higher numbers of young people in jobs.

Most of us will have to work longer than our parents or grandparents did, but how much longer is not clear. Why? Because there are so many variables, including how our health, productivity and savings culture evolve. But the best current guesses are not as alarming as you might think. As part of the National Transfer Accounts project, economists in over 50 countries are trying to predict the impact of the ageing population on public finances. One forecast is that developed countries could cover the costs of the longevity revolution by putting off retirement by two to two and a half years each decade until 2050. Given that the average

65-year-old in the rich world can now expect to live into her mid-80s, that is hardly a recipe for soldiering on like Stakhanovites until our last breath.

To make working longer as painless as possible, the workplace must become more welcoming to people in later life – and that is starting to happen. Forward-thinking companies are trying to make recruitment less ageist. Some are using algorithms that filter out biases; others are interviewing job candidates over the phone instead of face to face. Credit Suisse, Morgan Stanley, JPMorgan Chase, Goldman Sachs and other financial companies have set up retraining or internship programmes for people with more than a few miles on the career clock. Barclays has opened up its apprenticeship schemes to over-50s, arguing that older interns have the life experience and social chops to make fine loan officers. The bank has also joined other leading British companies, including Co-op and Boots, in signing a government-backed pledge to publish age data on their workforces and boost the number of over-50s on the payroll by 12 per cent by 2022.

As the tide starts to turn in favour of older workers, employers everywhere are coming up with inventive ways to make work more appealing in later life. Banks such as Santander, Heritage and Westpac now allow employees to take leaves of absence to care for grandchildren or elderly relatives. In the United States, CVS runs a 'snowbird program' that lets older staff from colder states in the north spend the winter months working at branches in warmer states in the south. The Marriott hotel chain encourages older employees to do shifts in roles that are less physically demanding: to cut down on heavy lifting, for instance, an engineer might spend one day a week working in the back office. Atlantic Health Systems, which is based in Morristown, New Jersey, runs an alumni club that allows retirees to return to the fold for up to 1,000 hours a year. In Japan, a growing number of companies, including the country's largest home builder, Daiwa House Industry, are raising or even abolishing their mandatory retirement ages. 'We think that it's our corporate responsibility to consider our employees' life planning in the future,' says Yoshio Saeki, Daiwa's general manager of human resources. 'We are trying to increase the options for workers.'

New ways of working that align with the strengths and aspirations of older people are also emerging. The gig economy, for example, offers precisely what many of us are looking for in later life: flexible, part-time work where career progression is not a priority and where money can be made by sweating an asset like a car or a home. A quarter of Uber drivers are now over 50 and the fastest-growing age group for hosts on Airbnb is the over-60s. One in four Americans who claim to work in the 'sharing economy' is aged over 55. Clearly, many gig workers take home too small a share of the pie, but if we can make the split fairer, gigging could be a real boon for people of all ages.

Another welcome shift is the rise of 'pretiring'. A decade ago, while running her own insurance brokerage in the US, Sharon Emek noticed a brain drain. Fewer young people were entering her industry, preferring instead to seek their fortunes on Wall Street or in Silicon Valley. At the same time, rigid working practices were driving many employees to retire earlier than they wished, taking their expertise, experience and élan with them. Emek's solution: make it easy for staff over 50 to go freelance and work remotely.

To that end, she launched Work At Home Vintage Experts (WAHVE) in 2010. Today, insurance companies can choose from her roster of 1,800 consultants with over 25 years of experience in fields ranging from policy rating to underwriting to claims adjusting. Everyone wins. The WAHVErs bid farewell to commuting and office politics and can work from anywhere – home, the beach, a bench in the park. They can put in a 50-hour week or just log a few hours here and there. Though welcome at any age, such flexibility is especially appealing to those who find their centre of gravity shifting away from work in later life. Many combine WAHVEing with caring for a loved one, moving to a warmer climate or devoting more time to their own projects.

Companies like hiring WAHVErs because they need little or no training. As freelancers they put a smaller dent in the payroll but are as productive and efficient as their younger, office-bound colleagues – sometimes more so. WAHVErs also have a knack for coming up with innovative solutions. 'They are more creative in solving problems because they have so much more knowledge and experience to draw on,' says Emek, who is 71. 'They also have amazing contacts and feel comfortable calling them up for information or to talk round a problem.' WAHVE recently expanded beyond insurance to add over-50s from the accounting industry to its roster of consultants.

Rather than moving older staff off site, other companies

are retooling the workplace to make it more congenial for them. BMW is a stand-out example. In 2007, the German carmaker set out to make one assembly line ageing-friendly at its flagship factory in Dingolfing. The result was 70 tweaks to the workstations. BMW introduced ergonomic chairs to allow some tasks to be performed sitting down; tables that adjust vertically to match each worker's height and thus guard against back strain; wooden flooring and weight-adapted footwear to protect joints; and flexible magnifying lenses to help those with weaker eyesight handle small parts. The company also altered working practices, with staff rotating across workstations to avoid burnout and taking part in regular exercise sessions to keep up the strength and flexibility that so often decline with age.

At first, the experiment provoked scorn from the plant's younger workers, who joked about the 'pensioners' line'. But BMW did exactly what you have to do to overcome ageism in the workplace: it ploughed on, and eventually won over the sceptics by delivering results. Within three months, the ageing-friendly workstations hit the quality target of 10 defects per million. Later, that figure fell to zero. Absenteeism for health reasons dipped below the plant average and productivity shot up. Even the young sceptics wanted to work on the new line and BMW went on to make similar changes in its plants in Germany, Austria and the USA.

～

Much more still needs to be done to make the working world a better place to age in. We need to revamp labour laws, pension rules and social welfare systems – all of which are currently based on full retirement in our 60s. Thanks to changes in compensation and benefit packages, the difference in the cost of hiring older and younger workers is narrowing, but that has to go much further. A good start would be abolishing age-related perks such as seniority-based pay and promotion, so that people are rewarded for the work they do rather than for how long they've been doing it. To make it easier to change jobs at any age we need to make lifelong learning the norm. Employers must learn to be more sympathetic to workers going through the menopause or suffering from the chronic diseases that are more prevalent in later life.

We also need to free ourselves from the straitjacket of working five days per week. Carlos Slim, a Mexican telecoms billionaire, and Richard Branson, the founder of Virgin, have both called for a three-day working week in later life to allow people to transition more gradually into full retirement. This makes sense, but why restrict it to later life? Why not follow the example set by Iceland and make part-time work easier at every age?

Indeed, with some experts predicting that automation could take over nearly a third of all labour by 2030, the time is ripe for a root-and-branch rethink of the place of work in our lives. Beyond putting food on the table and keeping a roof over our heads, work has much to recommend it at any age. Studies have shown that doing a job that delivers the right amount of stress and stimulation boosts health and well-being. Being laid off after the age of 58 can knock three years off your life expectancy. Freud put work up there with love as a pillar of mental health. Many people, including me, derive immense pleasure and meaning from their work. 'I can't get old; I'm working,' said George Burns, a comedian who performed into his late 90s. 'I was old when I was twenty-one and out of work. As long as you're working, you stay young.'

If only it were that simple. Not all jobs are created equal. Many are a lot less fulfilling than cracking jokes or writing books. When was the last time you heard someone rave about working in an Amazon fulfilment centre? Many jobs are simply too taxing to perform in later life, which is why you don't find many George Burnses in the ditch-digging world.

In a broader sense, however, work is now failing us. For a start it is poorly distributed: some have too much, others too little, and the same person can be overworked one day and underworked the next. Even those who love what they do often find their jobs onerous. Modern work culture is making many of us sick and unhappy with its long hours, stress, insecurity, technological distraction and endless sitting.

The most damning indictment of modern work, however, is that it no longer delivers on its basic promise to put enough money in our pockets. Productivity growth is sputtering across the developed world, despite herculean efforts to squeeze more and more output from workers, and, in many countries, average wages have flatlined. Nearly two-thirds of children living below the poverty line in the United Kingdom belong to working households. Work is no longer the engine of social mobility it once was. Everywhere, graduates are struggling to find jobs worthy of their degrees and millions of young adults are living at home with their parents, or putting off starting families, because the only work they can find pays too little to strike out on their own. According to Benjamin Hunnicutt, professor of leisure studies at the University of Iowa, young Americans are losing faith in work altogether: 'They are not looking to their job for satisfaction or social advancement.'

That is not a problem on the island of Okinawa, a Blue Zone off the eastern coast of Japan. There, the locals have no word for 'retire' because they do not suddenly go from productive to unproductive, from maker to taker, in later life. Instead, they are animated throughout their lives by what they call *ikigai*, a Japanese concept that translates roughly as 'a reason to get up in the morning'. This raison d'être can be anything – work, art, family – and can change at different stages of life.

We should take a leaf from the Okinawan book by encouraging everyone to find their own *ikigai*. How? By giving us all the freedom to blend working, volunteering, learning, resting, childrearing, having fun, creating, mentoring and caregiving in the way that suits us best at every age. Imagine how that would transform lives. How it would ease the pressure to nail down a career or spouse before the first wrinkle or grey hair appears. How it would unleash the potential in every generation.

Above all, how it would completely change our image of ageing.

CHAPTER 5

IMAGE: AGEING GETS A MAKEOVER

Whoever controls the media, the
images, controls the culture.
—ALLEN GINSBERG

Let me walk you through a candid-camera prank that went viral across the Arab world.

A frail, elderly woman dressed in a floral housecoat shuffles into a pharmacy in Beirut, the capital city of Lebanon. She approaches the counter at the back and asks for Viagra. The pharmacist, who is in on the prank, looks at her with feigned disbelief. 'Viagra?' he says.

'Yes, Viagra,' says the woman, with the matter-of-fact tone of someone ordering a tube of toothpaste.

'Who is it for?' asks the pharmacist.

'For my man,' says the woman. 'He is older than I am.'

The pharmacist looks amused, and slightly alarmed. He asks if her lover has health problems or takes other medication, and the woman replies: 'No, he is a Tarzan.'

She wants the most powerful dose of Viagra and asks if her beau can take four of the little blue pills at the same time. 'Of course not. Do you want to kill him?' exclaims the pharmacist.

Her deadpan reply: 'No, I don't want to kill him: he's still good in bed.'

Watching the clip, even with no knowledge of Arabic, you can see why it racked up millions of views on social media in Lebanon and beyond. The reactions of the real customers in the pharmacy are comedy gold. They squirm, they smirk, they giggle and guffaw. They exchange looks of disbelief, disapproval, disgust. One squeezes his eyes tightly shut as if trying to erase from his mind the image of octogenarians indulging in chemically enhanced sex. Another crosses herself and mutters, 'May God help us all.' When the elderly woman asks a young man if Viagra really is all it's cracked up to be, he dissolves into laughter. 'How would I know,' he says. 'I'm 20 years old!'

The clip comes from a hit Lebanese TV show called *Ich Ktir*, or *Live Long*. Its premise is simple: secretly film seventy- and eighty-somethings carrying out pranks that play with age stereotypes. The 30 episodes screened since the launch in 2016 have included elderly people buying pregnancy tests, shopping for high-end laptops and posing as shaky-handed medics charged with taking blood samples from terrified patients. One featured an old couple inspecting lingerie in a park. Revolutionary stuff in a country where cosmetic surgery is de rigueur and fresh, young faces dominate television.

The producer of *Live Long* is May Nassour, a 43-year-old

Lebanese with a penchant for mirrored sunglasses and high heels. When we meet up over minted lemonade at a café in Beirut, she tells me the show has a dual purpose: to make people laugh and to torpedo the stigma against ageing. 'When you are older, people think you have no more role in the society – you are inefficient, you have nothing to say or contribute, you are boring and miserable and unattractive – and that is so unfair because it is not true,' she says. 'For the first time on Lebanese TV we showed people in their 70s and 80s being funny and playing pranks and in situations where they have power over other people – and that changes perceptions.'

Change is just what the doctor ordered. Ageing has a serious image problem, and not just in Lebanon. In our youth-obsessed world, to grow older is to vanish. Unlined faces and young bodies monopolise the visual landscape, from advertising and social media to movies and television. To make matters worse, when older people do get some airtime they are often rendered as boring clichés. Complex, nuanced characters in later life, especially female ones, have seldom been a staple of Hollywood movies. Now in her early 60s, Juliet Stevenson, an English actress with a rich body of work behind her, sees the road ahead narrowing: 'As you go through life it gets more and more interesting and complicated, but the parts offered get more and more simple, and less complicated.' In 2016, when Getty Images, a leading stock photo agency, used web-crawling technology to explore images of older people online, it found them routinely depicted as more alone, less happy and more sedentary.

Or else engaged in stereotypical activities such as knitting, cuddling a grandchild or sipping tea in bed. Rebecca Swift, Director of Creative Insight at Getty, was chastened by the findings. 'It showed that we are just not visualising older people with the same richness and diversity that we use to visualise younger people,' she says. 'Instead of representing ageing in a genuine way we are reinforcing stereotypes.'

This matters to more than just image curators like Swift. What we see in movies and advertising, on television and online, shapes how we feel about ourselves and our place in the world. When older people are ignored, or dished up as caricatures, ageing becomes anathema to everyone. There is also a cramping effect on those already experiencing later life. If you routinely witness your generation reduced to narrow, unappetising stereotypes, your inclination to age boldly wanes. Bungee jumping, starting a new business, falling in love, backpacking round Asia, even just being happy – anything that fails to fit the Older Person Script feels like less of an option.

Ageist stereotypes can even curdle into self-fulfilling prophecy. It is well documented that exposure to racist and sexist assumptions causes ethnic minorities and women to perform less well in tests. Ageism has a similar effect. Studies have shown that encountering unflattering age stereotypes can cause older people to walk, talk and think more slowly. In an experiment at the School of Kinesiology and Health Science at York University, researcher Rachael Stone asked older test subjects to climb a flight of stairs. Later, she had them repeat the exercise after reading a fake article on how ageing erodes stair-climbing ability. On every measure, from speed to accuracy to balance, their performance worsened.

Something similar can happen with memory. The message coming at us from all sides is that later life is a bewildering blur of 'senior moments'. Result: as we age we frequently assume our memories are worse than they actually are. That leads to relying on aides-mémoire, such as a cookbook when making a favourite recipe or GPS when driving a familiar route. And that delivers a double whammy: First, it slows us down unnecessarily, reinforcing the myth that ageing is all about cognitive decline. Second, it can cause our memory to degrade through disuse.

Thankfully, though, the mind-over-matter effect can work in the other direction. The science shows that just believing we have slept well not only makes us feel more rested but also gives us a cognitive boost. Experts call this 'placebo sleep'. Something similar can happen with ageing. Studies show that those with a more upbeat image of growing older tend to look after themselves more. They perform better on memory and motor control tests. They can walk faster and stand a better chance of recovering from disability. They also live an average of seven and a half years longer. 'If we can get people to think about ageing in a much more positive way and not as this inevitable cascade of decline then we could start to see really impressive feats of function in older people that wouldn't be just exceptions to the rule but would just be, "Well, that's what older people do now,"' says Joe Baker, the kinesiologist we met earlier.

The point here is that we can, to some extent, think

ourselves into ageing better. This may even be true when it comes to warding off the most frightening illnesses. When researchers at Yale University studied people with a gene variant linked to dementia, they found that those with a favourable view of ageing were 50 per cent less likely to go on to develop the disease than those with a gloomy view. Becca Levy, a professor of epidemiology and psychology and the lead author in the study, held up the results as a call to action: 'This helps make the case for implementing a public health campaign against ageism.'

How can we give ageing an image overhaul? By sharing the visual landscape more evenly among the generations. By depicting later life in all its nuance, richness and variety. By shining the spotlight on those who are grabbing the longevity revolution with both hands and redefining what 'older' looks like. The good news is that all of the above are happening around the world.

$\sim$

Live Long has given ageing a better name in Lebanon. After two hit seasons, the cast are now so famous they struggle to prank the public without being recognised. 'People come up all the time wanting an autograph or a selfie,' says Nassour. 'Many fans tell them the show has changed how they feel about ageing.' To tap that shift, brands are scouring Lebanon in search of older models to feature in their advertising and Lebanese production companies are hunting for seniors to front TV shows in genres ranging from comedy to cooking.

The template they have in mind is the 86-year-old star of

the Viagra sketch. Her name was Jeanne d'Arc Zarazir, but everyone in Lebanon knew her simply as Jaco. She was a gifted prankster, keeping a straight face even as those around her surrendered to fits of laughter. Viewers saw her pose as everything from a rapper to an AK-47-wielding commando. Joie de vivre was her calling card and she had a knack for making later life seem enviable. When she died in 2017, news bulletins carried loving tributes and replayed her highlights from *Live Long*. One obituary described her as 'the funniest woman in Lebanon'.

By chance, I was the last person to interview Jaco before her death. When I arrived at her home in Beirut, she was frailer than she had been on *Live Long*. Her skin was almost transparent, her legs were riddled with sores and she was walking with a stick. But she still greeted me with the same smile – wry, mischievous, faux innocent, a tooth missing in the middle – that made her a TV star. It was a day of stultifying heat and her three cats were snoozing on the shady patio. We sat on an outdoor sofa and my first question elicited a bolt of coquettish wit. When I tried to confirm her age, she shot back: 'How old do you think I am?' Halfway through our chat, a doctor dropped by to check on those leg sores. As he counted them aloud – one, two, three – Jaco laughed softly and asked: 'Are you counting my scabs or my cats?'

Jaco found TV stardom in her 80s after an unremarkable life. Apart from a brief stint working as lady-in-waiting to the wife of a Lebanese president in the early '60s, she earned her keep by renting out the top floor of her house. No marriage, no children, no career. Yet the seeds of *Live Long* were always there: throughout her life, Jaco refused to be boxed in by age. 'I have never thought about whether I was young or old,' she told me. 'I have been content my whole life because I have just made the most of whatever age I was at the time.' That message resonated beyond the small screen. Throughout her brief TV career, fan mail poured in from across the Arab world. A young woman in Tripoli, a city in northern Lebanon, wrote: 'You have inspired me to stop worrying about my age. I am going to enjoy growing older now. Thank you!' When I asked Jaco, whose real name translates as Joan of Arc, if she was a role model, an ironic smile crept across her face. 'If I am, then it is only by accident,' she said. Either way, she clearly understood the toxic grip of ageism – and the power of shows like *Live Long* to loosen it. 'When you only ever see the young living life to the full then you suspect that growing older must be awful – and if you suspect growing older is awful then it will be awful,' she told me. 'We did a good thing by showing another way to age.'

Live Long is not alone in trying to present a bolder portrait of later life. Under Swift's stewardship, Getty Images is now leaning on photographers to file more images of older people doing things that go beyond the stereotypes of wise grandads and knitting grannies. She wants more stock shots of them using new technology, launching a company, exercising and playing sports, dancing and flirting, or even just laughing. She wants more images of middle-aged women doing more than motherhood. 'As a business we are starting to realise that we have a powerful voice and that we should be using it to represent the amazing diversity and possibilities of ageing,' says Swift. 'We want to have images with more colour, more dynamism and more activity to challenge the old stereotypes and give people the courage to age in their own way.'

Photographers hoping to fill that brief would do well to hang out with Paulina Braun. After a decade working on social and arts projects, the soft-spoken 34-year-old morphed into Poland's leading crusader against ageism. Like Nassour in Lebanon, she is on a mission to help both young and old make the most of our longer lives. 'I want to challenge the idea that ageing is a problem and that it means becoming useless and invisible,' she tells me. 'Showing older people doing things not normally associated with older people is a good way to do that.'

To see what that means I hop on a plane to Warsaw where Braun is throwing a party on the lakeshore at Wilanów Park. Towards the end of the evening, four Polish rappers put on a show that will later be described on social media as 'epic'. Clutching microphones close to their mouths, weaving among the small crowd with hip-hop swagger, they spit out lyrics like bullets. The fans, fuelled by beer and vodka shots, merge into a single, ecstatic monster, arms stabbing the air in unison, mouths firing lyrics right back at the performers. With rain pouring through the leaky roof, everyone is soaked and nobody cares.

If you're picturing a sea of youngsters, try again. The guy manning the decks is in his 80s and many of the revellers are sporting silver hair. At the very front, close enough to be hit by stray spittle from the rappers, three elderly women are swaying in time with the teens and twenty-somethings, laughing, punching the air, shouting rude words from the songs.

It is a surreal tableau that knocks me off balance. My first thought is a blast of weapons-grade ageism: What on earth are those oldsters doing in a sweaty mosh pit at their age? What if they have a fall and break a hip? My next thought puts things right: They're having fun like everyone else so why shouldn't they be here? I can easily picture Jaco in the middle of that madding crowd. When I recount this thought vector to Braun, she nods approvingly. 'That is exactly the kind of response I'm aiming for,' she says. 'You have the ageist reaction first and then you start to question it.'

Braun is always finding new ways to put older people in the public eye. She hosts intergenerational dance parties like the one at Wilanów Park everywhere from schools and hospices to nightclubs and town squares. She runs senior speed-dating events and an academy where older people learn to DJ. She also set up Poland's first casting agency for the over-60s. Everything she does is pushed out through social media and the traditional press. The morning after the Wilanów party one of the eighty-something women from the mosh pit appears on national television in a segment on the surprising things older people get up to in the summer. Thanks to Braun's casting agency, mature faces are popping up more frequently in Polish music videos, advertisements, films and YouTube clips – and they do so as characters rather than caricatures. In a recent commercial for Redd's beer, an eighty-something woman comes up with a cheeky ruse to jump a long queue at a beach bar: she pretends to faint, prompting everyone to rush to her rescue. The final scene shows her triumphantly sipping an ice-cold brew in a deckchair. You feel Jaco would approve. Another ad, shot like a beautiful piece of art-house cinema, shows an elderly couple outwitting the Grim Reaper with brushes and paints bought from Allegro, a leading Polish online retailer.

Braun's prizefighter is an 80-year-old bon vivant named Eryk Mroczek. He rides shotgun in her media interviews and attends all her dance parties, often sporting a pair of Jack Nicholson shades. Her casting agency recently landed him a plum role in a Polish film. Though he clearly loves the spotlight, he regards himself as a foot soldier in the war against ageism. 'Seeing me having fun can change the image people have of ageing,' he says. 'It can inspire them to make the most of their lives whatever age they are.'

Thanks to Braun, jobs once monopolised by youth are opening up to the not-so-young. A seventy-something graduate of her Senior DJ Academy is now a fixture on the Warsaw clubbing circuit. In my youth I would have run a mile from a DJ past pensioner age, but today's clubbers seem more open-minded – and not just in Poland. Ruth Flowers, a retired shopkeeper in England, learned how to spin records at the age of 68, dubbed herself DJ Mamy Rock and went on to play the biggest clubs and events in Europe, including the Glastonbury festival, before her death in 2014. Every week, Sumiko Iwamuro, aka DJ Sumirock, reigns over a trendy club in Tokyo's red-light district. She is 82.

The party at Wilanów Park has DJ Roman, a retired

electrical engineer in his 80s. When he spins the decks, the dance floor fills with people of all ages throwing shapes to 'Boys Boys Boys' and other classics from the 80s and 90s. The scene reminds me of the Roubaix velodrome, where it was hard to guess a cyclist's age on the track. What you notice first on the dance floor at one of Braun's bashes is people's clothes, their style, how they laugh and move, rather than their age, which makes a big impression on the younger party-goers. Beata, a 22-year-old student, came to Wilanów Park for the rappers but fell for the older crowd. 'I always think old means boring but the women here are so elegant and everyone is crazy and having fun,' she says. 'It makes me feel like "old" should not be such a dirty word.'

Even the performers are whistling the same tune. After the final encore, as the crowd – young, old, middle-aged – dissolves into the Warsaw night, I fall into conversation with one of the rappers. His stage name is Ero and tonight he is clad in the hip-hop uniform of beanie and baggy trousers. He is 36 years old.

Is it weird belting out foul-mouthed rap to a crowd studded with people who look like your grandparents? I ask. Does it send the wrong message to your fans? Does it kill the buzz?

He takes a drag from a bottle of beer and thinks for a moment. Then he shakes his head. 'Not at all, because age is a number that people care less and less about nowadays,' he says. 'You can be 18 or 80 – what really matters is what you bring to the party.'

$\sim$

One thing older people bring to the party nowadays is money. Having built up savings, and buoyed by solid pensions and surging property prices, many have cash to burn. Not all, of course: plenty are just scraping by or living in outright poverty. But as a cohort, this generation of over-50s is loaded. They make up a third of the UK population yet hold nearly 80 per cent of its wealth. By 2020, households headed by over-60s could be spending \$15 trillion worldwide. Even if the financial prospects for future generations seem less rosy, this moment in history is tailor-made for recasting ageing in a more favourable light. Why? Because money commands respect. It bestows power. Money talks.

And the world is listening. Wherever you look, pop culture is opening up more caricature-free space for older people. Singapore's National Day Parade now features a 'silver section' for performers over the age of 60. The video for Miley Cyrus's song 'Younger Now' looks like a party Braun might throw, with couples of all ages dancing up a storm. A television channel in the Netherlands is preparing to launch the world's first over-60s version of *The Voice*, the all-conquering sing-off show.

Cinema and television are also making more room for older characters who go beyond the cardigan-clad clichés of yesteryear. From Silver Screen in Europe to Legacy in the United States, festivals featuring films about all aspects of ageing are thriving. In 2018, the French movie *I Got Life* was hailed round the world as a breakthrough for portraying a woman in her 50s grappling boldly and amusingly with ageing, sexism and the menopause. That same year,

Girlfriends premiered on British television, with three sixty-something actresses playing the kind of juicy roles that Juliet Stevenson pines for. More actors are also landing action-hero roles later in life. Storm, Wolverine and Black Lightning were all played by forty-somethings; Tom Cruise is accepting impossible missions in his 50s; Liam Neeson is channelling his very particular set of skills in his 60s. Some action-film franchises are now built around older casts, with stars like Helen Mirren, Bruce Willis, Sylvester Stallone and Arnold Schwarzenegger duking it out with the bad guys in the various instalments of *Red* and *The Expendables*.

Over the last decade the average age of Oscar winners has risen across all acting categories. In 2018, the winning lead actor and actress, as well as those in supporting roles, were all aged between 49 and 60. Frances McDormand took the best actress gong for her gritty portrayal of a foul-mouthed, grieving mother in *Three Billboards Outside Ebbing, Missouri*. She described putting her un-Botoxed, 60-year-old face on the silver screen as a public service. 'I'm really interested in playing my age,' she said. 'I like being my age. I kind of have a political thing about it.' In the same Oscar season, Lesley Manville, then 61 and a losing nominee as best supporting actress for her role in *The Phantom Thread*, hailed a sea change in the pop-culture depiction of later life. 'You can have a lover at 60. You don't have to be shoved in a corner in a cardigan doing knitting,' she said. 'That's because film and television-makers realise that there is a huge audience of women who want to go to the cinema or turn on the telly and see stuff that doesn't alienate them, that embraces them, that isn't just about gorgeous twenty- or thirty-somethings, that represents their lives.'

To court that older dollar, brands must find new ways to address and portray ageing consumers. This is a big ask. Advertising and marketing are dominated by twenty- and thirty-somethings and many boardrooms remain wedded to the belief that the only market worth pursuing is the youth market. There is also a lingering suspicion – which studies have shown to be false – that older consumers are so stuck in their ways as to be impervious to advertising. According to the Boston Consulting Group, fewer than 15 per cent of companies have a specific business strategy for the over-60s. Nearly 70 per cent do not take rising longevity into account when planning sales and marketing.

The result is a whole lot of advertising that either ignores or patronises anyone over 40. Even campaigns aimed at older consumers are packed with younger models and actors. Many more cars are bought by the over-50s – remember those ageing suits – but when was the last time you saw anyone with grey hair in a car ad? Such ageism can backfire. Whenever I see a teenager modelling clothes clearly aimed at someone my age I feel a flash of annoyance. Crest discovered that nothing irks older consumers more than being pushed into a ghetto when its toothpaste for over-50s flopped. Bridgestone learned a similar lesson when it launched golf clubs aimed at pensioners.

Thankfully, though, brands are starting to wise up and move with the times. Amazon and Netflix now profile their customers based on taste rather than chronological age. A recent campaign by Kiehl's, an international skincare company, hit back at the notion of being defined by how old you are on paper. Its tagline was 'Act Any Age', and the video featured people across the generations dancing gleefully in front of purple balloons showing the age they feel.

Other brands are experimenting with age-blind advertising. A recent Virgin Holidays commercial features people of all ages charging into the ocean on a tropical beach. The 'Me. By me' campaign by clothing retailer TK Maxx shows shoppers of every generation trying on garments in sunny Cape Town.

Saga, Britain's best-known brand for the over-50s, has completely changed its tune. Long the butt of unflattering jokes about ageing, it relaunched its flagship magazine in 2017 with the slogan: 'We are not a brand for old people, we're a brand for people who are getting on with life after 50.' The ads for blended food and stairlifts were moved from the body of the magazine into a pull-out leaflet and replaced with more aspirational copy. The editorial tone is now more upbeat, with articles on exercise, travel, careers, shopping, romance and sex. The man behind the shift was Matt Atkinson, a trim fifty-something who competes in Ironman competitions and runs 60 miles a week. 'In the past we were reinforcing negative stereotypes about ageing,' he said at the time. 'Our aim now is to talk about ageing in a way that inspires our readers to think of themselves as bigger rather than smaller.'

Even beauty and fashion brands, which often seem genetically in hock to youth, are starting to embrace people from Planet Later Life. Many now use older women to hawk cosmetics, flooding the visual landscape with the lived-in faces of Charlotte Rampling, Helen Mirren, Twiggy, Jane Fonda, Ellen DeGeneres and Diane Keaton. Older models are also becoming a fixture in fashion catalogues and on catwalks. H&M, a global clothing giant, hired a 60-year-old woman to model its swimsuits. The face of Spanish chain Mango is also in her mid-60s. The star turn of 2017 London Fashion Week was a 72-year-old with a silver bob. Ten years her senior, writer Joan Didion has modelled for Céline. Nor is it just older women grabbing the spotlight. My favourite example of the trend for later-life models is a Chinese actor and performance artist called Deshun Wang. In 2015, at the age of 79, he broke the internet and was dubbed 'the world's hottest grandpa' when he strutted down the catwalk topless at Chinese Fashion Week. In his YouTube clips, he looks confident, sexy and like he's having the time of his life – everything I hope to be at 79.

As well as striking looks, these older models have something else in common: they are not pretending to be young. They are at ease with being and looking older, which means they can be role models both for their peers and for younger people seeking a reassuring vision of their own future selves.

~

When it comes to overhauling the image of ageing, social media is a godsend. The Web now bristles with depictions of later life conceived, curated and controlled by those who are actually in it. Mary, Josie and Teresa – aka the Golden Sisters – have racked up millions of views for the YouTube videos of them chatting amusingly about pop culture over lunch. Since parlaying her passion for raver clothes into online stardom at the age of 85, Helen Ruth Van Winkle has amassed more than three million followers on Instagram, fronted an ad for Smirnoff vodka and become the muse for makeup brand Urban Decay. In Asia, people are using social media to upend the traditional view that later life has to mean moving in with your children and devoting all your time to looking after the grandkids. Ms Q, a retired schoolteacher, backpacks round her native China in her 70s. 'Why do elderly Chinese people have to do housework, and look after their children and grandchildren?' she says. 'We should have our own lives.' As tech-savvy as any millennial, she chronicles her travels online and stays in touch with her family via video calls. A short film about her trip to Quanzhou, a city in southeastern China, drew more than 11 million views and helped spark a national debate about ageing. Many Chinese took to social media to hail Ms Q as a role model for later life. 'An independent, enchanting woman ... her age is not an issue,' wrote one. 'I hope I can be like her when I'm old,' said another.

In neighbouring Japan, Tsuyoshi and Tomi Seki, a sixty-something couple who go by the moniker Bon and Pon, are using Instagram to put a fresh spin on later life. More than 700,000 followers of all ages lap up quirky photographs of the pair wearing simple clothes in matching colours and styles. Propelled by their online stardom, which comes garlanded with hashtags such as #greyhair and #over60, the couple have also published books about the joys of later life and launched a range of clothes and accessories. In a less commercial vein, Kimiko Nishimoto is shaking up the Japanese view of ageing with slapstick selfies that go viral. My favourite shows the eighty-something hung out to dry on a washing line. Others feature her wiping out on a bicycle; wrapped up in a bin liner; being run over by a speeding car while reading a newspaper; smiling through the bars of a cage dressed as a gorilla.

Is there a danger that older people are being repackaged for the amusement of younger ones? Sometimes, perhaps. Most of those YouTube videos of seniors smoking weed for the first time or guessing how sex toys are used come with a young interviewer asking leading questions out of shot – and thus strike a patronising note. But many others do not. People like Nishimoto, Ms Q and the Golden Sisters are clearly no one's patsy. They are having a ball – and entirely on their own terms.

At the same time, millions of older people with zero celebrity cachet are filling up social media with images of themselves doing things that reduce the ageist stereotypes of yesteryear to rubble: splashing through mud on an obstacle course; wearing cool clothes; running a food truck; fixing a motorbike; playing Xbox; volunteering in Africa; studying for a big exam; dancing the night away. Each may only be seen by a handful of followers yet the numbers are irrelevant. What matters is that every image – even the traditional ones of cuddling grandchildren or knitting – adds another brushstroke to a portrait of later life that is rich, textured and specific – and therefore dignified. A portrait that says: 'Younger is not always better and ageing my way can be pretty wonderful.'

The tail is now wagging the dog. When I ask Swift what informs Getty's rethink on ageing, she answers with a single word: Instagram. 'Nowadays older people are taking charge of their visual language in a way they never have before,' she says. 'We see how they want to be visualised and how they visualise themselves and that's giving us some really good cues on how to produce our own imagery.'

~

As we overhaul the image of ageing, we would do well to remember the words of Germaine Greer: 'Nobody ages like anybody else.' Not everyone can be Wang or Jaco. We may not have the looks, talent, temperament, connections or health to follow their lead. To avoid portraying ageing as a game of winners and losers, we must depict it in all its shades. That means toasting the superagers without turning them into an unattainable gold standard. Those working to redefine what 'older' looks like understand this. Even as Braun cuts a swathe through the Polish media, seasoning her patter with catchphrases such as 'older is better' and 'it's cool to be old', she is careful to acknowledge the pitfalls of ageing. 'Along with the good stuff there is also loss, illness, death, tough stories,' she says. 'Ageing is not just dancing and partying.'

Creating an honest, inclusive image of ageing means depicting decline, disability and suffering in ways that reassure and dignify – rather than blame – those enduring them. It also means shining more light on the ordinary, humdrum moments that make up life at every stage. Ageing, after all, is not a binary choice between dazzling and drooling, between winning at Instagram and wasting away in a nursing home. 'What we really need is many more images of the ordinariness in between those extremes,' says Lorna Warren, a sociologist and expert on ageing at the University of Sheffield. 'Most of us spend most of our lives being mundane and we should embrace that. Sometimes I just want to be mundane fifty-something Lorna slacking around in her track bottoms. It's not boring; it's not shameful; it's the stuff of the majority of our lives. We should have space to be mundane as we get older.'

The truth is we are only just beginning to rebrand ageing. In every prank on *Live Long*, Jaco and her friends hold all the cards and have the last laugh, which is a welcome leap forward. But even as they poke fun at ageist assumptions they also trade in them. In other words, by playing on stereotypes about older people – they are sexless, techno-illiterate or have shaky hands – the show brings those same stereotypes to mind. In an ageist world, the line between laughing *with* Jaco and *at* her remains a fine one.

We are on the right track, though, not least because many of those updating how we see ageing are doing so with a sense of humour. Laughter is a potent tool for changing minds, toppling stereotypes and puncturing the status quo, which is why authoritarians and dictators hate being laughed at. Sometimes ageing sucks and finding mirth in the darkness can ease the burden. When Phyllis Diller quips: 'I'm at an age when my back goes out more than I do', we can all laugh – and maybe feel a little less worried about growing older.

That is why the longevity revolution is fuelling a boom in ageing-based humour. In Japan, the doyen of this trend is 66-year-old Yoshihiro Kariya, who delivers his high-energy stand-up routine dressed in a red tailcoat and sporting a rakish ponytail. Fans, mainly in their 60s and 70s, lap up his cruel quips about everything from death to disease to dwindling libidos.

My favourite example of later-life gallows humour comes from Diane Hill. Working with an artist in Coventry, England, the 56-year-old came up with a series of tongue-in-cheek emojis showing the less-welcome aspects of ageing. One depicts a woman wincing with back pain. Another is a bottle of memory pills. A third is a blingy character who represents 'spending the kids' inheritance'. The icons are known as 'emoldjis' and could soon be popping up on a smartphone near you.

Having a sense of humour can even help us age better. Laughing boosts the immune system, reduces pain and combats stress. A study done by psychologists at the University of Akron in Ohio revealed that people with a good sense of humour lived about eight years longer than their crabbier siblings. As George Bernard Shaw put it: 'You don't stop laughing when you grow old, you grow old when you stop laughing.'

What made Jaco so compelling was that she never stopped laughing. She made the most of ageing by embracing its many upsides, while accepting the drawbacks with equanimity and her trademark wit. Even the Shakespearean decline of the final lap failed to dim her lightness of spirit. The human body can be a sorry sight at the end of life, and seeing Jaco's up close and personal shook me more than I expected. Even as I relished her company, I felt unnerved, even repelled, by her physical state. Towards the end of our meeting, Jaco caught me peeking at a scab on her shin. She held my gaze, her expression tender, forgiving. She laid a hand on mine. 'It happens, ageing. *C'est la vie.* You just have to get over it and embrace all the good that being alive can bring you at every age,' she said. Then, in a flash, that famous smile returned. 'And if that doesn't work, just go to the pharmacy and get yourself a double dose of Viagra.'

I want to go out of this world just like Jaco: laughing at the dying of the light. Whether in movies, television, social media or advertising, seeing more and more people thriving in later life makes it easier to do just that.

As I gathered my things to leave her sun-soaked patio in Beirut, Jaco prepared to join her cats in a siesta. I put a final question to her: What one thing in the modern world has made ageing better for you? She thought for a moment and then pointed to the smartphone in my hand. 'There is your answer,' she said. 'I would not be sitting here with you now were it not for all this new technology.'

Food for thought in a world that tells us that tech belongs to the kids.

CHAPTER 6

TECHNOLOGY: iAGE

Technology is the campfire around
which we tell our stories.

—LAURIE ANDERSON

Shirley Curry starts every morning the same way: by making a cheerful beeline from her bed to the living room. Assembled there, in a corner of her small apartment in Rocky Mount, Virginia, is a shrine to online gaming. The tools of the trade are all present: a keyboard, two monitors, an external hard drive and router, a headset microphone and video camera, a wind-up timer and a smartphone. Tucked among the gadgets are bits of analogue bric-a-brac – a globe of Jupiter, a small ceramic house, a pink stuffed dog for wiping screens. Red and white Post-it notes bearing messages from her fans are scattered around like bunting at a summer fair. After switching on the power, Curry settles in for a shift that can last up to 18 hours.

132

Her first port of call is YouTube. To get in the zone, she watches videos of other gamers in action followed by her own exploits from the day before. Then she starts playing. Her game of choice is *Skyrim*, which unfolds in a richly imagined world of warrior monks and esoteric scrolls on a planet called Nirn. Her avatar is a young travelling merchant named Katamet. Curry was hooked from her first session. 'It's like being in a movie where you can do whatever you want to, go wherever you want to,' she says. 'It's just so beautiful that I fell in love with it immediately.'

Back in the honeymoon period, she played *Skyrim* for up to 12 hours at a stretch, completely unhooking from the outside world. 'I was like a zombie,' she says. Today, her gaming is far more regimented because the outside world is always awaiting her latest dispatch from Nirn. She plays in bursts of 40 minutes or an hour (hence the timer), recording every skirmish and raid, every discovered bag of treasure, every trek through the undergrowth, along with her own real-time commentary. She then renders the video and uploads it to her 250,000 subscribers on YouTube. Though she occasionally gets up to go to the bathroom or do chores, most of her day is spent glued to the chair. She even eats at the keyboard. To a non-gamer like me, her routine looks like a fresh circle in Dante's Hell. But to people like Curry it's manna from heaven. 'Oh, I love it,' she says. 'I'm totally addicted.'

Time for a thought experiment: What image have you formed in your mind of Curry? A teenager with facial piercings? A twenty-something in denial about her student debt? A thirty-something coder gone rogue? The truth: none of the above. Curry has no facial piercings, no student debt and knows nothing about coding. And she is 81 years old.

Curry, who took up gaming in her 60s, has faced plenty of ageism along the way. When she first came out online as a senior citizen, the backlash was swift and savage. Other gamers accused her of being a teenaged impostor. A sound engineer claimed she was using a device to alter her voice. When eventually it became clear that she was in fact a senior citizen, the trolls ramped up the vitriol. 'There were a lot of vulgar, nasty comments about my age,' says Curry, wincing at the memory. 'People were telling me, "Get off here, you don't belong on here, you're too old for this!"'

Over time, though, the haters faded away and her age became part of her brand. Fans christened her 'Grandma' and themselves her 'grandkids'. Media outlets lined up to interview the 'gaming granny'. Curry, who has the wit and warmth of a late-night radio DJ, was happy to play along and now boasts an online following that many gamers would give their right thumb for. One fan recently posted a message that spoke for many: 'Thank you grandma your videos are awesome and like a gift everyday.'

Curry's rise to YouTube stardom is further evidence that we are entering a golden age of ageing. Technology is a great leveller, not least because the only physical prowess needed is sitting in front of a screen and wielding a keyboard or gamepad. Though youthful looks remain the hard currency in the more selfie-driven corners of the Web, many online interactions are text-based and thus put a premium on the very traits that tend to improve with age: knowledge, social acumen, a way with words. The online world also offers the chance to reinvent ourselves in ways that never existed in the past, which dovetails with the desire to spread our wings or make a fresh start that often comes upon us in later life. As well as being 50 years younger than Curry, Katamet is also male.

The slowing down that occurs as we grow older can also be a secret weapon online, even in the gaming world. While her age delivers novelty value, what really fuels Curry's celebrity status on YouTube is her unhurried style of play. She leads her fans through the abandoned forts and teeming markets of Nirn like a gentle, genial Virgil. Compared to the fast and furious videos uploaded by younger gamers, her clips are long and a little plodding. 'I play slow and notice every little thing in the game, and talk about how pretty this or that is, and people like my commentary because I sound so natural,' she says. 'To many people I think my slowness is a breath of fresh air.'

Curry is the tip of a growing iceberg. As technology becomes more and more central to modern life, cyberspace is ageing right along with the population. My generation, despite growing up in the pre-internet era, now spends almost as much time online as our children. Since 2010, the proportion of American over-65s on social media has more than tripled, with many doing much more than just looking at family photos on Pinterest: they're gaming, teaching and taking courses, hunting for romance, crowdsourcing, leading campaigns for social reform, lobbying governments, launching startups, playing the stock market, writing blogs, selling or showing off their artwork. My 77-year-old mother takes her iPad everywhere.

Perhaps because chronological age means even less online, both young and old share the same love–hate relationship with technology. In a recent online survey in Britain, 89 per cent of 18–24-year-olds said the internet was an indispensable part of their lives. No surprise, there, but guess what the figure was for over-65s: 84 per cent. When my mother comes to visit, she racks up more screen time than my teenaged daughter. The same survey also found that young and old feel equally overwhelmed by the rapid minting of new technologies.

Curry certainly feels the downside of being an online brand as keenly as any millennial. These days she has to spend more time interacting with fans than playing her beloved *Skyrim*. 'I used to get in my game and play for hours and hours,' she says, wistfully. 'I don't have time to play just for myself anymore and I miss that a lot.' All that online toil has also crowded out exercise. No more treadmill in the gym across the hall. No more strolls round the neighbourhood. Some days Curry doesn't even leave home. 'I've fallen into the same trap as a lot of people,' she sighs. 'It can happen at any age.'

∼

The stereotype of the older person flummoxed by technology in the workplace is also heading for obsolescence. A survey of more than 4,000 IT professionals carried out by Dropbox showed just the opposite: the over-55s were less stressed by tech than were their younger colleagues. Researchers at North Carolina State University have shown that programmers enhance their knowledge and skills over time – and that those in their 50s often know as much (or more) about the latest software platforms as their twenty-something rivals. When Jean Pralong, a professor of business at Rouen Business School in France, analysed the work performance of 400 people with similar educational backgrounds ranging in age from 20s to 60s, he found that older workers mastered new technology just as quickly as younger ones.

Ron Ayers is a case in point. After a long career designing bomber aircraft and missiles, he channelled his knowledge of aerodynamics into building absurdly fast cars. One of his creations set a diesel land-speed record by hitting 350 miles per hour in 2006. Now, he is designing a car that can travel along the ground at 1,000 miles per hour. The launch is scheduled for 2019, when Ayers will be 87. When asked how he keeps up with all the new science and gadgetry, he replies simply: 'I've evolved with the technology.'

Barbara Jones, the insurance agent we met earlier, does the same. At the age of 69, she is every inch a digital native, active on Facebook and quick to turn to Google to answer questions that pop up in daily life. Her iPhone is packed with apps and flashes up the scores from her favourite sport, US college football. She used Craigslist to buy the partner desk that now serves as the dual-monitor workstation in her apartment in Arizona. And she likes to bond over tech with her gamer grandson. 'I haven't got a clue about gaming,' she says. 'But I know enough that we can talk about computers, you know, what we like and what we don't like.'

To land work in the cut-throat world of consultancy, Jones

has to stay on top of the latest technology in the insurance industry. When I catch up with her, she is on her way to mastering a complex new management system called Epic. 'It's really an amazing piece of software, so advanced, but that's not a problem for me,' she says. 'The agency's tech guy would tell you I'm ahead of the curve and picking it up faster than some of my younger colleagues.'

Jones has the advantage of having spent many years rolling with the technological punches. When she was in her 20s, her then-husband filled their home with gadgets, including the first Apple Mac computer. Years of working in sales and retail exposed her to wave after wave of technology. As we saw earlier, the human brain does well when asked to learn new skills in a similar field later in life. But how about tackling tech when you are older if you don't have the pedigree of someone like Jones? Is that a lost cause?

Of course not.

Arianna Huffington was in her early 50s when she first dreamt of harnessing the Web to spread news and opinion. At the time she was a writer with a limited grasp of technology, but that did not stop her. She learned what tech she needed to learn and made up the shortfall by hiring the right geeks. In 2005, at the age of 55, she launched the *Huffington Post*, now one of the most successful news and commentary blogs in the world.

Okay. Maybe you're thinking that early 50s is not that old to get down with the tech. After all, Steve Jobs oversaw the launch of the iPhone at the same age as Huffington created her world-beating blog. But how about later in life?

To find out, I drop by Senior Planet on the west side of New York City. Billed as the first 'stand-alone community center dedicated to leveraging the power of technology to improve the way we age', it serves up online information and advice on everything from health and dating to travel and fashion. It also teaches computing to rank beginners. When I turn up for a class one evening, I find precisely the kind of scene that is so rare in the archive at Getty Images: a dozen students, ranging in age from 62 to 83, building websites on iMacs. The classroom is buzzing like a beehive. Every so often someone cries out 'Shussssshhh', but to no avail: spirits are riding too high. One pupil is itching to build a website to display artwork without having to go through a gallery. Another has plans to sell jewellery online. A third aims to set up a news site devoted to farming in Africa. The woman at the iMac beside mine is 80 years old and eager to grow her coaching business by moving it online. 'At my age I'm looking for the best way to bring my talents to the world and that means mastering the technology that's out there,' she tells me. 'And besides, it's fun learning something new – it's like being at school again!'

Apart from me, the only person under 60 in the room is the teacher, Kin Chan. He is 26 years old and dressed in a red T-shirt bearing the Senior Planet slogan, 'Ageing with Attitude'. Though he explains everything clearly and without a whiff of condescension, the class gets off to a faltering start. Some pupils are struggling with the basics. One cannot find a simple Start button. Another double clicks the mouse when a single click is called for. When asked to open their accounts in an online platform, a third finds himself locked out. 'Please write your passwords down in your books!' says Chan, a hint of exasperation in his voice.

Before long, though, everyone starts making progress – and it occurs to me that maybe the setbacks the students suffered at the start of the evening arose not because they are hamstrung by age but because the technology is unfamiliar to them. The other day I watched a TV show where teenagers were invited to operate gadgets from yesteryear – and they were mystified. Some could not work out how to play a record on a turntable, lifting up and inspecting the stylus as if it were the stem of an exotic plant. Others blanched when asked to tune a manual radio. The tone of the show was light and whimsical, along the lines of: 'Oh, isn't it amusing to see digital natives foxed by analogue technology.' There was no handwringing about the cognitive failings of an entire age cohort. And yet when someone over 50 struggles with any kind of gadget, ageism rears its ugly head. We tut, we exchange knowing glances, we blame it on their advanced years.

This is wrongheaded. The truth is that everyone faces a learning curve when confronted with unfamiliar technology. How well you climb that curve depends more on your attitude and aptitudes than on your age. That is what studies of learning show. It's also what Chan has observed during two years of teaching at Senior Planet. 'When it comes to learning new technology, age really is just a number,' he says. 'Personality and brainpower, and the amount of interest you have in computers, matter much more than how old you are.'

Remember Kimiko Nishimoto, Japan's queen of the slapstick selfie? She picked up a camera for the first time at the age of 72. Her compatriot, Masako Wakamiya, a retired banker, started using computers in her 60s and later taught herself how to write software code with online tutorials. Frustrated by the dearth of mobile video games for the elderly, she eventually designed her own. Based on a traditional Japanese doll festival, and played and narrated at a slower pace, her brainchild, *Hinadan*, earned her an invitation to Apple's annual developer conference at the age of 82. Wakamiya is now an evangelist for harnessing technology in later life, zooming round the world to give interviews and speeches. On her website she posts vlogs from her travels and tutorials on how to make art using Excel.

Learning about people like Wakamiya, along with hanging out at Senior Planet, is making me more sanguine about my own ageing in a world where technology is constantly changing. Chan feels the same. 'One major lesson for me is that no matter how "behind" you are compared to the rest of the world in something, you *will* catch up as long as you try,' he says. 'It's very reassuring.'

Yet that message takes time to sink in. Even at Senior Planet – where every poster, every email, every brochure rams home the idea that ageing should be embraced – students sometimes blame their advancing years when learning something takes longer than they would like. Rather than let that self-inflicted ageism go unchallenged, Chan counterpunches by citing the 92-year-old with Parkinson's who graduated from both his basic and advanced computer courses with flying colours: 'She blew my mind with how much she learned!'

～

Technology can give us wings in later life, making it possible to engage with the world in ways that transcend our ageing bodies. Right up to the end, Jaco used Facebook and YouTube to build a following across the Arab world. At Nightingale House, a nursing home in London, 93-year-old John Rich keeps up with global events by surfing news websites on his iPad. He also cyber-travels to far-flung destinations. Using Google Earth, he has visited the streets of Steglitz, the neighbourhood in Berlin where he grew up, and toured the back roads of Somerset, the English county that was his home for many years. Top of his current to-visit list: the Seychelles, the Caribbean and sundry golf courses in the United States. 'Google Earth is incredible,' he says. 'I can be sitting here in my chair and travel anywhere in the world.'

Ida White uses her wings to help others. Born in New York, she lived most of her adult life in the US Virgin Islands, working as a schoolteacher, guidance counsellor, radio host and political activist. Now in her 80s, she lives in Orlando, Florida, but stays in touch with her adopted homeland through social media. On Facebook, she offers advice to her nearly 700 friends, many of them former pupils who call her 'teacher' or 'Miss White'. After hurricanes laid waste to the islands in 2017, she used her experience in disaster management to dole out tips on how to cope with the aftermath. 'Age is not the first thing people notice on

Facebook and that can be liberating,' she says. 'Instead of worrying about how old I am, I can just be myself.'

The online world is still a long way from being an age-blind utopia. Like sexism, homophobia and racism, ageism is never far from the surface in cyberspace. Sometimes Paulina Braun's posts on Facebook and YouTube draw nasty remarks about seniors. Many older gamers still hide behind fake profiles to avoid the ageist bile. Curry only chose to come out of the closet when she found herself chatting more and more with her fanbase. 'I wanted people to know me for me because I wanted to know them,' she says. 'There's no sense being on there chatting with people if you don't know who anyone else is – that's just silly.' She has a point. Experimenting with online personas can be fun and liberating, but not if you always feel obliged to pretend to be younger than you are. To harness the full potential of cyberspace, everyone must feel equally welcome there.

~

After chatting with Curry, I stumble across another surprising way that technology might help us with ageing. You can now summon an artificially aged self-portrait on a smartphone or hang out with a convincing avatar of an older you in a virtual reality simulation. While this sounds like harmless fun, studies show it can help narrow that 'fundamental emotional disconnect' between your present and future self – and that can inspire you to plan better for later life, exercise more, procrastinate less and even behave more ethically.

When I ask Curry if she would like to spend some quality time with a virtual version of her future self, she laughs. 'At my age, I think I already am my future self,' she says. 'I'm happy and content with who I am now, and where I'm at.' Hearing those words from anyone, young or old, always lifts my spirits. But hearing them from Curry, who has 30 years on me, brings to mind a question that has been scraping at the back of my mind since that hockey tournament in Gateshead: has she found happiness because – or in spite – of her age?

CHAPTER 7

HAPPINESS: MINDING LESS, ENJOYING MORE

Grow old along with me!
The best is yet to be ...

—ROBERT BROWNING

It's a bright Sunday morning in early spring, and a dozen women are picking their way through the streets of Sagunto, a sleepy port on the eastern coast of Spain. A generation ago, their mothers would have been heading to church for a couple of hours in the company of priests and paintings of the Virgin Mary. But these women, aged between 50 and 70, are en route to a very different kind of ritual: they will spend the day spraying graffiti onto walls in the centre of town.

The expedition feels like a hen party – raucous, festive, laced with mischief. 'What if someone we know sees us?' cries one of the *grafiteras*, with mock concern. 'I'm more worried about the police because I'm too old to spend the night in a prison cell,' says another. When a third announces that her family have christened her 'Graffiti Granny', everyone roars with laughter.

The women are taking part in a street-art workshop for older people and I am one of the group. Yesterday we learned about the history of graffiti around the world and looked at photographs of works by famous practitioners such as Banksy, ROA and Escif. We designed our own signatures, or tags. We also created stencils of flowers, cats, castles, dresses and laboratory beakers.

Dressed in smocks, overalls and mismatched second-hand garments, we eventually arrive at a wall on the banks of the dried-up River Palancia. Large, blank and cream-coloured, it's a dream canvas for a *grafitero*. With masking tape, we create rectangular frames on the smooth concrete. We then pull on face masks and start spraying in a kaleidoscope of colours – pink, teal, tan, cobalt, green, yellow, orange, white, red, black. We paint our hands, tags and stencils, along with slogans such as '¡*Viva Sagunto!*' Before long our murals resemble a chaotic collaboration between Jackson Pollock and Jean-Michel Basquiat. 'This is way more fun than going to Mass,' says one woman, eliciting cheers and more laughter.

Though Sagunto, like many Spanish towns, is festooned with graffiti, much of it political, some of it rude, locals gather to gawk at our anarchic murals. Two young women carry-ing a supersize pan of paella stop to take photos, as does a middle-aged cyclist in Lycra. 'We should get Granny to do this sometime,' says a father to his toddler. 'It looks like much more fun than watching soap operas.' An elderly woman returning from Mass in her Sunday finest wanders up and down the pavement, inspecting the art, posing questions, touching the paintwork, picking up unattended spray cans to test their weight. 'It's all so beautiful, especially in this spring sunshine,' she says. 'I always thought graffiti was for young people but seeing this makes me want to try it myself.'

The workshop is the brainchild of Lara Seixo Rodrigues, a thirty-something architect from Portugal. After seeing older people entranced by a street-art festival in her home country, she decided to teach them how to paint the city walls themselves. Since then she has run graffiti workshops for the over-50s everywhere from Portugal and Spain to Brazil and the United States. Many participants have physical impairments. Some arrive with Zimmer frames. Others suffer from dementia. The oldest so far has been 102.

As we hurl paint at the wall in Sagunto, Seixo Rodrigues tells me her aim is not to discover a silver-haired Banksy. 'This project is about so much more than just art,' she says. 'It's about smashing ageist stereotypes by getting older people out into the streets where they often feel unwelcome. It's about living life to the full and not worrying about what others think.'

Earlier we saw how ageing can make us more socially adroit, more at ease with other people. Now here comes another piece of good news: it can also make us more at ease with ourselves. As we age we tend to become more comfortable in our own skin, reconciled to our strengths and weaknesses, more accepting of the slings and arrows of outrageous fortune. We eventually realise we're never going to win Wimbledon or fly the Space Shuttle or earn a Rhodes scholarship – and, actually, we're okay with that. The fear of saying or doing the wrong thing, so common and so crippling in early life, starts to fade. What others think of us comes to matter less than living on our own terms. Ann Landers, the legendary agony aunt, laid out this shift in black and white: 'At age 20, we worry about what others think of us. At age 40, we don't care what they think of us. At age 60, we discover they haven't been thinking of us at all.'

Not everyone follows that route. Some of us shake off the yoke of other people's opinions early in life. John Lydon, for example, gleefully offended everyone from the monarchy to the media to his own mates while fronting the Sex Pistols in his early 20s. On the other hand, some of us, no matter how old we get, never stop fretting over how others see us. If we let it, though, ageing can make us masters of the subtle and satisfying art of minding less.

Sometimes, practising that art rubs people up the wrong way. Twenty-five years ago, I was not always thrilled by my grandmother's blunt appraisal of my clothes, hair and early career decisions. Today, my own children wince at my dad jokes and dad dancing. But that seems a small price to pay when you consider how deliciously liberating minding less can be.

Deep thinkers have always known this to be true. Two and a half thousand years before Facebook invented the Like button, Lao Tzu, the founder of Taoism, intoned: 'Care about people's approval, and you will always be their prisoner.' Virginia Woolf made a similar observation in the early

20th century: 'The eyes of others our prisons; their thoughts our cages.' Even Dr Seuss, the children's author, joined the chorus: 'Be who you are and say what you feel, because those who mind don't matter and those who matter don't mind.' Much of the self-help industry rests on the same principle.

Minding less offers welcome release from sweating the small stuff. It gave Albert Einstein the courage to dress as he pleased. 'I have reached an age,' he once remarked, 'when, if someone tells me to wear socks, I don't have to.' It can also make it easier to do the big stuff like leaving a bad marriage, quitting a prestigious job or ending a toxic friendship. In her TED Talk, novelist Isabel Allende, then in her 70s, waxed lyrical about no longer feeling obliged to tiptoe round other people's expectations. 'I don't have to prove anything any-more,' she said. 'I'm not stuck in the idea of who I was, who I want to be or what other people expect me to be. I feel lighter.'

That lightness certainly makes being a cartoonist easier for Mac. Some of his work, like the editorial stance of the newspaper where it appears, annoys people, and he faces the occasional roasting on social media. But these days the brickbats bounce right off. 'In the old days I wanted to please everybody, so if I got a letter from a reader saying, "Bloody hell, what a waste of time you are on the paper and why don't they bring the last bloke back who was much better, blah blah blah", I used to take it so personally and get desperately hurt about it,' he says. 'Now I just take it in my stride because I know you can't please everybody and that's okay.'

Of course, the tendency to mind less can go too far. Not caring at all about what other people think can lead to selfish, hurtful behaviour. When dementia or other forms of severe cognitive decline erode people's impulse control, the results can be mortifying. In the right dosage, though, minding less is a ticket to living the life you want to live. When asked to pinpoint the best thing about ageing, Oprah Winfrey replied: '. . . being able to be free to be and do whatever you want to.'

Such freedom can be a godsend in cultures that put a premium on 'saving face' and fitting in with the group. Just ask Park Dae-Hyun, who spent nearly 30 years doing an accounting job he loathed in Seoul. When we meet up for lunch at a restaurant in the South Korean capital, he sticks out a mile from the groomed, dark-suited salarymen swarming around us. Dressed in grey chinos and an open-necked shirt, he looks like he has not combed his hair for a couple of days. As we settle down to warm bowls of Instagramable *bibimbap*, he tells me why he spent so long in a job he hated.

As the first person in his family to attend university, he felt duty-bound to shelve his childhood dream of running a restaurant in favour of a steady pay cheque. What kept him returning to the office, month after month, year after year, was the fear of upsetting other people – a fear that runs deep in many Asian cultures. In Korea, standing out from the crowd is so frowned upon that the words 'my' and 'I' are often used interchangeably with 'our' and 'we'. Park felt nauseated whenever he contemplated how others would react if he swapped his calculator for a chopping board. 'I was paralysed by the fear of upsetting people,' he says. 'My parents, my wife, my son, my friends, my colleagues, even the neighbours – I was so worried about what all of them thought.' True to the Ann Landers dictum, however, that fear began to wane in his 40s. The turning point came one day when he found himself chomping through a second-rate *bibimbap* at his desk. 'I suddenly thought, *You know what, I really don't mind anymore what everyone else thinks,*' he says. '*I refuse to spend the rest of my life doing boring work and eating bad food.*' A few months later, not long after his 51st birthday, Park quit his accounting job and is now learning how to make proper *bibimbap* at a local cookery school.

Embarking on a new career later in life is seldom a piece of cake. Park still does freelance accountancy work to make ends meet. Though he and his wife have cut back on their spending, they may have to move from Seoul to a smaller city to afford a restaurant of their own. 'You have to make sacrifices but that's okay because you're following your dream,' says Park. 'My advice to anyone thinking of changing careers is: Just go for it. You will find a way to make it work.'

When I ask if ageing has turned him into a different person, Park puts down his metal chopsticks to think for a moment, running a finger along a fresh knife scar on his left thumb. 'No, if anything I am more myself now than I ever have been,' he says. 'Ageing has given me the confidence to live for me rather than for other people.'

Minding less can also serve the greater good. Some people have changed the course of history by stepping up to say the unsayable or do the undoable in later life. Rosa Parks was 42 when she refused to give up her seat on that bus in Montgomery, Alabama. Today we need that willingness to rock the boat and speak truth to power more than ever. Why?

151

Because we live in a world ruled by bullshit and branding, where spin trumps sincerity, where the pressure to perform is relentless, where online echo chambers insulate us from views that contradict our own, where Twitter mobs police opinions, jokes and language, where the keys to the kingdom are handed to those who find the most marketable way of saying what everyone else wants to hear. One remedy for this culture of conformity is to have more people around who are prepared to speak their mind because they mind less what others think of them – and that is exactly what the longevity revolution can deliver. As Oliver James, a prominent British psychologist and psychotherapist, puts it: 'That bluntness, that refreshing authenticity you find in older people, is hugely to be valued.'

～

Sagunto is a conservative place, and the *grafiteras* are revelling in raising eyebrows and ruffling feathers. Graffiti is usually the preserve of young tearaways playing night-time cat and mouse with the police. A few weeks before the workshop, a local teenager was fined for tagging a train carriage. Though the town council has sanctioned our art-making, the sight of older women doing a Banksy in broad daylight is jarring. 'It's good for people to see us out here having fun and doing something a bit outlaw,' says one *grafitera*. 'It breaks down the stereotype of older people being boring and invisible.' Another is delighted when a colleague fails to recognise her behind her mask. 'He's known me for 26 years and he's in shock,' she says. A third is pleased to be stirring things up on the home front. 'I wanted to bring my grandson along to watch me paint in the street,' she says. 'But his mother felt it would set a bad example for him.'

Did she consider eschewing the workshop to placate her daughter-in-law? I ask.

She shakes her head. 'To be honest, I really don't care what she believes,' she says. 'While I'm out here having fun, she can stay at home worrying about what the neighbours think.'

Towards the end of the workshop, a husband turns up and hovers on the edge of the crowd, scowling. 'I don't like this at all,' he tells me. 'Sure, what my wife is doing here might look nice but it's also a provocation and an invitation to others to indulge in the kind of graffiti that is just mindless vandalism.' He points to a nearby wall where the word 'penis' is daubed in black paint. Then he wanders over to his wife, who is struggling to hold a stencil in place, and announces that the paella is ready back home. Without turning to face him, she hisses a retort that sums up the workshop's carefree spirit: 'Let the paella wait!'

～

Spain is as famous for fiestas as it is for paella, and the *grafiteras* are in full party mode: minding less is clearly a lot of fun. I can easily imagine Jaco grabbing a can of spray paint and joining in the merriment. But the laughter in Sagunto brings a more serious question to mind: Are these women always as gleeful as they are torching stereotypes on this sunny Sunday morning, or is this workshop just a mini-vacation from otherwise sad lives? Every *grafitera* I put this question to echoes the answer Shirley Curry gave me: I am happy with my life. Some of the older ones say they are happier than they have ever been.

My first reaction when I hear this is: Have they inhaled too much spray paint? After all, ageing often goes hand in hand with things that would seem to militate against happiness: the loss of vigour, fertility and youthful looks; slower cognition; the death of loved ones; disease; time's winged chariot hurrying near. Popular culture certainly reinforces the idea that old equals sad. Think of all those stock photos of glum oldsters in the database at Getty Images. Or the surly seniors, from Archie Bunker to Grandpa Simpson to Larry David, who populate TV sitcoms. From codger, crone and curmudgeon to hag and fogey, the English language is peppered with words for an ill-tempered older person but none for a happy one. In the medical world, older people suffering from low mood are less likely to be offered psychotherapy because depression is often regarded as a natural part of later life. In a survey conducted by the AARP, formerly known as the American Association of Retired Persons, 47 per cent of respondents aged 18–39 said it is 'normal to be depressed when you are old'.

But is it?

We all know someone who is miserable in later life. Maybe several someones. But are they the norm? And is their unhappiness an inevitable by-product of ageing? Thankfully, the answer to both questions is No. Ageing is not a one-way ticket to Planet Sad. Far from it. In that same AARP survey, only 10 per cent of over-60s described old age as a depressing stage of life.

While ageing takes a toll on the body, mental health generally improves as we grow older. Anxiety, depression and perceived stress go down and we get better at being present and in the moment, which is linked to greater well-being. Even as the probability of dying goes up, our fear of death often diminishes – and that applies right up to the very end. When researchers compared blog posts written by the terminally ill with essays by healthy people asked to imagine being near death, they found the former to be more upbeat. Being more honest because you mind less what others think of you can also reduce cognitive dissonance by bringing your actions into line with your beliefs. 'Most people think that old age is all doom and gloom,' says Dilip Jeste, distinguished professor of psychiatry and neurosciences and director of the Center for Healthy Aging at the University of California, San Diego. 'In reality, that is not the case.'

Studies bear this out. Researchers at the University of Chicago found that our odds of being 'very happy' rise 5 per cent every 10 years. In national surveys, British adults report the highest levels of happiness and life satisfaction after the age of 60. Even Pete Townshend confessed to feeling more cheerful in his 60s than he was when he wrote that line, one of the most ageist in the pop music canon: 'Hope I die before I get old.' Across the world, longitudinal studies suggest that happiness follows a U-shaped curve, bottoming out in middle age and then rising again from our 50s. Even those afflicted by poor health and poverty tend to follow the same pattern. What's more, scientists have found evidence that chimpanzees and orangutans ride a similar U-shaped curve, suggesting that a happiness boost in later life might be coded into our primate genes. 'It appears to be a very deep phenomenon,' says Andrew Oswald, professor of economics and behavioural science at Warwick University in the UK. 'One of the great social science puzzles.'

Thanks to the grip of the old-equals-sad stereotype, this comes to many of us as a complete surprise. Goethe, a full-bore ageist in early life, was amazed to find out later that 'that which one wishes for in youth, one finds in old age'. Tolstoy also found later life to be a long way from the Rothian massacre he had feared. 'Do not complain about old age,' he wrote. 'How much good it has brought me that was unexpected and beautiful. I concluded from that that the end of old age and of life will be just as unexpectedly beautiful.' Ellen Glasgow, an American novelist, was bowled over by how her spirits rose in later life. 'In the past few years, I've made a thrilling discovery,' she wrote. '... that until one is over sixty, one can never really learn the secret of living. One can then begin to live, not simply with the intense part of oneself, but with one's entire being.' Frank Lloyd Wright, an architect who lived to the age of 91, once observed: 'The longer I live, the more beautiful life becomes.'

Lim Kyoung Sook knows the feeling. Now in her mid-60s, she has worked for 11 years as a guide at the Hanok Village in Jeonju, one of the top tourist attractions in South Korea. Visitors flock here to admire the period houses topped with peaked roofs and swooping eaves. The latest trend is for young Koreans to wander round the neighbourhood clad in the ornate costumes of the Joseon dynasty. Even on an ordinary working day the narrow streets are jammed with punters munching on skewers of barbecued chicken or posing for photographs. I meet Lim at the 500-year-old palace at the end of her seven-hour shift. Dressed in an elegant maroon tunic, she is slim, brisk and blessed with a megawatt smile worthy of the cheeriest emoji.

She tells me that ageing has bestowed upon her two unexpected gifts. First, an inner calm that makes her a better tour guide. Second, more happiness than she ever imagined possible. 'When I was young I believed the stereotype that older people are unhappy, so it has been a really lovely shock to discover the stereotype is completely wrong,' she says, unleashing that smile. 'I'm happier than ever now.'

Even the knowledge that we are moving closer to death need not dampen our spirits – if we face up to it. Research has shown that confronting mortality – at any age – spurs us to make the most of what life we have left. That is why 'death meditations' have been central to so many cultures throughout history: Japanese, Chinese, Islamic, Buddhist, Hebrew, Egyptian, Indian, Hellenic, Roman. According to a Bhutanese proverb, the secret to happiness lies in contemplating death five times a day. 'Analysis of death is not for the sake of becoming fearful,' says the Dalai Lama, 'but to appreciate this precious lifetime.' Similar thinking lies behind the Tikker, a digital watch that estimates your life expectancy and then counts down, on your wrist, the time you have left. The company slogan: 'Make every moment count'.

Of course, it is easier to contemplate death when you stand a decent chance of dying well – and thankfully our chances of doing so are rising. Around the world there is a move to de-medicalise and de-institutionalise the end of life, to take it out of the hands of the experts and give it back to those going through it. That means letting us decide, as much as possible, where, when, how and with whom we spend our final lap. When that happens, the result is usually a better death. Study after study shows that when people with end-stage cancer or heart disease stop medical treatment and move into a hospice they not only endure less suffering at the end but also live longer.

Long before death comes, however, life can get smaller as we age, leaving us with fewer things to do and fewer people to do them with. But while that sounds like a recipe for sadness, it is often just the opposite. In our younger years the natural tendency is to cast the net as widely as possible in order to build networks and garner experience and knowledge. But studies show that from around the age of 50 we tend to narrow the lens, training our attention on what really matters, which can mean letting go of people, activities and routines that no longer light us up. This is not loss; it is pruning, streamlining, putting quality before quantity. You may have fewer relationships, yet those you do have are more fulfilling. 'Older adults typically report better marriages, more supportive friendships, less conflict with children and siblings and closer ties with members of their social networks than younger adults,' says Karen Fingerman, a professor of human development and family sciences at the University of Texas, Austin.

Sometimes that pruning goes too far and leaves us isolated

in later life. The loneliest age group in the UK is the over-75s, two-fifths of whom tell researchers that television is their main form of company. An AARP survey found that 35 per cent of American over-45s are lonely. But although loneliness is miserable, and may even take the same toll on our health as being obese or smoking, it is not an inevitable corollary of growing older. Much of the social isolation seen in the later years is less the fault of ageing itself and more a function of modern life: changes in family structure, consumerism, income inequality, working culture, housing, technology. That is why loneliness is a scourge in every generation. The second loneliest age group in the UK is 21–35, and one in five young British mothers always feels lonely. Loneliness is almost twice as common among Americans aged 45–49 as it is among those aged over 70, and the loneliest age cohort in the United States is 18–22-year-olds. When the British government recently appointed a minister to tackle social isolation, the guiding principle was 'young or old, loneliness doesn't discriminate'.

Nor is being alone always the same as being lonely. Another benefit of ageing is that we learn to enjoy our own company more – and therefore feel more desire for solitude. I notice this in my own life. Even though I still love to socialise, I derive increasing pleasure from just hanging out with myself. Things – such as dining solo in a restaurant or going for a long walk alone – that once struck me as sad or dull or weird now feel like a treat. 'Solitude is a great source of pleasure to many people,' says Oliver James, the psychologist. 'It should not be conflated with isolation.' In other words, a 'smaller' life can mean a richer life.

When I ask Lim if her life has shrunk, she nods – but with no trace of sadness. 'I have more time to myself, which I really enjoy,' she says. 'I have found the right balance between being alone and being with other people.'

~

What is going on here? As the founding director of the Stanford Center on Longevity, Laura Carstensen has devoted her life to studying how ageing changes us. Her own research, along with studies by other academics, has shown that the human mind – regardless of gender, income, social class or ethnicity – develops a sunnier bent in later life. Carstensen calls this the 'positivity effect' of ageing.

As we age, our amygdalae – the two small almond-shaped regions of the brain that regulate the fight-or-flight response – react less and less to negative stimuli. That means we experience fewer unhappy emotions. Other studies have shown that ageing tilts our gaze towards the brighter side of life. For instance, when asked about a movie they have seen, older people are more likely to respond with praise ('the acting was wonderful' or 'the soundtrack was great') than with criticism ('the plot was full of holes' or 'the ending was a let-down'). As we age, we become less prone to letting one setback – a row with a friend or a workplace slight – taint our view of an entire day. Memory also takes on a rosier tint: from our early 40s, we start to recall more upbeat images than downbeat ones.

None of this means that in later life we bury our heads in the sand. Ageing is not the biological equivalent of soma, the happy drug used to numb the citizenry in *Brave New World*. On the contrary. When shown a series of images, people of all ages triage their attention in the same way, spending more time looking at the unpleasant pictures than at the pleasant ones. Nor do we ever lose the capacity to feel grief, regret, sorrow, envy, shame, anger, fear. As we age, we still see the clouds; we just get better at handling the emotions they elicit and at pinpointing their silver linings. In other words, we become more resilient. After Hurricane Katrina ripped through the Gulf Coast of the United States in 2005, leaving millions homeless, researchers studying the aftermath found that the oldest survivors were coping better emotionally than were the younger ones.

No one is sure why the positivity effect occurs. It might be nature's way of helping us cope with the prospect of dying. Or it could be that upbeat grandparents improved our ancestors' chances of survival in the distant past. Another theory is that because the world is a hazardous place, it pays to be more attuned to its darker side when we are wet behind the ears. 'When we are younger we orient towards the negative because that information just has more value,' says Carstensen. Once you've been round the block a few times, you can relax a little – and pay more attention to the lighter side.

Others think surviving into later life brings relief and a feeling of achievement. That might explain why most people respond with a firm No when asked if they would push a button to roll back the decades and relive their youth. We may miss how our bodies looked, felt and performed in our salad days, but few of us would sacrifice all the life lived since then, the secrets and stories, the triumphs and mishaps, the laughter and tears, to start all over again. Writing this book makes me realise I feel the same. I loved my 20s and 30s but have no desire to relive them. Doing so would feel like slithering down the longest serpent in snakes and ladders. Partly because I remember the anxiety of trying to find myself and my place in the world as a younger man. But also because I treasure all the experiences – good, bad and ugly – that have made me who am I today. Author Anne Lamott nailed it when she observed that a big benefit of being older is 'we contain all the ages we have ever been'.

The natural slowing down that comes with ageing may also fuel the positivity bounce. In the 19th century, Søren Kierkegaard, the Danish philosopher, observed that 'most men pursue pleasure with such breathless haste that they hurry past it'. In the roadrunner culture of today, when every moment feels like a race against the clock, pleasure-destroying haste is endemic – which explains why a backlash is underway across the world. I have spent more than a decade travelling the world to promote the Slow movement, which teaches that doing things less quickly often means doing them better and enjoying them more. Taking a 'slow' approach to life does not mean withdrawing from the world but rather experiencing it more vividly. As Mae West observed: 'Anything worth doing is worth doing slowly.'

Putting that into practice is not always easy. Not only is the adrenaline rush that comes from living fast hard to give up, but the taboo against slowness runs so deep that even when we do yearn for a gentler pace we often feel too guilty, ashamed or afraid to shift down a gear. Yet those who embrace the deceleration in later life come out happier in the end. Take John Talbot, a high-school chemistry teacher in Chicago. A natural athlete, he prided himself on living in the fast lane, playing lots of sports, partying hard and always running instead of walking up the stairs. When that vigour began to wane in his 40s, he rebelled. 'I hated the idea of slowing down, hated it, hated it, hated it,' he says. 'The first time I caught myself walking instead of running up the stairs I immediately sprinted the rest of the way two steps at a time.' Over the years, though, he has come to terms with his own deceleration – and learned to savour the benefits. At the age of 58, he now takes time to stop and stare. 'I'm happier because I'm living with more presence,' he says. 'When you slow down you start to notice all the things you miss when you're in a hurry all the time.'

There is always more to discover in the world – and in ourselves. That's why the happiest people usually cultivate a healthy restlessness in later life. Sure, they look back, savouring moments from their personal highlight reel, feeling the odd pang of nostalgia, but they are not stuck in the past, or in a rut. Instead, they follow the advice of French philosopher Henri Bergson: 'To exist is to change, to change is to mature, to mature is to go on creating oneself endlessly.'

Our default setting as we age should be the slogan that The North Face uses to sell its upmarket outdoor apparel: 'Never Stop Exploring'. Every one of us is a work in progress, and seeking out new experiences moves that *oeuvre* closer to fruition. With the right spirit, growing older can therefore mean colouring in rather than erasing yourself. As we saw earlier, David Bowie never lost his drive to explore and experiment, even as cancer drove him into an early grave – and that went hand in hand with embracing ageing. 'If you are pining for youth I think it produces a stereotypical old man because you only live in memory, you live in a place that doesn't exist,' he said. 'I think ageing is an extraordinary process whereby you become the person you always should have been.'

I love the idea of becoming the person I always should have been. Seen through that Bowie lens, ageing suddenly looks more like a bonus than a burden. It stops being a dreary slide towards the tomb to become instead an adventure or a quest – like a video game where there is always a surprise round the next corner, another level to reach, more shades and textures to discover, a chest full of treasure waiting at the heart of the maze. Rather than rotting, you are ripening; rather than losing the person you once were, you are finding your true self. 'Why is it good being old?' asked poet May Sarton at the age of 70. 'I am more myself than I have ever been.'

Turning the 'Never Stop Exploring' motto into life tips is easy: Grasp the nettle. Step out of your comfort zone. Learn new stuff. Look forward more than backward. Hang around people who are different from you. Take a course. Read widely. Keep up with the news and cultural trends. Build – rather than rest – on your experience.

～

Exploring can be scary but it pays to feel the fear and do it anyway. Seixo Rodrigues sees participants arrive at her graffiti workshops hobbled by their own ageism, convinced they will never master the box cutter or the stencil. Before long, though, they're tracing, cutting and stencilling like seasoned professionals. 'They completely change in a couple of hours,' she says. 'They put aside their walking sticks and jump to it.'

Towards the end of our workshop in Sagunto, when the murals are almost finished, a young police officer pulls up in his squad car. The *grafiteras* cheer and whoop as if he were a stripper. 'Officer, officer,' one coos. 'Have you brought handcuffs?' Another offers up her wrists coquettishly. Even the cop joins in the laughter.

This is the positivity effect in action, and it feels wonderful. But then something happens that sends my spirits plummeting. The trigger is a brief chat with a teenager shooting photos of us on her iPhone. I ask if the images will soon be up on Instagram and she shakes her head. 'They are for my grandmother,' she tells me. 'She might like to give this a try.'

When I ask why our workshop is not worthy of Instagram, she remains silent, squirming a little. I gently rephrase the question, but then wish I hadn't because her reply stings. 'I need to be selective about the photos I post on Instagram because I'm trying to get more followers,' she says. 'And, you know, I don't want to be offensive or anything, but older people just aren't that attractive.'

Even on this day of public high jinks, of smashing stereotypes, channelling the positivity effect and cultivating the art of minding less, her words are a dagger to my middle-aged heart. Why? Because I fear she might be right.

CHAPTER 8
ATTRACT: SWIPING RIGHT

*After 40 nobody is young, but one can
be irresistible at any age.*

—COCO CHANEL

Donna McGuffie was never a pageant girl. Even though she grew up in the southern United States, where beauty contests sit in the cultural pantheon alongside Bibles and barbecues, she never dreamed of being crowned Miss Anything. It wasn't just that she was too short, even in heels, to take part. The very idea of women sashaying in ballgowns and bikinis in front of a panel of judges left her cold. 'I never went to a pageant, let alone entered one,' she says. 'I thought they were silly. You know, why you wanna do that? If you're cute, you're cute; you don't need to walk on a stage and have someone confirm it for you.'

McGuffie is telling me this shortly after winning an international pageant in Las Vegas, Nevada. A sparkling crown

166

sits on her perfectly coiffured hair. The winner's sash is draped over her ballgown. A trophy nestles at her feet like an obedient dog. As fellow contestants come up for a hug or a photo, she laughs and brushes away tears like a giddy schoolgirl. 'This doesn't happen to someone like me,' she says, ramping up the southern twang for comic effect. 'I'm five foot tall and from Alabama!' She is also 65 years old.

We have already seen how the longevity revolution is changing everything from the Web to the workplace. The same is now happening with the rules of attraction. We are in Las Vegas in 2017 and McGuffie has just won the first-ever Ms Senior Universe pageant, beating a field of rivals aged from 61 to 94. 'When I was growing up, being beautiful meant being the young blonde with the pretty tan and the long legs, but our definition of beauty is absolutely broadening now,' she says. 'People are beginning to realise that you can be beautiful and attractive at any age.'

If that is true then Vegas has yet to read the memo. Before watching McGuffie win her crown, I go for a stroll down the legendary Strip. Giant screens flicker with ads for burlesque shows and erotic circuses. Vans advertising 'Girls Direct To You' idle garishly in the traffic. Cards for strippers and prostitutes lie scattered on the pavement like leaves on a forest floor. Here and there, topless hunks and babes wearing little more than thongs and nipple tassels hand out leaflets and pose for cheeky photographs with the tourists. It is a veritable buffet of flesh – all of it young. No wrinkles, no liver spots, no grey hair, no cellulite, no varicose veins, no unsightly bulges, no sagging skin. Even older performers, such as Céline Dion, have been retouched in their concert posters to look pre-ternaturally youthful. As I settle into my seat to watch the Ms Senior Universe pageant, the words of that teenager in Sagunto come floating back into my mind: *Older people just aren't that attractive.*

This is not a new idea. The Nambikwara people of Brazil have one word for both old and ugly and another for both young and beautiful. In Ancient Greece, Aristophanes dismissed women of a certain age as 'dirty old bags' who can only offer men 'vinegar dregs and a beard and bad breath'. More than a millennium and a half later, Roger Bacon, a Franciscan friar who helped pioneer the scientific method, opined that men start losing their looks after reaching their 'peak at the age of 40'. In Chaucer's *Canterbury Tales*, the Wife of Bath identifies youth as a *sine qua non* for hotness: 'Age that comes to poison everything, has taken all my beauty and all my pith.'

Trying too hard to conceal the effects of ageing could also provoke the harshest scorn. Racine, a 17th-century French playwright, mocked an older character for striving to make herself look young and attractive: 'She took care to paint and to adorn her face to repair the irreparable outrage of the years.' In a similar vein, a French print from 1800 shows two older women at their toilette. One is putting on a fake bosom, the other retouching lines around her wrinkled eyes. Their younger maids look out at us with expressions of amused pity.

With so much bile aimed at older faces and bodies it comes as no surprise that the earliest texts in the medical canon promised to preserve the appearance of youth. The Edwin Smith papyrus set the template nearly 5,000 years ago with a 'recipe for transforming an old man into a youth'. Combining the recommended ingredients yielded a paste to be stored in a coffer of semi-precious stone. With its grandiose claims and breathless tone, the accompanying text reads like an ad for a modern-day cosmetic, right down to the vague claim to efficacy in the final line: 'Anoint a man therewith. It is a remover of wrinkles from the head. When the flesh is smeared therewith it becomes a beautifier of the skin, a remover of blemishes, of all disfigurements, of all signs of age, of all weaknesses which are in the flesh. Found effective myriads of times.' In the 5,000 years since then, human beings have roamed far beyond lotions and potions made from fruits and flowers in the quest to look young. Cleopatra took a daily bath in soured donkey milk; women in Elizabethan England laid thin slices of raw meat on their faces; French aristocrats washed their skin with red wine in the years leading up to the Revolution. Others have tried to ward off Racine's 'irreparable damage' by ingesting or smearing on ingredients worthy of a witch's brew: crane eggs, crocodile faeces, monkey brains, lion fat, spider webs, earthworms, coral, frogspawn, scorpion's oil, urine, beeswax or moor mud.

Some even sacrificed their lives on the altar of youthful looks. In 16th-century France, Diane de Poitiers, a mistress of King Henry II, was fêted for her smooth, porcelain complexion, with one courtier noting admiringly that she remained 'as fresh and lovable' as a 30-year-old, with skin 'of great whiteness', into her 60s. The secret to her beauty regime? Downing a daily cup of gold chloride and diethyl ether that eventually killed her. Talk about suffering to be beautiful.

Plus ça change. Today, both men and women take human growth hormone in the hope of staying fresh and perky despite warnings that doing so might increase their risk of coming down with heart disease, type 2 diabetes and some cancers. With millions more turning to chemical and surgical interventions ranging from facelifts and Botox to microdermabrasion, chemical peels and dermal fillers, the global anti-ageing industry could soon be worth $300 billion a year. Wrinkle panic is also setting in younger than before. A few years back, 'anti-ageing' cosmetics for tweens popped up on the shelves at Walmart. Scarlett Johansson, an actress famous for her peaches-and-cream complexion, was already using anti-wrinkle creams by the age of 20. 'It's hard not to feel under pressure,' she said. 'Everybody in Hollywood is just so damn beautiful.' Translation: beauty and youth are so tightly linked that you cannot have one without the other.

No wonder we greet the arrival of our first wrinkle or grey hair with a shiver of existential dread. Or that we use apps such as Visage Lab to rejuvenate our online photographs. Or that we rejoice when someone thinks we are younger than we are. I am just as susceptible to this as anyone else. A little while ago I uploaded a photo of my face to one of those websites that estimate your age. When the algorithm said I looked eight years younger than I was at the time I practically turned a cartwheel. Ashton Applewhite, the anti-ageism campaigner we met earlier, gives me a sympathetic smile when I tell her this story. People often praise her for looking younger than her 65 years. 'It's very, very hard not to take it as a compliment on the basis of internalised ageism,' she says. 'There is nothing wrong with trying to look your best but it's a problem when your goal is to look younger. The goal is health, not youth.'

Loosening the link between 'looking good' and 'looking young' may be the hardest challenge facing the longevity revolution. After all, we are hardwired to find youth, and the fertility it implies, attractive. The frisson we feel when confronted with dewy skin, glossy hair, full lips, white teeth and a lithe body is nature's way of keeping the human race going. As Simone de Beauvoir put it: 'It is the tendency of every society to live and to go on living: it extols the strength and fecundity that are so closely linked with youth and it dreads the worn-out sterility, the decrepitude of age.'

That would explain why art has always celebrated young beauty. Why Hippocrates took time off from laying the foundations of modern medicine to develop a sideline in anti-wrinkle potions. Why once you hit 50 pretty much everyone under 30 looks a little bit beautiful. It might also explain our uncanny ability to guess a person's age from their appearance or smell.

But there is a big difference between admiring youth and making it a prerequisite for being attractive. When we create a cult of young beauty everyone suffers: older people are shamed for no longer making the grade, while younger ones feel they are losing market value with each passing day.

A first step to dismantling that cult is to make age-shaming taboo – and the world is moving in that direction. In 2016, a *Playboy* Playmate of the Year named Dani Mathers went to a gym in Los Angeles to exercise her young and much-photographed body. While in the changing room, she spotted a naked 71-year-old woman beside the showers. She found the spectacle so comically repellent that she took a picture with her phone. Below the photo, she wrote a caption: 'If I can't unsee this then you can't either.' She paired that image with a shot of her 29-year-old self, eyes twinkling with mock horror, hand over mouth as if stifling a laugh, and uploaded the montage to Snapchat.

What was going through her mind as she pressed Send? Perhaps she felt herself following safely in the crone-shaming tradition that stretches back to Erasmus, Plautus, Ovid, Homer and Horace. Maybe she thought her montage would elicit the same laughter and applause that greeted the plays of Aristophanes more than 2,000 years ago. If so, she was wrong. Very wrong. When her post hit the public channel in Snapchat, the backlash was instant and fierce. 'This is a hate crime,' cried one Twitter user. 'Shame on you,' howled others. Many called for Mathers to be fired from her modelling jobs, banned from gyms, thrown in jail.

As the social media storm intensified, she went into damage-limitation mode, issuing a public apology, signing up for counselling and enrolling in an anti-bullying course. Yet still the law went after her. To avoid a jail sentence for invasion of privacy, she eventually cut a deal for three years' probation and 30 days of community service removing graffiti around Los Angeles. She was banned from using a mobile phone anywhere that people might be in a state of undress and from posting images of others online without their express permission. She also had to foot the bill for Showering Older Woman to buy a new backpack to replace the one seen in the photo.

What can we take from this story? First, that attitudes are changing for the better. Aristophanes would have been utterly baffled by the price Mathers paid for her Snapchat sneer. Today, though, mocking people for having older bodies – or for failing to look like Mathers – is moving beyond the pale.

Even industries that were once proudly ageist now have to watch their step. In the early days of commercial air travel, airlines hired young flight attendants and then filled their marketing with images of foxy 'stewardesses'. Remember those lascivious tag lines from National: 'I'm Laura. Fly me nonstop to Miami.' Many airlines now permit their cabin crew to carry on working into their 50s and beyond, but old prejudices die hard: the models they use in advertising remain young and wrinkle-free. In 2017, while delivering a speech at a dinner in Ireland, Akbar Al Baker, the chief executive of Qatar Airways, poked fun at the paucity of nubile flight attendants on US airlines. Their passengers, he said, were 'always being served by grandmothers', boasting that 'the average age of my cabin crew is only 26'.

Again, the backlash was swift. Leading industry figures rounded on Al Baker. Like Mathers, he was forced into a grovelling, if slightly unconvincing, public apology, claiming his remarks had been 'careless' and did not reflect his 'true sentiments'. 'For the cabin crew serving aboard all air carriers, professionalism, skill and dedication are the qualities that matter,' he said. 'I was wrong to imply that other factors, like age, are relevant.'

The more we hear that age is not relevant the better, but the pillorying of Mathers and Al Baker does not mean ageism is dead and buried, not by a long shot. Sexist, homophobic and racist remarks are also verboten nowadays, yet sexism, homophobia and racism are all alive and well. There is often a gap between what we decry in public and what we think and do in private. Surely Mathers cannot have been the only person in the world who laughed at her Snapchat montage. Nor is it hard to imagine that others quietly shared her revulsion at the sight of a 71-year-old woman in the nude. By the same token, Al Baker is not the only airline executive – or passenger – ever to complain that flight attendants are too old.

And yet the needle is moving.

Another promising sign is that the term 'anti-ageing' is coming under fire like never before. Consumers and bloggers have chafed against it for some time now. 'Treating age as something that needs "curing" is pointlessly demoralising for anyone over 30,' says Jane Cunningham, founder of britishbeautyblogger.com. 'Beauty is not one thing, it's many things.'

That thinking went mainstream in 2017 when *Allure*, the leading beauty magazine in the US, announced with much fanfare that it would stop using the expression 'anti-ageing' altogether. The cover model that month was Helen Mirren, looking radiant, cool and wrinkled in a very unwrinkled white dress by Carmen March. In her editor's letter, Michelle Lee made a case for growing older that went beyond rethinking what we see in the mirror. 'I'm not going to lie and say that everything about ageing is great. We're not the same at 18 as we are at 80. But we need to stop looking at our life as a hill that we start rolling uncontrollably down past 35,' she wrote. 'Repeat after me: Growing older is a wonderful thing because it means that we get a chance, every day, to live a full, happy life.'

Lee then zeroed in on looks. 'I hope we can all get to a point where we recognise that beauty is not something just for the young,' she wrote. She argued that all of us can do our bit to bring about that change by altering the way we speak. 'Language matters,' she wrote. 'When talking about a woman over, say, 40, people tend to add qualifiers: "She looks great ... for her age" or "She's beautiful ... for an older woman". Catch yourself next time and consider what would happen if you just said, "She looks great ... "'

Lee is not some Canute ranting alone on the sidelines. Four months before her *cri de coeur*, actress Julia Roberts, then 49 years old, was named the World's Most Beautiful Woman by *People* magazine. Older women are increasingly scoring jobs as catwalk mannequins and ambassadors for beauty brands. Carmen Dell'Orefice is racking up *Vogue* and *Cosmopolitan* covers in her 80s and a record number of fifty- and sixty-somethings modelled clothes at the 'Spring 2018' shows in London, Paris, New York and Milan. Even the legendary Pirelli calendar, for so long the home of young babes in the buff, is moving in the same direction.

Shot by Annie Leibovitz, the 2016 edition featured portraits of women, all but one fully clothed, fêted for their accomplishments in fields ranging from the arts and business to sports and journalism. They were a jumble of sizes, ethnicities – and ages. The subtext was clear: Youth is not the only route to Planet Attractive: you can also get there via presence, personality and having a story to tell. 'One of the stereotypes I see breaking is the idea of ageing and older women not being beautiful,' said Leibovitz. Pirelli upped the ante in 2017 by featuring clothed, unretouched women aged from 28 to 71 and putting the fight against ageism at the core of its promotional campaign. 'As an artist,' said Peter Lindbergh, the photographer that year, 'I feel I'm responsible for freeing women from the idea of eternal youth and perfection.' One of his models, the actress Kate Winslet, insisted on showing the back of her hands because she loved the way they had changed as she aged into her 40s. 'People are constantly trying to make us look a softer version of 40, or a more youthful, fresher version of 50,' she said. 'Isn't it okay to just be 40 or 50 or 60?'

More and more the answer to that question is Yes – for women and men. As the broader push for diversity nudges non-white, transgender, disabled and plus-size models into the limelight, modelling agencies for older people are springing up all over the place. One example is Oldushka, whose name is a portmanteau of 'old' and 'babushka', the Russian word for grandmother. Based in Moscow, it grew out of photographer Igor Gavar's hobby of shooting the street style of pensioners in Omsk, his hometown in Siberia.

Today Oldushka has 18 male and female models aged 60 to 85 on the books, and their faces adorn magazine spreads and advertising campaigns across Russia. Gavar is on a crusade to demolish ageist stereotypes and change the very meaning of the word 'attractive'. 'I wanted to show that older people are capable of working in the fashion industry and that they can be beautiful, with their wrinkles and grey hair,' he says.

Many are proving that point by turning themselves into style and beauty influencers on social media. The Instagram account where seventy-something Linda Rodin posts photos and videos of herself wearing hip clothes and hanging out with her poodle, Winks, in Manhattan has over 100,000 followers. Her rivals include fifty-something Anna Dello Russo (1.4 million followers), sixty-something Sarah Jane Adams (157,000 followers) and eighty-something Helen Ruth Van Winkle (2.3 million followers). Older men, from fifty-something Nickelson Wooster (750,000 followers) to the sixty-something David Evans (24,000 followers), are also turning heads on Instagram. These sultans of social media are helping to broaden the definition of attractive by being completely at ease in their older skin. Rodin, for example, has never coloured her hair and eschews Botox and fillers. Wooster is lined and grey-haired. 'It's less about age and more about spirit,' says Gwen Flamberg, beauty director at *Us Weekly*.

Is all this just a storm in a media teacup? No, because role models matter. When we see people like us toasted in public we find it easier to accept and celebrate who we are.

That goes for race, gender, sexuality, colour, body type – and age. Growing older feels less troubling to me whenever I see a shot of Jeff Goldblum or Daniel Day-Lewis looking sexy as hell. McGuffie feels a fillip every time she comes across a photo of someone like Mirren or Rodin. 'They make it easier for the rest of us to be and look our own age,' she says. They also make growing older seem less hellish to the young. A 24-year-old can look at Dello Russo or Deshun Wang and think: *Yeah, I could be like that when I'm that age.*

Out in the real world, beyond the catwalks and curated confines of social media, the definition of 'attractive' is widening. Many women now lift weights because strong is the new skinny, while others aspire to match the curvy derrieres sported by celebrities such as the Kardashians, Nicki Minaj and Iggy Azalea. Conchita, an Austrian drag queen, won the 2014 Eurovision Song Contest sporting a golden gown and a full beard. A year later, the internet fell in love with the 'dad bod'. In 2018, in Germany, a transgender model appeared on the cover of *Playboy* magazine for the first time ever. 'Culture does a lot in training the eye to find certain things erotic or attractive,' says Alexander Edmonds, a professor of anthropology at the University of Edinburgh. 'And those standards change over time.'

Adriana Corte agrees. The 62-year-old has lived her whole life in São Paulo, Brazil. Svelte, stylish and blessed with a dazzling smile, she always drew admiring glances in the street – until the compliments dried up in her 40s. Two decades later, though, she is starting to see a change. 'People have begun looking at me again,' she says. 'Now I often have younger people, men and women, stopping me in the street to compliment my outfit or my hair or my general look.' The other day a teenaged girl asked if she could take her photograph and upload it to her own Instagram account. 'She told me I was the most attractive woman she'd seen all day,' says Corte.

When it comes to female beauty, the new holy grail is a healthy glow rather than the perfectly smooth skin of youth. 'Women's expectations of how they want to look as they age have changed,' says Elisa Simonpietri, scientific director for Vichy Laboratories at L'Oréal. 'We are no longer fixated with wrinkles.' Rebecca Valentine sees the same shift occurring in the advertising industry. Launched in 2012, her Grey Model Agency now has 300 older men and women on the books. 'We all love to gaze upon beauty and that will never change, but our concept of beauty as we embrace our multicultural and wonderfully diverse community is changing,' she says. 'Aspirations now stretch beyond youthfulness and flawless skin, to wisdom, experience and a life well lived. The view of wrinkles is changing: now clients are looking for radiant complexions and don't mind the lines.'

It's worth repeating that last part: *don't mind the lines*. Though it may sound shallow or trivial, it actually heralds what Helen Mirren called, at the launch of the 2017 Pirelli calendar, a 'cultural shift'. After all, learning to live with wrinkles, seeing them as, in the words of Mark Twain, reminders of 'where smiles have been', might be the first step towards finding them attractive.

The same goes for grey hair. Attempts to stave off

follicular whitening go way back. The Assyrians recorded treatments for banishing silver locks in 1500BC and henna has been a cosmetic staple across the Middle East since the time of Ancient Egypt. In the latter part of the 20th century, washing that grey right outta your hair became de rigueur for women in the West. Half the contestants at the first Ms Senior Universe, including McGuffie, visit a colourist. Debora Price, the gerontologist we met earlier, thinks all this hair dyeing reinforces ageism. 'No woman in her mid-40s is grey, even though they're all grey,' she says. 'All the women of the earth are involved in this massive conspiracy to stop young people realising that what's happening to them is completely normal. Teenagers think grey is for grandmothers, so when it happens to them in their 30s it's panic stations.' But now the tide shows signs of turning.

Celebrities ranging from Kim Kardashian to Rihanna to Kate Moss have recently sported grey hair. Sarah Harris, the thirty-something beauty editor of British *Vogue,* has silver locks, as do all those older influencers on Instagram. Across the world women in their 20s, 30s and upwards are cancelling appointments with their colourists and then chronicling the resulting transformation in books, blogs and YouTube videos using hashtags like #greyhairjourney. French journalist Sophie Fontanel recently turned her voyage to the grey side into a zeitgeisty book called *Une Apparition.* Not long after its publication, Angela Buttolph, a British beauty columnist, announced that '... grey hair is no longer about "letting yourself go". It's edgy, it's chic, it's aspirational, whatever your age.'

Yet if Mirren is right that a cultural shift is underway then it is only just beginning. Most of the women getting credit for redefining older beauty still fit a pretty limited definition of pulchritude: they are tall, slim, white, symmetrical, able-bodied. They also tend to be affluent enough to tap the best dermatologists, personal trainers, nutritionists, chefs, makeup artists and photographers. In some cases their images are touched up to make them look younger. The danger is that we end up creating a fresh set of impossible expectations. In the same way as super-geezer athletes can turn ordinary mortals off exercise, über-lovely oldsters can end up demoralising the rest of us. Not everyone can age like Mirren or Day-Lewis. 'I'm glad they're showing older models more now but it's still a very narrow definition of beauty that just puts pressure on all the other people out there who are ageing in a way that most people do,' says Shanthony Exum, a thirty-something graphic designer and rapper based in New York. 'We won't take a real step forward until we start showing everyone in the media.' To that end, she runs the Every Body Project, a style blog that celebrates a much broader range of shapes, sizes, races and ages. She photographs people she finds visually interesting in New York and then uploads them along with a short comment from her or a quote from the subject. The older men and women on her blog are stylish and arresting – you want to meet them – but they seldom look like mainstream models.

The project is a welcome reminder that looks are only ever part of what makes someone attractive. We are drawn to others by their courage, eloquence, intellect, achievements, kindness, wisdom, character, imagination, creativity, élan and sense of humour – most of which ripen as we age. What makes you attractive is not having exactly the same face or body at 45 or 55 or 65 that you did at 25; what matters is filling the years in between with the kind of rich experiences that make you someone people want to be around. In other words, becoming the person you always should have been may be the best way to boost your attractiveness score. Or, as Eleanor Roosevelt put it: 'Beautiful young people are accidents of nature, but beautiful old people are works of art.'

～

That is very much the spirit driving the rise of senior pageants. Before we go any further, though, it's time for some full disclosure: I have never been a fan of beauty contests. Even when the participants say all the right things about world peace and the environment, even when they are highly educated, even when they insist that they feel in no way objectified, pageants strike me as retrograde. They weaponise female beauty and turn us into judgemental voyeurs. Sitting in a 5,000-seat theatre in Las Vegas, watching the contestants for Miss Universe 2017 (maximum age: 28) strut their stuff in swimsuits on the stage, made me feel like a delegate at a Peeping Tom convention.

Senior pageants are striving to plough a different furrow. Their aim is to celebrate the content of a woman's character over the contours of her body. At the inaugural Ms Senior Universe pageant in Las Vegas, the judges' handbook comes with a stern warning: 'Remember, women come in all sizes, heights and shapes.' The 15 contestants live up to that description – and there is no bikini moment. 'Are you kidding me?' says McGuffie, laughing. 'Swimsuits would have been a deal-breaker.'

With under 100 people in the audience, most of them family and friends, the contest itself has a relaxed, amateur charm, like an early round of *Britain's Got Talent*. We watch the contestants parade in national costumes and then in formal wear. We see them sing, dance and recite poetry. We hear each give her philosophy of life in 35 seconds. 'I dream big. I aim high. I act bold. To dream the impossible I begin to make it possible,' declares one. There is also a healthy dollop of self-deprecating humour. One contestant sings a tongue-in-cheek song about forgetting where she left her keys. Halfway through the pageant, a Joan Rivers impersonator takes to the stage to deliver a stream of jokes about loose vaginas and leaky bladders.

Every contestant has lived a full life and that comes through in their brio and joie de vivre. These are women with stories to tell, with much more to offer the world than a well-turned ankle, women you want to be around. After McGuffie is crowned, and with spirits running high, one of the organisers announces from the stage that we have made history today, and that from these humble beginnings the Ms Senior Universe pageant could go on to conquer the planet. 'The world is changing,' says Ms China, who is 61. 'People are now ready to see older women as attractive.'

My first thought on hearing this: I hope you're right. My second: What about men?

Traditionally, guys have suffered less pressure to look youthful. Ageing is said to give us gravitas and make us look 'distinguished'. While Hollywood ruthlessly blackballs female actors in their 30s, their male counterparts, from George Clooney to Pierce Brosnan, go on playing the 'silver fox' roles into their 50s and beyond. Across the public sphere, males get away with ageing in ways that women can only dream about.

That does not mean men are immune to the pressure to look young. We can also feel deflated by our greying or thinning hair, sagging skin and thickening waists. The Web is full of photos and videos of me from more than a decade ago, a constant and poignant reminder that I'm ageing in a world – and an industry – that prizes youth. I have no plans to go under the knife, but like a midlife-crisis Romeo on Tinder I've been guilty of using publicity shots that are several years out of date.

To explore my own fear of becoming less attractive with each passing birthday, I set up a meeting in London with David Evans, the 63-year-old star of the Grey Fox blog. We meet at the Royal Society of Arts, which is housed in a handsome Georgian building near Trafalgar Square. On its walls hang 18th-century paintings of portly men in powdered wigs. Tall, trim and dapper, Evans strides in as if fresh from a GQ photoshoot, his outfit a sharp take on the modern man about town: khaki jacket over a blue-and-white-striped shirt, grey-blue linen trousers, brown shoes. You could easily imagine a twenty-something rocking the same look.

Evans makes 63 look attractive because he is utterly at ease not only with his grey hair and lined face but with the idea of ageing itself. 'When I think of "old" I think of beautiful old buildings and objects because it's not a pejorative word for me,' he says. 'You can't live your life wishing you were 10, 20 or 30 years younger – that's just a very sad situation to be in because you're overlooking all the advantages of being where you are now. If you look at ageing positively rather than continually hankering after what used to be or what could have been, you see that life does get better as you get older.'

Does that include looks? I ask.

Evans nods. 'I feel no pressure to look younger. I feel very proud of my age, of my grey hairs, of my lines – to me they're signs of maturity, distinction, intelligence.' Then he adds, with a laugh: 'And even if they're not, that's how we ought to see them.'

Spending time with people like Evans, poring over photos of older models and attending senior pageants is having an effect on me. I have stopped avoiding mirrors because what I see in them no longer plunges me into a slough of despond. George Orwell once said that at the age of 50 everyone has the face they deserve. I am now 50 and I agree. My face looks older than it did 20 years ago and I'm okay with that. Sure, there are times, usually after a late night, when what I see in the mirror looks a little too Lucian Freud for comfort. But generally I feel good about the face staring back at me. We change as we age, and every phase has its pros and cons. My face, marked and sculpted by years of laughter, love and learning, looks more interesting to me now, like I am becoming the person I always should have been.

Singer Pat Benatar is more than a decade my senior yet her take on looking your age makes more and more sense to me. 'Every laugh line, every scar, is a badge I wear to show I've been present, the inner rings of my personal tree trunk that I display proudly for all to see,' she says. 'Nowadays I don't want a "perfect" face or body; I want to wear the life I've lived.' Like Benatar, I'm enjoying the story my face tells at 50 rather than pining for the way it looked at 25. Will I still feel the same 10 years from now? Who knows. What I can say is that right now I'm looking forward to evolving into my own version of Evans in my 60s, Deshun Wang in my 70s and maybe Sir David Attenborough in my 90s. The better I feel about growing older, the better I feel about looking older, and vice versa. Nor am I alone: Botox is far more popular among the under-40s than the over-60s.

~

As I embark on my sixth decade, I find myself fretting more about my wardrobe than my wattle. Is my future full of cardigans and corduroy? Am I doomed to wear the bottoms of my trousers rolled? Such questions are only partly motivated by vanity because there is evidence that dressing 'old' can be bad for your health. Researchers at Harvard University have shown that older people who wear what they feel is 'age-appropriate' clothing to work report more injuries and age-related illnesses than those who wear the same uniforms as younger colleagues. Their conclusion: 'Clothing can be a trigger for ageing stereotypes.'

Does that mean everyone over the age of 40 should make

a beeline for the teen section of their nearest clothing outlet? Definitely not. Some outfits can make even the fittest fifty-something look like mutton dressed as lamb. But the world is changing in ways that give us many more sartorial options in later life. When I ask Evans if there are still hard-and-fast rules on what older men can wear, he shakes his head. 'I see no reason why an 85-year-old man can't wear a pair of jeans, a printed T-shirt and a pair of Converse,' he says. 'It's how the clothes are cut and how he wears them that matters.' The same goes for women. When it comes to choosing an outfit or an accessory, the only question that matters to all those older female Instagrammers is: Does this work for me as I am now? 'You get to know your body with time, what makes you look and feel the best,' says Rodin. Iris Apfel, a ninety-something fashion designer and model, agrees. 'I don't think that age should dictate what you wear or how you can wear it,' she says. 'I think it depends on the person: there are old people at 35 and young ones at 94.'

Which brings us right back to the idea that chronological age is no longer the true measure of a person, that attitude matters much more than birthdate. It remains to be seen how far we can push this shift, especially where it relates to what we consider attractive, but at least our compass is now pointing in the right direction.

∼

Back in Las Vegas, the Ms Senior Universe contestants are sharing a triumphant post-pageant drink at a bar inside the casino at Planet Hollywood. They sit together in a colourful sea of crowns and gowns. Though passers-by toss glances our way, I notice that nobody makes a detour to crash the party. If this were a Miss Universe gathering it would be crawling with guys seeking dates, pictures and phone numbers. Caught up in their own whirlwind of laughter, gossip and raillery, the Senior pageanteers seem unfazed by the lack of attention, which gets me thinking. Is being attractive in later life less about goosing your prospects in the mating game? What happens to romance as we grow older? What does ageing mean for love, lust and libido?

CHAPTER 9

ROMANCE: THE HEART HAS NO WRINKLES

People are wrong to think that we no longer fall in love when we grow old – we grow old when we stop falling in love.
—GABRIEL GARCÍA MÁRQUEZ

What comes to mind when you think of a hot, steamy affair? Middle-agers frolicking on a sandy beach? Sixty-somethings doing the *Kama Sutra* on satin sheets? Eighty-five-year-olds making out in the back row of the cinema? Probably none of the above. Mention butterflies-in-the-stomach romance or earth-moving sex, and most of us picture young couples of airbrushed beauty. From television to Hollywood to advertising, the message is always the same: passion belongs to youth. Anyone who bends that rule faces a fusillade of jokes about cougars and Viagra.

This is not new. Many cultures have regarded sex in later life as immoral and sinful, a gateway to blindness, insanity and early death. Frisky seniors were mercilessly mocked in the plays and poems of Ancient Greece and Rome. Aristophanes warned that bedding a postmenopausal woman was 'like sleeping with death' and Juvenal poked fun at septuagenarians who couldn't get it up or keep it down. Fourteen hundred years later, during the Renaissance, Erasmus took time off from his lofty musings on the human condition to troll older women who 'still play the coquette'. Medieval literature, commedia dell'arte and English Restoration comedy all made ruthless fun of sex-crazed seniors. Even Niccolò Machiavelli, when he wasn't pondering how to win and wield political power, joined the chorus. A line from *Clizia*, a play he wrote in 1525, made it clear that hanky-panky should be left to the young: 'An old soldier is a hideous thing; an old lover even more hideous.'

Growing older not only knocked sex off the menu: even falling in love in later life was seen as unnatural. In Boccaccio's *Decameron*, written in the 14th century, Count Guido is gobsmacked when his elderly king falls head over heels: 'I find it so novel and extraordinary that you, who are already old, would fall passionately in love, that it almost seems a miracle.' Three centuries later, an Italian proverb warned that 'Anyone who falls in love when he is old should be put in the stocks'. Even just stepping out on the town was frowned upon if you were past a certain age. In early Europe, the words of Horace, the Roman poet, were widely quoted: 'The fleeces shorn near famed Lucera are fit work for you; not yours the dance-band

and the red, red rose, nor the cask drained to its last dregs.' In other words, leave the cavorting to the young.

The belief that we outgrow – or should outgrow – romantic passion is still with us today. I carry it around myself. When I see an older couple sharing a tender moment, my heart warms. *Oh, look, how sweet,* I think to myself, *still together after all these years.* It never occurs to me they might be struggling to keep their hands off each other, or in the honeymoon period of a fresh fling. And no wonder: though people have always fallen in love and had sex in later life, the taboo against doing so runs deep. That's why Jaco's Viagra prank on Lebanese TV went viral. It's also why the forty-something protagonist of Michel Houellebecq's novel *The Possibility of an Island* refers to his own sexual machinations as 'the repellent insistence of an old fart who refuses to give up the ghost'.

Much like the poets and playwrights of yesteryear, modern pop culture reflects and reinforces the pressure to hang up our romantic spurs past a certain age. Apart from the trope of ageing Lotharios bedding younger women, how often do you see a movie or a play or read a novel about older people enjoying a *grand amour,* let alone good sex? Just look at how the contestants on romance-based reality TV shows such as *The Bachelor* and *The Bachelorette* are almost always under 35. In online forums for a recent season of *Love Island,* indignant fans rounded on the twenty-something female contestants for looking too old. 'The one with all the tattoos looks about 40,' exclaimed one. When another tried to imagine what a *Love Island* for over-40s would be like, a third fan weighed in: 'No! Eww! Feel sick just thinking about it!'

Insisting that sex and romance are for the young hurts all of us. It cranks up the pressure to achieve sexual nirvana or find Mr or Ms Right early in life. It sharpens our dread of ageing by painting the later years as a romantic and erotic wasteland. It makes it harder to enjoy the fruits of love throughout our lives. It also narrows our definition of what sex can be.

The good news is that things are changing. As lifespans lengthen, the taboo against love and lust in later life is coming under review. One reason is there are now many more older people in the dating market. Why? More of us are living longer, to be sure. But we are also looking at the longevity figures, then at our partners, and asking: 'Do I want to spend all the years left to me with this person?' Even though overall divorce rates have fallen in many countries, older couples are splitting up in record numbers. The divorce rate for the over-60s has doubled in the US and tripled in Britain since 1990. The dating site Match.com reports that its fastest-growing age group is 53–72-year-olds, who already make up more than a quarter of its members. Most of these lonely hearts are diving back into the dating pool without shame – and often with the blessing and backing of family and friends.

Take Inés Hidalgo, who ran a small tobacconist's in Madrid with her husband for more than three decades. When he left her widowed at the age of 55, she feared spending the rest of her life wearing black and being celibate. After all, that's what her mother and grandmother had done. It is also what widows have traditionally been expected to do in many cultures, from Spain and Russia to Greece, Italy and Mexico.

But Hidalgo decided to turn her back on black. She felt she might live another 30 years and didn't want to spend that time cloistered away like a nun. 'The world is changing and it is more okay now to go on enjoying life when you are older,' she says. 'The traditional idea that at a certain age you must retire from pleasure just seems a bit ridiculous now.' A little more than a year after her husband's death, and with a helping hand from her children, Hidalgo uploaded her profile to an online dating website. Before long, her inbox was full of messages from men eager to chat.

When we meet on a hot, sultry evening in July, she is getting dolled up for her first date with an engineer called Ernesto. He has suggested meeting in a sherry bar and then strolling round the Plaza Mayor. An hour before their rendezvous, Hidalgo's small apartment on the outskirts of town is a diorama of date-night mayhem. Steam from the shower fills the bathroom. Rejected outfits lie draped across the bed and pots of makeup stand open on the dressing table. The pop song 'Despacito' is playing at full volume from a radio somewhere in the kitchen. 'Whenever I meet a man for the first time like this I feel nervous, of course, but I also feel alive,' Hidalgo tells me. 'And if there is no spark then it's no big deal: there are lots of other men out there.'

By the time she is ready to hit the town she looks chic, fun and confident in her favourite polka-dot dress and red lipstick. What would her mother or grandmother have made of her late-life coquetry? I ask.

She pauses for a moment to consider the question. 'Well, they would certainly be surprised because for their generation many doors closed after a certain age,' she says, checking her hair in the hallway mirror. 'But I also think they would be envious that things are changing: after all, the capacity for love never dies, so why not enjoy it as long as you can?'

As I watch Hidalgo striding in her heels towards the metro stop, I try to imagine what it is like to fall in love later in life. My gut tells me it's sweet yet lacking in the pyrotechnics of young romance. Thankfully, my gut turns out to be completely wrong.

This becomes plain the moment I encounter Lily Crawford and Jack Payton, two divorcees who met while online dating in their late 50s. After a few weeks of exchanging emails and chatting on the phone, they agreed to do lunch at a restaurant halfway between their homes in England. What happened next can only be described as a *coup de foudre*. 'It was the most bizarre experience,' says Payton. 'We got out of our cars and just ran towards each other and hugged like we'd known one another for years.' He pauses for a moment, still marvelling at the memory. 'When you get older you think things like that are just for young people, but there we were in this car park looking into each other's eyes thinking, *What just happened?*'

Next came a whirlwind courtship worthy of a Mills and Boon novel or an episode of *The Bachelor*, complete with candlelit dinners, dancing till dawn, outings to the theatre, walks by the sea, a trip to New York – and lots of hot sex. Listening to them talk about their romantic fireworks, I catch myself wondering: *Is this for real?* These people were nearly

60 when they met. Maybe they've just forgotten the intensity of falling in love when you're young. Crawford brushes aside my scepticism with a complicit chuckle. 'I know exactly why you feel that way because I felt the same,' she says. 'But what I discovered, and it's been quite a revelation, is that meeting someone in later life is exactly like meeting someone in your teenage years or your early 20s,' she says. 'All those feelings – the butterflies in your stomach, the trembling, the excitement of getting ready for a date – they're just the same, and possibly even greater.'

Okay, so the heart can still skip a beat in your 60s. But what about later? Can romance hit the same heights after 70? Turns out it can. Crawford was partly inspired to date again by seeing her own widowed mother land a boyfriend at the age of 92 and live out her final years in lovestruck bliss. 'She was behaving just like a teenager and they had so much fun together,' she says. 'I thought, *If you can have that at her age then you can have it at any age.*'

Persuading people that romance is age-blind is not easy in a world in thrall to youth, which is where people like Marina Rozenman, a Paris-based writer, come in. When she was a teenager, her 71-year-old grandmother started a passionate affair with an 81-year-old neighbour. It changed Rozenman's view of romance forever. 'Falling in love at any age became the norm to me,' she says. 'I understood from that day that while the body grows old, the heart beats the same until the end.'

Rozenman set about tackling the cult of young love within her own social circle. To comfort friends suffering in bad relationships or fearing they might never escape Planet Single, she trotted out the story of her loved-up granny. Her message: it's never too late to find love, even the love of your life. 'My granny's story had a kind of power and everyone took it home as if it were a magic potion,' she says. 'It cheered them up and reassured them because they thought, *Phew, if love can happen right up till the end, then I have time*.'

In her early 30s, Rozenman decided to share that potion more widely by writing a book about falling head over heels in later life. She spent two years travelling around France to interview people in their 70s, 80s and 90s. While the project lacked the glamour of her day job, which was writing celebrity profiles in *ELLE* magazine, it solidified her conviction that romance never gets old. 'All the people I interviewed talked about love and sensuality in a way that made me feel almost envious,' she says. 'I learned that when you start a new love affair, even late in life, it is simply a love affair, and age really doesn't matter.' Her book, entitled *Le cœur n'a pas de rides* (*The Heart Has No Wrinkles*), made a splash when it appeared in 2012. Rozenman gave scores of media interviews, often flanked by her granny. They told the public to be bold, to seize the day, no matter what your age. 'Even if you are 80, and someone gives you butterflies in your stomach, go for it,' says Rozenman. 'Even if it only lasts two months, it's worth it.'

Of course, not everyone is in the market for new love in later life. Many of us are growing older with a partner. What does ageing do to a long-term relationship?

That depends. Obviously many couples fall apart over

time. But for those who stick together ageing can help the relationship ripen. Over the years, couples tend to argue less because they find ways to iron out or finesse their differences. Many discover that growing older under the same roof brings them closer, fanning rather than extinguishing the romantic flame.

Take Daisy and Michael Shaw, who are looking forward to celebrating their 60th wedding anniversary in Dallas, Texas, with their four children, 10 grandchildren and six great-grandchildren. They met at a drive-in in 1961 and tied the knot after courting for a few months. Michael then landed a job in the oil industry and Daisy became a schoolteacher. Like many couples, they had their ups and downs.

'Some of the downs were very down, but we worked through it,' says Daisy. 'Partly because that's what you did in those days, but also because there really was something worth fighting for there.' The adrenaline rush of their early courtship has evolved into something richer and more textured today. 'There is so much shared history and understanding and respect built up over the years – you know the other person to their core and they know you in the same way, and that's such a wonderful feeling,' says Daisy. 'The other day I saw Mike outside explaining something to a courier and he looked so gentle and I just felt this incredible rush of love for him. I was literally swooning like a 16-year-old at the kitchen sink.'

Though Mother Teresa was herself single, she was clearly on to something when she observed that 'love is a fruit in season at all times, and within reach of every hand'. Learning that romance deepens as you grow older, or that you can fall hard for someone at any age, is already making me feel better about ageing. But what about sex? Again, my gut tells me the prognosis is poor, that ageing is a ticket to relentless sexual decline. But again my gut is wrong.

Studies show that sexual desire can carry on throughout life. Clearly, the body changes. Erections become less frequent and reliable, women can suffer from vaginal dryness and both sexes take longer to warm up and reach climax. In a performance-obsessed world where non-stop nookie is the gold standard, that all sounds catastrophic, but it need not be, not by a long shot. As the novelist Erica Jong observed: 'Sex doesn't disappear, it just changes forms.' Even as it becomes less frequent and frenetic it can carry on being just as pleasurable, if not more so. On his 80th birthday, Georges Clemenceau was taking a walk on the Champs-Elysées in Paris when a beautiful young woman strolled past. Without missing a beat, the French statesman turned to his friend and sighed: 'Oh, to be 70 again.'

Though sex tends to be a minority pursuit in advanced old age, surveys in Britain show that 80 per cent of sexually active men between the ages of 50 and 90 are satisfied with their sex lives. The figure for women is 92 per cent. Yet when these numbers were released, many reacted with tittering disbelief or with the same 'yuck' reflex most of us feel when contemplating our own parents getting it on. David Lee, one of the authors of the study, was surprised neither by the findings nor the public reaction. 'There's this misconception that sex belongs to young people,' he says. 'The reactions of the young to older people having sex range from humour and disgust to disbelief that the over-50s are having it at all.'

Thankfully, that misconception is now being challenged – even in the courts. In 1995, a 50-year-old woman named Maria Ivone Carvalho Pinto de Sousa Morais checked into a hospital in Lisbon, Portugal, to undergo surgery for Bartholinitis, a painful vaginal condition. The doctors botched the operation, leaving her with permanent nerve damage. She suffered from incontinence, depression and chronic pain and was unable to sit, walk or have sex. Eventually, in 2013, after nearly two decades of legal wrangling, a Portuguese judge awarded her damages. A year later, however, a higher court slashed her payout by a third. One reason given for the cut: harm was done to Morais at 'an age when sex is not as important as in younger years'. In the past, such reasoning would have been read as conventional wisdom, but today it sparked a public outcry. Commentators and social media users lambasted the court for its ageist assumption that sex belongs to the young. 'My 50th birthday is coming up soon,' one woman tweeted. 'Will someone give me a No Entry sign to place on my vagina?' Others accused the court of sexism given that Portuguese men have been awarded much higher damages after medical mistakes robbed them of the ability to have sex. One critic warned of 'Taliban jurisprudence'.

The hue and cry led to a new legal precedent that speaks volumes about how our expectations for later life are rising. In 2017, the European Court of Human Rights overturned the ruling in Portugal, criticising it for reinforcing the 'traditional idea' that women should no longer need or desire sex once their childbearing years are finished. 'This breaks a suffocating taboo,' said one Portuguese pundit. 'The message is loud and clear: sex can be important at any age.'

The truth is that older people are not only having sex, but often enjoying it more. We have already seen how ageing delivers dividends that compensate for the ebbing away of physical vigour everywhere from sports to work. Now we can add the bedroom to that list. In the younger years, sex can be hampered by worries over performance, looks, self-esteem, emotions. But that anxiety often melts away over time. As we age, we become more confident and better acquainted with how our bodies work – both prerequisites for good sex. This is especially true for women, who often find it easier to reach orgasm in their 40s than in their 20s. As we age we build up our knowledge of how to pleasure others, and our greater social acumen gives us an edge in romance and seduction.

Ageing also reduces and eventually removes the risk of pregnancy, which can make heterosexual couples feel more relaxed between the sheets. Feminist icons such as Jane Fonda, Nancy Friday and Betty Friedan have praised the menopause for freeing women up to be more sexual. At the same time, drugs such as Viagra and Cialis can do wonders for erectile dysfunction, which can strike men at any age but is more prevalent after the age of 40.

Nine years into their relationship, and despite a long campaign by Crawford's sons to keep them apart, she and Payton both feel they're having the best sex of their lives. But getting there meant conquering their own ageism. 'Early on we said to ourselves, "This will only work if we don't worry or think about how old we are,"' says Payton, who is now 67. 'If we'd hung onto the old "we're 60, we shouldn't be doing this, or that", it would never have worked. But we forgot our age and it worked so well. We had sex, the lot, we did everything that kids do with no inhibitions, and it worked so well.' When I ask Crawford, who is 69, if Payton still rocks her world between the sheets, she giggles like a giddy debutante. 'Oh, absolutely,' she says. 'We are still operating!'

The much older couples that Rozenman interviewed also raved about *le grand frisson* they felt in bed together. 'We are living an exquisite moment,' said one woman. 'We are living a waking dream. It is miraculous, magic, magnificent. Whenever I touch his shoulder, it is ecstasy on his face. Our bodies attract each other. Our mouths never stop finding pleasure together.' Heck, if that's what the future holds, then growing older suddenly looks a lot less bleak.

Of course, getting naked in front of a new partner can be unnerving at any age – and even more so when you feel past your physical prime. One way to calm the jitters is to deploy that old slayer of ageism: humour. Payton and Crawford eased their way into bed together by poking fun at what might – or might not – occur once their clothes were off. 'Before it happened we were joking and laughing about it a lot,' says Payton. 'When you're a couple of washed-up old farts having a laugh it just doesn't matter as much and the sex ends up being more relaxed and fun.'

Even the physical slowing down that occurs as we age

can be a blessing in disguise. Women often complain that younger men are too fast in bed: too quick to get aroused, too rushed to notice or decipher the needs and desires of their partners, too eager to rack up as many orgasms as possible. By slowing them down physically, ageing can help men be more attentive, which is why some sex therapists think males hit their sexual prime in middle age. Removing the swinging-from-the-chandelier acrobatics, and the performance anxiety that often results, can also open up space for deeper intimacy and sensuality, more play and tenderness – a bonus for lovers of any age. Later in life, when erections are harder to come by, many couples find other ways – using toys or extended foreplay, for instance – to make the earth move without penetration.

In another survey, sexually active Britons over 80 reported more sexual and emotional closeness than those between 50 and 69. This is especially so for long-term couples who build up intimacy over the years. Some research suggests the best sex happens between partners who have been together for 15 years or longer. Of course, all that familiarity – waking up side by side day after day, sharing a bathroom, rowing over household chores – erodes the thrill of the honeymoon period. But in a strong relationship it also clears the way for the three key ingredients of good lovemaking: honesty, communication and closeness. Or, as Mark Twain put it: 'Love seems the swiftest, but it is the slowest of all growths. No man or woman knows what perfect love is until they have been married a quarter of a century.'

That chimes with the experience of David Evans, the Grey

Fox, who married his wife 40 years ago. 'The red-hot passion and many-times-a-night thing peters out but is replaced by something deeper, less frantic and more meaningful,' he says. 'Instead of the wham-bang-thank-you-ma'am, it's more sensual, with more warmth and contact – and to be honest, in many ways it's better.'

Michael Shaw agrees. 'When you're young, it's all about the physical release or notches on the bedpost,' he says. 'But that's crazy: it's like standing in front of a buffet and only sampling one dish.' Now in their 80s, the Shaws make love at a more leisurely pace, taking time to explore, savour and connect. Their long, shared history adds an extra frisson. 'When we make love we're bringing the memories of a life-time of sharing a bed together,' says Daisy. 'That can just turbo-charge the whole experience.'

While people like the Shaws build on or fine-tune what they have always done between the sheets, others find that ageing inspires them to rewrite the romantic rule book altogether. Witness the numbers turning to same-sex relationships for the first time in later life. The phenome-non is now so common among women that psychologists have coined the term 'late-blooming lesbian' to describe it. Researchers are starting to think sexual identity might be just as fluid in middle age and beyond as it is in adoles-cence. Lisa Diamond, an associate professor of psychology and gender studies at the University of Utah, suspects that ageing itself broadens our sexual palette. 'What we know about adult development suggests that people become more expansive in a number of ways as they get older,' she says. 'I

203

think a lot of women, late in life, when they're no longer worried about raising the kids, and when they're looking back on their marriage and how satisfying it is, find an opportunity to take a second look at what they want and feel like.'

Megan Cartwright, a paralegal in Toronto, fits that model to a tee. In her youth she occasionally found other women attractive but never went as far as sleeping with one. 'I made out with a few girls at parties but I just put that down to raging hormones and too much beer,' she says. 'I thought of myself as straight and that was that.' At 25, she married and had three children. Bobbing along in the slipstream of family life, and happy in bed with her husband, she felt zero erotic interest in other women. Those same-sex fumblings in the college dorm were filed away, along with that nose piercing in Tijuana, in a drawer marked Teenaged Moments of Madness. But then her marriage fell apart, and she found herself back on the market one week before her 45th birthday.

Like many middle-agers, Cartwright was terrified by the prospect of dating again. She worried about how her children would react to a new partner. She also fretted about her appearance – the wrinkles, the cellulite, the scar left by a Caesarean delivery. To boost her confidence, she hired a professional photographer to take her profile pictures. The shoot changed everything for two reasons. First, it made Cartwright feel sexy again. 'I was so self-conscious at first that I couldn't even look into the camera,' she remembers. 'But then we sat down and looked at some beautiful portraits of older women like Helen Mirren and I just thought, *Well, if it's okay for them to be sexy, why can't I?* and the shoot went great from there.' Second, towards the end of the session, Cartwright caught herself checking out the female photographer. She went home with her head spinning. 'Later that night, when I was filling in my first online dating profile, I came to the section asking what I was looking for and without even really thinking about it I ticked the box for women,' she says. 'I don't know if the desire to be with a woman was always there or if it was something new, but either way my 45-year-old self was confident enough to own it.'

The first few months of online dating were a rollercoaster and Cartwright endured her share of wackos and weirdos: the one who wept every time she mentioned her ex-husband; the one who could not stop brushing her hair; the one who went to the bathroom before dessert and never returned. But eventually she struck gold in the form of a schoolteacher called Naz. 'The attraction was instant,' says Cartwright. 'It was electric.' After a couple of dates they tumbled into bed together. A dreamy expression washes over Cartwright's face as she remembers her first lesbian experience. 'It was hot, it was sweet, it was sensual, it was raunchy – it was just everything I hoped it would be,' she says.

The fling with Naz fizzled out but it made Cartwright feel a whole lot better about ageing. 'What I realise now is that when you're young you just don't have the experience or the self-awareness or the guts to say, "This is who I am, this is what I need, this is what I want for myself,"' she says. 'You gain all that stuff as you get older and it allows you to spread your wings.'

That boldness has spilled from the bedroom into the rest of her life. Cartwright recently started rock climbing and learning Spanish – two things she never imagined taking up in her late 40s. 'I used to be really bummed about getting older but now I see things differently,' she says. 'Ageing can actually be a gift if you go on learning about yourself and finding new things to enjoy.'

Jürgen Schroeder is on the same page. He was a faithful husband to his high-school sweetheart in Munich, Germany, until her death three years ago. Their marriage was solid, and they raised four children together. 'We had a good life so I never strayed,' says Schroeder, who is an electrician. 'But it also helped that I had very little confidence with women.' This is a stunning admission. At 64, Schroeder is a fine-looking man, tall and trim with a shock of silver hair swept back like an ice-cream sundae. He laughs easily and has the seducer's gift of always looking fascinated by what others have to say. In photographs from his younger days he looks like a Teutonic Cary Grant. But Schroeder never saw it that way. Teased at school for being chubby, he carried on feeling unattractive even after he had shed the puppy fat. It was only in his 50s that he began to feel sure of himself in female company. When bachelorhood struck at the age of 61, he was ready to make up for lost time. When I meet Schroeder at a noisy café in Munich, the first thing he says is: 'The best thing about ageing is the confidence you develop.' Then he tells me he is juggling three girlfriends, ranging in ages from 47 to 68, all of whom know of each other.

Are you sleeping with all three? I ask.

'Oh, yes,' he says, with a cat-got-the-cream grin. 'With each woman it is different but it is the best sex I have ever known.' Like many people in later life, Schroeder is widening, rather than narrowing, his sexual repertoire. With one girlfriend he is exploring light bondage, with another it's costumes and role-playing. The third recently persuaded him to attend his first sex party.

The biggest surprise for Schroeder, though, has been discovering the heady joys of romance. By his own admission, he was never one for wooing with chocolates, flowers or poetry in his youth, but now he could give Casanova lessons. He slips *billets-doux* into his girlfriends' purses and sends them WhatsApp audios of him singing love songs. He cooks them ambitious Italian meals and his foot rubs are legendary. 'I have learned that when it comes to erotic pleasure between two people the most intense thrills are in the mind,' he says. 'The brain is the most important sexual organ.'

And, as we have already seen, the brain is like a fine wine: in many ways, it gets better with age.

∿

Popular culture is making more room for the idea of sexual passion among the not-so-young. Tapping into growing demand from older readers, authors of romantic fiction, from Nora Roberts to Emma Miller, are publishing novels built around characters over 40. Television is moving in the same direction, with more shows featuring older people falling in and out of love. In *Grace and Frankie*, the lives of two seventy-something couples are blown apart when both husbands leave their wives – to live together as a gay couple. *Mum*, a British comedy-drama, has won rave reviews for its bittersweet depiction of a middle-aged woman stumbling towards a love affair with a man the same age. The 2017 movie *The Wife* opens with a frank sex scene between Glenn Close and Jonathan Pryce, who were both aged 70 at the time. Off-screen, meanwhile, older celebrities such as Jennifer Lopez, Madonna, Sam Taylor-Johnson, Julianne Moore, Robin Wright and Jennifer Aniston are tearing up the dating rules to step out with much younger men. Brigitte Macron is 24 years older than her husband, the current president of France.

Time for a caveat: the last thing we want to do is replace the taboo against 'wrinkly romance' with the expectation that everyone be hot to trot right up till their deathbed. Making the most of the longevity revolution means being free to choose, without guilt or shame, the role played by love, romance or sex in your life. Many will want them front and centre. Some may prefer to dabble from time to time. Others will be content to let them fade away altogether.

History is replete with examples of people relieved to find themselves ageing out of romantic and sexual turbulence. When someone asked the elderly Sophocles in the fifth century BC if he was still capable of falling in love, he replied: 'Hush! If you please: to my great delight I have escaped from it, and feel as if I had escaped from a frantic and savage master.' A century later, Isidore of Seville, an early Christian scholar, praised ageing for freeing 'us from the most violent of masters . . . it smashes the force of lust, it increases wisdom, and it grants wiser counsels.' Even today, when the cultural pressure to be sexual, or at least coupled up, is immense, people are standing up for their right to be neither. Some feminist thinkers, from Germaine Greer and Gloria Steinem to Diana Kurz and Nancy Miller, credit the menopause with freeing women from sex.

Younger people are putting their own spin on that message. Shanthony Exum recently released a rap song hailing the joys of being single in later life. It was called 'Paper Mache (Single AF)' and the funky video starred a 60-year-old woman. 'I want to change that narrative around being single when you're older,' says Exum. 'We need more stories about older people who are leading rich, interesting lives without being partnered.'

As long as you are not lonely, there are clear benefits to being single in later life. You have more time and energy for yourself. You do not have to share a bathroom, chocolate or the remote control with anyone else. You call the shots.

You can also give more of yourself to the world.

CHAPTER 10

CARE: WE, NOT ME

When you stop giving and offering
something to the rest of the world, it's
time to turn out the lights.

—GEORGE BURNS

Rubbish is a big problem in Lebanon. It's everywhere. Piled in the streets and on beaches. Floating in the sea. Lying loose in ditches. Blowing through parks and across farmland like tumbleweed. Littering sometimes feels like the national sport, with locals merrily tossing plastic bottles, wrappers and other trash from cars and buses. When the temperature soars, the rancid smell of decomposing waste hangs in the air.

Garbage graduated from being a problem to a crisis in 2015. That was when Lebanon closed its main landfill site with no alternative at the ready. Result: households and businesses began dumping waste all over the place. By 2017, the trash mountain near Beirut airport was attracting enough seagulls to pose a threat to planes taking off and landing. Unwilling, or unable, to find a new home for the illegal dump, local officials sent in hunters to shoot the birds out of the sky.

Most Lebanese put this shambles down to the failure of their political class to rebuild their country following the end of the long civil war in 1990. Today, Lebanon is hobbled by corruption, mismanagement and sectarian squabbling. Protesters fed up with the rubbish crisis taunt the nation's politicians with the slogan 'You Stink'.

Small wonder, then, that private citizens have stepped into the breach, setting up non-profit schemes to tackle the garbage problem. Who is spearheading the pushback? Lebanese millennials are doing their thing on social media but the country's most fêted anti-trash warrior was born long before anyone had heard of flash mobs or crowdsourcing. Her name is Zeinab Mokalled, and she is 81-years old.

On a hot, hazy day in the middle of summer, I drive up into the hills of southern Lebanon to meet her. She lives in Arabsalim, a small town near the border with Israel. The trip from Beirut serves up a microcosm of the country's environmental woes. Every road is lined with trash, some bagged, the rest scattered, all of it stinking in the July heat. Even the olive groves, the backstop of the local economy for centuries, are dotted with plastic bags that flap in the wind like toy flags. In the middle of this desert of debris, Arabsalim stands out like an oasis of tidiness, a little slice of Switzerland. Okay, so it's not quite that immaculate – visitors still toss garbage out the window as they drive through – but by Lebanese standards the town is startlingly tidy.

On the outskirts, I spot a single-storey building with a corrugated metal roof. Paintings of trees, flags and the sun adorn the whitewashed walls. A sign in French and Arabic reads: 'Recycling'. I get out to investigate. The inside is crammed with boxes and sacks overflowing with paper, glass and plastic. A man named Mohamed Mazraani is fiddling with a machine that grinds plastic into pellets. When I tell him I am visiting from London he gives me a so-what shrug: foreigners come here all the time, he tells me. He brightens up when I ask about Mokalled. 'She has put Arabsalim on the map,' he says, making a sweeping gesture with his arms. 'She made all this happen.'

When I finally reach her home, Mokalled, a former schoolteacher, is waiting in the breezy living-room. A tray piled high with assorted baklava sits on the table like a cruise liner ready to sail. She is dressed modestly in a salmon-pink hijab. Her voice is so soft that I have to lean forward to hear her, yet there is enough steel in her manner that you know she does not suffer fools gladly. As she pours me a cup of dark, sugary tea, I ask how she became an eco-celebrity in Lebanon. The question makes her chuckle in a way that seems almost girlish. She takes a sip of tea and then rewinds back to the Israeli occupation in the 1980s and 1990s.

It was a time of great hardship in southern Lebanon, she tells me. With the fighting and bombings, many public services in Arabsalim ground to a halt. Rubbish piled up all over town, attracting flies and rats and posing a risk to children playing outside. By 1995, Mokalled decided enough was enough. At the time, she was nearly 60, an age when

Lebanese women, especially in the Muslim community, are expected to be easing into a quiet grandmotherhood. Mokalled, by contrast, was morphing into an environmental warrior.

She wanted to do much more than just remove rubbish from the streets – she wanted to make Arabsalim the first place in Lebanon to recycle domestic waste. Since the town had no mayor or municipal government, her first port of call was the local governor, who brushed her aside. 'He said to me: "What are you thinking? Arabsalim is not Paris,"' she recalls. 'That was when I knew I had to do something myself.' What she did was start a recycling revolution.

Mokalled began by sorting her own trash and then persuaded a dozen other local women to follow suit. Together, they split the town up into sectors and went door to door to win more converts. It was tough. Lebanon did not yet have a single plant for recycling household waste and locals told the women they should be at home cooking for their families instead of trying to save the planet. But Mokalled's merry band of rubbish rebels persevered, using their own cars to collect the sorted trash until one of their number scraped together the cash to buy a beat-up old truck. Mokalled gave over her backyard as a storage area and scoured the country to find companies willing to start recycling household waste. As more families in Arabsalim signed up, the women created a non-government organisation named *Nidaa Al Ard* (Call of the Earth), which helped attract funding from home and abroad.

Corruption has always been a hindrance. Remember

that machine for grinding plastic in the recycling depot? Originally one just like it was sent from Europe but vanished en route, with only the instruction manual arriving in Arabsalim. Rather than give up, however, Mokalled found a savvy local mechanic who used the manual to build a replacement from scratch. 'It has been a long and constant struggle and we have made many sacrifices,' she says.

Eventually the women pulled together enough money to build the recycling depot, buy a new truck and hire Mazraani. Today, the citizens of Arabsalim collect two tons of plastic, the same amount of paper, and one ton of glass for recycling every month. Their efforts have been copied elsewhere in Lebanon and inspired other green projects locally. These days, many homes in Arabsalim use solar power to heat their water and there are plans afoot to set up a composting scheme.

It all adds up to a remarkable achievement that has turned Mokalled into a figurehead of the green movement. She has won international awards and features regularly in the media. But you can tell celebrity is of zero interest to her. What matters is doing the right thing. 'I wanted to do something for my homeland, for the environment and for my people,' she says. 'It was a very strong calling that I felt.'

I ask if age played any part in hearing that call. She nods. 'When you are younger you are generally busy with work and family,' she says. 'When you are older you can focus more on your own projects and ambitions.'

Was it just by chance, then, that her project turned out to be for the greater good? Could she just as easily have ploughed her energy into setting up a private equity firm or an online betting company? Or is there a natural link between ageing and altruism? Mokalled ponders this for a moment. 'I believe very strongly that we should seek to give back at every age, but the urge to do so seems to get stronger as we grow older,' she says. 'Maybe as we age we become more altruistic.'

This stops me in my tracks. Can it be true? Do we really become more eager to help others and give back as we grow older? Does ageing nudge the selfish gene into recession? My inner sceptic immediately starts listing the many people who seem to disprove the theory. Bernie Madoff was certainly not thinking of the greater good while running the biggest Ponzi scheme in American history at the age of 70. Nor has US President Donald Trump shown much sign of a philanthropic surge in later life. True, Ebenezer Scrooge, literature's patron saint of misanthropes, eventually embraced altruism – but only after being scared half to death by three ghosts.

At the same time, young people can also feel a strong drive to help others. Look at all the millennials setting up social enterprises that put purpose before profit or the young plutocrats of Silicon Valley creating philanthropic foundations to funnel their wealth into noble causes. When choosing where to work, many younger people favour employers that promote good works.

The yawning wealth gap between the generations casts further doubt on Mokalled's theory of a special bond between ageing and altruism. Many retirees are now sitting on enviably large nest eggs thanks to perks that are no longer within reach of most people under 40: property ownership, free education, rock-solid pensions, stable employment. Are older voters rising as one to demand sweeping reform and redistribution? The hell they are.

And yet Mokalled is clearly on to something. Even if older voters show little appetite for backing policies that would redistribute wealth across the generations, what they do in daily life speaks of altruism. Around the world, people tend to donate more time and money to good causes after the age of 35. In Britain, the over-60s are twice as likely as the under-30s to give to charity, and Americans over 55 rack up 3.3 billion hours of volunteer work every year. Around the world, many charities, big and small, could not survive without the unpaid labour of older citizens.

How to explain this? One theory is that it is easier to give back when we are older because we have more to give: more money, time, skills, experience. But that does not account for studies showing that the impulse to put purpose before personal gain in later life is just as strong regardless of income, education or health.

Enter a second theory: ageing itself triggers a deeper, existential shift. Erik Erikson, a prominent psychoanalyst, coined the term 'generativity' to describe the 'ability to transcend personal interests to provide care and concern for younger and older generations'. He reckoned this altruistic urge comes upon us somewhere between the ages of 40 and 64. Lars Tornstam, a sociologist, agreed. He invented another word, 'gerotranscendence', to express how growing older makes us feel less interested in material things and more connected to other people. Others argue that the sharper awareness of death that comes with ageing spurs us to care more for others. In his book, *A Year to Live*, Stephen Levine points out that 'when people know they are going to die, that last year is often the most loving, most conscious, and most caring – even under conditions of poor concentration, the side effects of medication, and so on'.

Bottom line: as we age, we mind less but care more.

Helen Dennis witnesses that shift every day. Based in California, she is the author of a syndicated column called 'Successful Ageing' and an expert in forging new career paths in later life. She has worked with over 15,000 people, from accountants and senior executives to engineers and factory workers, and believes that Mokalled is spot-on. 'It just seems to be a natural part of our life trajectory,' she says. 'As you realise your time here is finite, those questions come up: Have I made a difference in the world, in my family, in my community? What footprint will I leave behind? What is my legacy?'

Plenty of research bears this out. One recent survey found that 85 per cent of US retirees over the age of 50 defined success as 'being generous' rather than as 'being wealthy'. Translation: climbing the corporate ladder or padding a pension pot becomes less important than helping people and projects that make a meaningful difference in the world. Simone de Beauvoir regarded serving a higher purpose in our later years as both a civic duty and an existential imperative. 'There is only one solution if old age is not to be an absurd parody of our former life,' she wrote in her 1970 book *The Coming of Age*. 'And that is to go on pursuing ends that give our existence meaning – devotion to individuals, to groups or to causes, social, political, intellectual and creative work.'

Studies show that helping others boosts the immune system, lowers blood pressure and enhances general well-being – all good news for ageing. It can also fuel that positivity effect we learned about earlier. The Chinese have a saying that goes: 'If you want happiness for an hour, take a nap. If you want happiness for a day, go fishing. If you want happiness for a year, inherit a fortune. If you want happiness for a lifetime, help somebody.' Saint Francis of Assisi agreed when he observed back in the 13th century that 'it is in giving that we receive'. Winston Churchill turned the same sentiment into an aphorism that often does the rounds on social media: 'We make a living by what we get; we make a life by what we give.' Even science backs this up now. Recent experiments using fMRI scans show that the act of giving stimulates the same happy regions of the brain that light up when we eat or have sex. This jibes with my own experience. Some of my happiest memories come from the volunteering I did in my youth, from feeding paralysed patients in hospital to working with street children in Brazil. The best part is I can now look forward to enjoying similar experiences even more in the future. Why? Because studies show that charitable giving delivers a bigger emotional kick in later life.

The bond between ageing and altruism is so well established now that some argue for another layer to be added to Maslow's hierarchy of needs. Call it what you like – philanthropy, legacy, transcendence – it adds up to the same thing: the human yearning to serve a cause larger than the self and to leave the world a better place than we found it.

This is good news for many reasons. It suggests we can look forward to finding more meaning and purpose as we age and torpedoes the idea that older people are a burden. It also means the longevity revolution can help make the world a better, less selfish place. Over the next two decades, US retirees are expected to donate $8 trillion – yes, trillion – to charities in cash and volunteer work. Some futurists think that, as the population ages, service to others could become the new status symbol of the global economy, arousing more admiration than fancy job titles and net worth.

∼

More and more people are lending credence to Mokalled's theory by following her example. Take 53-year-old Jacki Zehner, the youngest woman ever to make partner at Goldman Sachs. Despite the riches on offer, she left the bank to devote her life to improving the lot of women and girls as the CEO of Women Moving Millions, a non-profit whose members pledge large sums to fund projects ranging from school building to documentary films. Older Canadians have raised millions of dollars to help grandparents care for children orphaned by AIDS in Africa. Grandmother Power, an activist movement created by Paola Gianturco, a seventy-something photojournalist, inspires women across the world to find ways to improve education, health and human rights for the next generation. Carol Fox has gone further by devoting her later years to rewriting the rules of philanthropy. She left a career in the art and museum sector to teach the new rich in China how to spend their money on charity. Now in her mid-70s, she jets across the globe to help channel funds into environmental, social and cultural causes that would have been ignored a few years ago.

Altruism in later life is now so common that there are even awards for it. Every year, the AARP gives a Purpose Prize to five Americans over 60 who do stand-out work for the social good. Recent winners have come up with ways to tutor prison inmates, help foster families, supply feminine hygiene products to a Kenyan orphanage and encourage girls to fall in love with science. Every backstory is a testament to the compassion, nous and experience that come with ageing. Robert Chambers won for founding More Than Wheels, a company that offers auto loans to the rural poor at low interest rates. As a car salesman, he had seen how hard it was for such people to find fair financing at dealerships. When he was honoured at the White House, Chambers said: 'I was old enough to know injustice when I saw it – and experienced enough to do something about it.'

Many climb on the altruism train while still at the top of their game in the workplace. At the age of 49, Michael Sheen scaled back on his acting work to lead a campaign to provide affordable credit to people on low incomes. Laila Zahed was around the same age and working as a clinical geneticist at a top hospital in Beirut when she began devoting more time to social projects. To teach middle-class Lebanese children about the culture of their immigrant maids, she wrote and published books on Sri Lanka, Ethiopia and the Philippines. In 2016, at the age of 56, she stumbled on a way to tackle two of her country's biggest problems – rubbish and refugees – at the same time.

More than a million Syrians have fled civil war in their homeland to seek refuge in neighbouring Lebanon since 2011. Many have been stuck here for years, living in make-shift camps or cramped apartments, surviving on hand-outs or odd jobs in the black market, subject to curfews, never knowing when or if they will return home. Zahed's idea: teach them how to turn plastic bags into artisanal goods.

Seven women are now signed up to her project in the Bekaa Valley, just across the border from battle-ravaged Syria. They collect plastic bags and then fold and cut them into strips to make a tough yarn. With that they crochet everything from handbags, pouches and bottle holders to tissue dispensers and placemats. From her home 70 kilometres away in Beirut, Zahed uses WhatsApp to discuss product design and sales tactics with the group. 'I have to make sure the stuff they are making is upmarket and saleable,' she says. 'Otherwise they will often produce things that are too flowery and tradi-tional.' Their colourful handiwork now sells in markets and on Facebook but Zahed makes no money herself. All profits go straight back into the project or to the crocheters, who, in a good month, might clear US$100, a handsome wage here.

When I arrive in the Bekaa Valley, five of the Syrian women are waiting for me in the basement of a spartan, ramshackle building. The air is stuffy and smells of masonry. Black tea and biscuits are laid out on a low table. After the warm welcome, the mood darkens as the women list the woes common to refugees the world over: The yearning for home. Thwarted ambitions. Physical discomfort. Violence and boredom. Anxiety about their children's future. Endless paperwork and crumbling self-esteem. The cold shoulder from locals fed up with so many uninvited guests in their midst. Only one topic brightens the mood: the plastic-bag project.

Amina Hafez Al Zouhouri fled to Lebanon with her husband and seven children in 2011. The 59-year-old was a seamstress back home, so signing up with Zahed was a no-brainer. Her husband, who has no work here, turns the plastic bags into yarn while she does the crocheting. 'The money is a lifesaver,' she says. 'But I also feel like I have my self-respect and dignity back again because I am working and being creative.' A wave of smiles and nods and hands-on-heart gestures washes round the room.

I feel like doing the same when I meet Zahed back in Beirut. She is slight, with short, brown hair, a toothy smile and the restless energy of someone with a long to-do list. Being in her company is a tonic; her drive to make the world a better place, and her conviction that ageing is about opening rather than closing doors, are electrifying. 'I am very happy running this crocheting project now, seeing how it helps these women, but who knows what will come next?' she says, flashing that big smile. 'I know something will come and I am curious to find out what it is!'

Hanging out with Mokalled and Zahed puts my own relationship with altruism under the microscope. I stopped volunteering in my 20s as work and then children took pole position. Though my career as a writer and speaker is animated by a desire to make the world a better place, I increasingly feel the urge to do more. Where do I start? I turn to Zahed for counsel. 'Don't overthink things,' she tells me. 'It's unlikely you'll dream up the perfect project while sitting at your desk. Just dive in, try stuff out, see what feels right. Keep an open mind and build one step at a time. I never in my life imagined setting up a project with plastic bags and Syrian refugees, but once you're out doing good things in the world one thing just leads to another.'

Others follow a more direct path to service in later life: taking the skills they have built up over the years and offering them up for free. That is the thinking behind Volunteers in Medicine, which runs nearly 100 medical clinics across the United States. More than 600 older physicians, nurses, dentists and social workers now handle 30,000 patient visits every year – without charging a dime. Dr Jack McConnell, the group's founder, called later-life volunteerism 'the wave of the future'.

It certainly feels that way at the Ruffin Family Clinic in Las Vegas. The bright, new facility on the edge of downtown is a godsend for the uninsured poor who flock here for free medical care. When I roll up on a weekday afternoon, Janet Maran, a 71-year-old nurse with short, silver hair and a stethoscope round her neck, is attending to patients. Brisk but friendly, she has been volunteering since her 60s and now puts in four hours every week at the Ruffin clinic. When I ask if growing older has made her a better nurse, she nods. 'I bring more humanity to the job now and have more awareness of how patients are coping,' she says. 'Instead of trying to make what I know fit every patient, I tailor my approach more to each individual.' Another example of how the patience and empathy that often come in later life can boost job performance.

Maran was bitten by the volunteering bug when her family responsibilities lightened. Since then she has branched out from medicine to serve in other ways. She gives English lessons and helps out in the dining room at a local shelter for homeless people and refugees. She also teaches qigong, an ancient Chinese exercise and healing practice, to cancer patients. Her motto is very much 'Never Stop Exploring'. These days she feels the itch to take up social activism. 'I've gotta maybe expand myself into that area next,' she says. Maran certainly has no plans to stop volunteering. Like many people in later life, she wants to keep on giving till there is nothing left to give. 'I just abhor the idea of a recreational retirement,' she says. 'All the bingo and outings and golf courses and dance classes – I would just die in that environment.' Of course, the choice is never either-or: you can do the salsa class or spend hours on the putting green and still give back in retirement.

$$\sim$$

Time for another caveat: Even if ageing sharpens the desire to give back, we must not paint later life as the only time for serving the greater good. Altruism can and should be cultivated at every age – and the longevity revolution can help with that. Why? Because the philanthropic urge is a little bit contagious. Studies show that when old and young work together on a life problem, some of the altruism of the former rubs off on the latter. You see this in action among those Syrian crocheters in the Bekaa Valley. When I ask what working with a middle-aged dynamo like Zahed has taught her, the youngest member of the group, 22-year-old Alaa Aslan Al Zouhouri, tells me: 'It has made me want to help others.'

To spread this healthy contagion, the different generations must cross paths in the first place – and the only way for that to happen is for people of all ages to start mingling a lot more than they do at the moment.

CHAPTER 11

MINGLE: ALL TOGETHER NOW

Associate with people who are likely to improve you.

—SENECA

Patrick Stoffer is building a farm for the future. Housed inside a shipping container devoid of both soil and sunlight, his miniature Eden looks like something out of a science fiction movie. Fixed to the stainless-steel walls are sensors monitoring humidity, temperature and carbon dioxide. Blue- and red-spectrum lights combine to bathe the tunnel-like space in an eerie, purple glow. Four hundred plants, including bibb and butterhead lettuce, hang from the ceiling on strips of rubber. From time to time, very clever software sprays nutrients stored in rows of plastic containers onto their exposed roots.

When I arrive, Stoffer is examining his crop. With his shaved head and trim beard, and with hip-hop blasting at full volume, he looks like an agronomical Moby. Though he can cultivate his high-tech garden from anywhere with his iPad, he spends up to 20 hours a week doing the farmer thing on site. He is on a mission to show the world how to grow fresh produce with almost zero waste. Recently, he took to the stage to explain at a local TEDx conference how hydroponic gardens like his can provide healthy food, rebuild communities and save the planet.

You might think a trailblazer like Stoffer, who is 28 years old, would launch his farming revolution in a big city, perhaps alongside a co-working space for tech startups. Think again. His shipping container sits on the grounds of Humanitas, a nursing home in Deventer, a small town in the middle of the Netherlands.

A few years ago, the director here set out to liven things up by offering free lodging to a handful of university students. In return, the youngsters agreed to spend 30 hours a month interacting with the elderly residents at the 150-bed facility. Result: the home is now a beacon for breaking down barriers between the generations. Academics and nursing home directors visit from around the world and similar schemes have been launched in France, Spain and the United States. Seniors and students are queuing up to live here, drawn by the glowing reports of generational mingling.

A programme to bring young and old closer together would have baffled our ancestors. Through most of history and across cultures, people of all ages rubbed along together in shared spaces whether they liked it or not: at home and on the farm, in parks and markets, at social gatherings and places of worship. Modern living has done much to undermine that. By their very nature, schools, nursing homes and retirement communities are all age ghettos. Along the way, urbanisation, individualism and falling birth rates have made the multigenerational family less common, even in societies that traditionally place a premium on filial piety, such as China, Japan and India. Panic over 'stranger danger' and the polarisation of the property market have driven a further wedge between young and old. I notice this age clustering in my own corner of London, where people tend to arrive in their late 20s or early 30s and then move out again in their 40s. The neighbourhood is so dominated by young families that it has been christened 'Nappy Valley'.

When the generations do rub shoulders, everyone benefits. As we have already seen, the young can become more altruistic. In the other direction, studies show that mingling with younger people boosts the health, happiness and self-esteem of older ones. They find it easier to share their experience and act on that later-life desire to give back to the world. They also stay more in touch with new ideas and trends. That is why Ms Q, the seventy-something Chinese backpacker we met earlier, makes a point of sleeping in hostels and touring with younger travellers. 'I talk with them and they have lots of fresh things to say,' she says.

At Humanitas, the students run workshops on everything from street art to wheelchair breakdancing to using a tablet. One staged an Xbox soccer tournament in the dining hall, while another raced a resident on mobility scooters and then uploaded the footage to YouTube. Stoffer, who is a mean cook, slips unfamiliar foods onto the menu where some, like hummus, become fixtures. The older residents have even learned a few drinking games, with one eighty-something now so good at beer-pong that everyone clamours to have him on their team.

Everywhere you look in Humanitas you see friendship blossoming across generational lines. Sunday dinner in the main hall is a cheerful affair with much fist-bumping between young and old. Two accordion players belt out classic tunes such as 'The More We Get Together' as Stoffer weaves among the tables, handing out his homemade cheese sticks, chatting and flirting as he goes. When he threw his first birthday party at Humanitas, even some of the more reclusive residents came along. These days, his closest friend here is Harry Ter Braak, a 90-year-old former barber with tidy white hair and a roguish smile. You often find the duo cooking together in the communal kitchen or shooting the breeze over a few beers. Ter Braak is a charmer, always on the verge of cracking a joke or play-tackling someone. 'We talk about girls and life in general,' says Stoffer. 'I hang out with Harry like I would a guy my own age.'

Marty Weulink knows the feeling. She lives in an apartment stuffed with the vintage doll prams she restores as a hobby. Everything from the lampshade and her iPad cover to the vase of roses and her outfit comes in her favourite colour, red. A highlight of her day is when Sores Duman, a communications student, drops by for a chat. With his porkpie hat, dark, curly locks and bone necklace, the 27-year-old could be a busker searching for a bed for the night. 'I adopted Sores because he looks like a beaten dog in need of a good meal,' laughs Weulink, who is 91. Early on in their friendship, she went out on her scooter to buy his favourite food – chicken and rice – from a local takeaway. Now she is learning online about his Kurdish background. When I drop by her flat the pair are chatting over tea, laughing at private jokes, nudging each other playfully. 'We just get along so well,' says Duman. Weulink beams, and winks at him. 'I am not aware of age with Sores,' she says. 'We sit and eat and have fun – it's just talking to someone you like talking to.'

Bringing in students has worked so well that Humanitas is always devising new ways to get more younger people through the door. The middle-aged members of a local billiards club now use the tables here and join in the home's activities and celebrations. Children from a nearby kindergarten come to play, draw and sing with the residents, and trainee chefs from a culinary school cook traditional Dutch dishes with residents from the dementia ward. A more recent scheme pairs up teenagers from poor families with a 'grandmother' at the home. A virtuous circle has taken hold: the generational mixing makes the residents happier, which helps attract more young people to Humanitas, and so on.

The students benefit from all this age mingling, too. The slower pace at Humanitas helps them rethink the speed of their own lives. 'In the outside world people want things as fast as possible but here you come through the front door and everything slows down – even the elevator,' says Stoffer. 'In here, if someone asks how your day went they really want to know and I like that. It has taught me to stop rushing through my own life and to pay more attention to the small things.' Another student, Sharmain Thenu, is showered with romantic advice by the female residents, who urge her not to rush into marriage. 'Being around the older women is teaching me to put myself first,' she says.

Of course, it's not all harmony at Humanitas. The students sometimes grumble when their hard-of-hearing neighbours crank up the volume on their television sets. Yet no one wants to turn the home back into an age silo. On the contrary, the older residents love the injection of youthful energy. Often they are rising for breakfast just as the students are returning from a night on the town. If one is spotted bringing home a new companion, everyone in the building knows by lunchtime. 'They love gossip,' says Stoffer. 'We bring the outside world into the home and give them stories they can share with each other and their families.' Ter Braak tells me this offers welcome relief from the standard nursing home chats about pills, pains and medical appointments. 'Letting young people live here was the best decision ever,' he says.

I feel inclined to agree. Pretty much every other nursing home I've visited has left me feeling down in the dumps – the heavy silence, the loneliness, the smell, the forced cheer, the sense of counting off the days till death comes. Humanitas is no holiday resort. Not all the residents are able – or willing – to engage with the students. There is suffering here, and loneliness, and there is death. But the overall atmosphere is light and upbeat. It helps that the home is well put-together. In the public spaces there are wooden floors, chandeliers and funky chairs, as well as good coffee machines and plates of biscuits. One room is done up

231

to look like a traditional Dutch bar, another like a beach scene. Residents can hang out on the roof terrace or pretend they are cycling through Amsterdam or Paris on the virtual reality exercise bike in the gym. The bathrooms are clean and the corridors free of that nursing home smell. But what keeps spirits so high is the generational mingling. I can easily imagine wanting to live here – in my 20s or 80s.

~

Mixing up the ages may well be the best antidote for ageism. When the generations mingle, older people are forced to rethink the lazy assumption that 'the young have never had it so good', while the young see that not 'all old people are the same'. Everyone learns that ageing has plenty of upsides and that people aspire to many of the same things throughout their lives: strong relationships, good health, learning, fun, meaningful work, independence, self-respect, helping others. Research shows we are less ageist towards people we know personally, and a major study in Australia found that the more contact younger people have with older ones, the more favourable their attitudes to ageing and the aged. 'It's segregation that enables stereotyping and discrimination,' says Ashton Applewhite, the anti-ageism campaigner. 'When all ages mix, it's the natural order of things: just as places with races living together are less likely to be racist, any place where ages mix together is going to be less ageist.'

You see that in action at Humanitas. Every student tells me the same story of arriving here riddled with ageism and then learning to embrace ageing and those who have done more of it than they have. 'I used to look at older people and see limits and feel pity, but now I see possibilities because I know they can do lots of things and they don't want pity,' says Duman. 'Now I feel it is possible for me to live a good life till the end.'

Generational mingling can work its magic on even the most inveterate ageist. Take Tom Kamber. Burly, balding and gregarious, the 50-year-old spent his teens and 20s campaigning for the homeless and working in social housing. But despite the noble CV, he was, like me, a card-carrying ageist. 'I thought of myself as a guy who wants to help people, but when it came to seniors I was a bit of a dick,' he says. 'I just felt a sense of mild annoyance about older people for walking too slowly on the sidewalk or for being cranky and crotchety, and I didn't really want to hang out with them.'

Raised in what he calls 'a sort of macho family', Kamber built his identity on physical prowess. He loves to cycle, sail and dance and worried that growing older would take all that away. 'I assumed that ageing would be bad and that I'd hit a point where I'd no longer be relevant to the world, nobody would care about me and I wouldn't be physically strong or attractive anymore and nobody would want to be around me,' he says.

The first dent in that fear came when Kamber gave private computing lessons to an 85-year-old woman named Pearl. At first her ignorance merely confirmed his worst suspicions about ageing. 'When I asked her to point her mouse at something on the screen she lifted up the mouse and pointed it,' he says, laughing. But Pearl proved to be a quick study. When she mentioned that the best years of her life had started after she turned 70, Kamber, who was 35 at the time, was astonished. He marvelled at her boldness and hunger for new experiences. 'It was a total revelation to me,' he says. 'I had always thought old people just moved to Florida to play bingo or golf.'

Inspired by Pearl, Kamber founded Senior Planet, the technology non-profit we visited earlier. Doing so made generational mingling part of his daily routine, yet still his ageism held strong. 'I have to admit that for the first few years I carried on thinking of older people as "other",' he says. 'They were a category I could help, but not identify with. It wasn't condescending but there also wasn't a lot of connection. They were like my customers.'

Over time, though, the intergenerational shoulder-rubbing did its thing. Hearing older people tell their stories, watching them meet with triumph and disaster and treat those two impostors just the same, eventually put paid to Kamber's ageism. He now has close friends older than his parents, some of whom hit the Latin clubs in Manhattan with him.

Like the students at Humanitas, Kamber has travelled a path the rest of us would do well to follow: moving from a fear and dread of ageing to the kind of understanding and optimism that help you take the rough with the smooth. He can now imagine himself as an older person without feeling his heart sink. He expects to carry on cycling, sailing and dancing for a few more decades – and is comforted to know that, when his body starts to wane, there will be other compensations. 'Not only do I feel much less worried about getting older now,

I'm really looking forward to it,' he says. 'Not like, "Bring it on, I don't want to be 50 anymore!", but looking forward to a sense of being in your own moment, comfortable in your own skin, of things slowing down in a good way, a certain peace and calm and a feeling of accomplishment and not being so stressed about what you haven't done or what other people think about you.'

~

You do not have to sleep, work or study under the same roof to benefit from generational mingling. Even just socialising can do the trick. Back in Warsaw, at the party in Wilanów Park, revellers of various ages are huddled round the dance floor, chatting over strawberry cocktails and bowls of fries. I spot Eryk Mroczek, with his trademark Jack Nicholson shades, leading one group in a raucous toast. I join them.

Benjamin Diamoutene, a gentle 25-year-old street dancer with a goatee, tells me that he and Mroczek have been firm friends ever since meeting two years ago at another of Paulina Braun's intergenerational dance events. Like seasoned drinking buddies, they reminisce about past benders and tease each other remorselessly. The other night they went clubbing to celebrate Mroczek's 80th birthday. 'He is such a party animal,' says Diamoutene. 'When I left the club at 3am he was still dancing and flirting with women.' Mroczek nods, smiles and then adopts an expression of mock pity. 'I'm sorry, because I know it's hard for you to accept that between us I'm the better dancer,' he says. The pair dissolve into laughter.

As more cocktails arrive, Mroczek whips out his phone to take a call from a fifty-something mate who is en route to the party. He gives him directions and then hangs up with a triumphant grin. 'He'll be here soon – and he's bringing two women with him!'

Diamoutene smiles indulgently, and then tells me that life in Braun's intergenerational world is not one endless party: there are tears, too. A few months ago, he went out dancing with a 67-year-old friend named Basia in Warsaw. Days later she was dead. 'A lot of people my age never really think about death but having older friends changes that,' he says. 'You realise that whenever you see a person or dance with them it might be the last time.'

Earlier we saw how an awareness of death can spur us to make the most of the time we have left. This is a welcome side effect of ageing that need not be confined to later life. After all, dying is not a remote, unpleasant thing that only old people do. It is a natural part of life that can come to anyone at any time.

To his surprise, Diamoutene finds that seeing older friends reach the end of their lives makes him less anxious about ageing. 'Obviously, it is very sad when someone dies but it also reminds you how lucky you are to be alive,' he says. 'Thinking that I am going to die one day does not make me worry more about ageing: it makes me want to live my life to the maximum.'

Welcome to another surprising benefit of the ageing population: death is carving out a more prominent place on the cultural radar. In Japan, bookstores now have separate '*shukatsu*' sections dedicated to pondering and planning the end of life, and the country's coffin makers offer try-before-you-buy deals to spark conversations about dying. English readers are gobbling up books with titles such as *Death: A Graveside Companion*, *The Chick and the Dead, Confessions of a Funeral Director* and *From Here to Eternity: Travelling the World to Find the Good Death*. Everywhere, people are watching YouTube shows like *Ask a Mortician*, joining online communities such as the Order of the Good Death and attending Death Cafés to chat about mortality over coffee and cake. You can even hire an end-of-life 'doula' to help plan your final exit.

To see if confronting death has the same effect on me as it does on Diamoutene, I download an app called WeCroak. It sends my smartphone, at random intervals, a message saying: 'Don't forget, you're going to die.' I then swipe left and am taken to a page with a quote about death by thinkers ranging from Lao Tzu and Pablo Neruda to Henry David Thoreau and Margaret Atwood. My first is from philosopher Martin Heidegger: 'If I take death into my life, acknowledge it, and face it squarely, I will free myself from the anxiety of death and the pettiness of life – and only then will I be free to become myself.' Heavy stuff to be wrestling with over breakfast.

I didn't think I would like the app but I do. It brings death to mind in a way that feels playful rather than morbid. Sometimes the messages are a mild irritant, like another software update from Adobe Reader. But often the invitation to pause and ponder the big picture gives me a lift. The other day a WeCroak notification popped up on my phone while I was struggling to read the print on a restaurant menu – and quietly raging against my older eyes. I swiped left to find a quote about the wisdom of not sweating the small stuff. It worked. All of a sudden my faltering eyesight seemed like a trivial worry that should not be ruining my evening. I asked the young waitress to walk me through the menu and then got on with enjoying my meal.

Whether I'll still be using WeCroak 10 or 20 years from now is another matter. The older we get, the fewer reminders we need that death is round the corner. Memento mori are more useful – and welcome – in our younger years, which is why most WeCroak users are under 35. But for now the app is still on my phone.

One way to channel WeCroak without a smartphone is to think of yourself as an 'old person in training'. At first blush, the phrase, coined by geriatrician Joanne Lynn, sounds odd, even a little cheesy, but then you realise it neatly describes a welcome conceptual leap. It reminds us that life is a long journey with many stages that will eventually end – if we are lucky – in a ripe old age, and that ageing and dying happen to everyone. It breaks down that barrier between our present and future selves, making it easier to accept who we are at every age. 'If we do not know who we are going to be, we cannot know who we are,' wrote Simone de Beauvoir. 'Let us recognise ourselves in this old man or in that old woman ... It must be done if we are to take upon ourselves the entirety of our human state.' Applewhite agrees. 'Being an old person in training derails shame and self-loathing,' she says. 'It frees us to become our full selves – ageful, not ageless – at whatever point in our lives we make this leap.'

That makes sense to me. Conceiving of myself as an old person in training is already making me think more about my life in the past, present and future. How did I get where I am today? What is important to me right now? Where do I want to go from here? Grappling with these questions makes the prospect of actually *being* an old person less scary.

Thinking of ourselves as old people in training can also deal a blow to ageism in general. 'It undoes the "otherness" that powers all prejudice,' says Applewhite. 'It makes room for empathy. It makes it easier to think critically about what age means in this society, and to push back against the discriminatory social structures and erroneous beliefs that attempt to shape our ageing.'

～

It is easier to become an old person in training when you spend time with people who are older than you – and the growing trend for mixing the generations is making that more likely. Some of this is driven by economic hardship. To save on rent, more young adults are boomeranging back to the parental home. Admittedly this can be a nightmare, but many find mixing up the ages works well. These days multiple generations of the same family are holidaying together more than ever before, and so many single career women now travel with their nieces and nephews that the industry has invented a term for them: 'PANK' means professional aunts with no kids.

It helps that the generations have more in common now. When I was young, my father seemed to live in a galaxy far, far away: he and I dressed differently, listened to our own music, watched our own TV shows. Though my son and I are separated by the same 30 years, we have much more in common culturally. We play sports together, listen to the same bands on Spotify and both love *Breaking Bad*. We use similar slang and would both be bereft without our iPhones. Even our wardrobes overlap enough to share clothes and shoes. No wonder children are happier to hang out with their parents than in the past: we're a lot less like embarrassing aliens from Planet Nerd.

Everywhere, the cultural walls between the generations are tumbling. Bands from yesteryear, from U2 and Kiss to the Rolling Stones and Earth, Wind and Fire, play to crowds of all ages. Back in the 1970s, the average age of a headliner at Glastonbury was 25; today it is 41. Burt Bacharach took to the famous Pyramid stage at the age of 87. The same is true in movies and television. *Star Wars* and *Stranger Things* both pull audiences from across the generations. That old battle cry from the '60s – Don't trust anyone over 30! – now seems out of step with the times. In recent years, and despite warnings that ageing is poison at the ballot box, young voters across the West have fallen at the feet of maverick politicians well past their 60th birthdays: Bernie Sanders in the United States, Jeremy Corbyn in the United Kingdom, Jean-Luc Mélenchon in France, Beppe Grillo in Italy.

Even the definition of 'cool' is becoming less ageist. In the past, to be older was to be square. Cool and young were two sides of the same coin. Today, that is less and less the case. All those lifestyle influencers smashing it online in their 50s, 60s and beyond are revered by people of all ages. On Instagram, the largest group of followers of the Grey Fox is 25–34-year-olds. In 2017, the youngest person on Trending Top Most's list of the 10 Coolest People in the World was aged 35, the oldest 77.

Or look at how Jungle Boogie, a rave paying homage to Sir David Attenborough, is taking university campuses in Britain by storm. Episodes of *Blue Planet*, the nonogenerian's ground-breaking nature documentary, play on screens behind the DJ and clips of his voice are dropped into tracks. Ravers take selfies with life-size cardboard cut-outs of the broadcasting legend and wear masks of his face as they dance to a medley of house, soul, funk and disco. 'He's kind of an icon among students,' says Louis Jadwat, the 25-year-old behind the rave. 'He's really popular.' And not just among students: people in their 30s and 40s come, too.

As the generations find more common ground, projects like the student lodging at Humanitas are multiplying. Berlin is now home to the world's first multigenerational LGBT housing project, where gay pensioners once persecuted by the Nazis live alongside millennial IT workers. In the United States, San Diego County hosts an annual Intergenerational Games where children and seniors compete in everything from frisbee to field hockey. Everywhere, schools are bringing older people into the classroom as mentors and playmates. Nursing homes in Britain now run Pimp My Zimmer programmes where children help residents personalise their walking frames with tinsel, string, knitted covers, football scarves and flowers.

Around the world, cities are opening playgrounds designed for people of all ages to have fun and exercise together. When I visit one in Barcelona, I meet three generations of the Ferrer family. The two children are clambering up and down the monkey bars pretending to be characters from *The Avengers*. Their mother is pedalling on a stationary bicycle. Oriol, the grandfather, is working out on an elliptical machine. 'In the old days I would have sat on a bench and watched my grandchildren play,' he says. 'Now we all play together.'

You find the same mingling online. People of all ages are sitting at screens and squaring off in everything from bridge, Scrabble and chess to *Halo*, poker and *Call of Duty*. Shirley Curry still hangs out with her old quilting group where no one knows the difference between Skype and *Skyrim*, but all those hours online have made her a confidante to many of her younger fans, some of whom are now friends. She regularly exchanges handwritten letters with one college student and video-chats with a young man who is helping her burnish her role-playing game. She is now planning a trip to the West Coast to meet up with her gaming BFF. When I ask the woman's age, Curry is flummoxed. 'I really don't know, to be honest, maybe mid- to late 30s,' she says. 'We Skype all the time and I really want to meet her badly because I think we'd get along great. It broadens your life having friends of different ages and I learn as much from them as they might pick up from me.'

The best way to build understanding between generations is to get children mingling with older people as young as possible. A fine example of this is the nursery that sits on the grounds of Nightingale House, the London nursing home we visited earlier. The three- and four-year-old pupils bump into the elderly residents all the time. They take tea together and share interactive storytelling sessions. Many of the pre-schoolers come from families who see the mingling as a way to make up for absent grandparents. When I drop by, a dozen children and residents are sipping grape juice and singing songs to celebrate Havdalah, a Jewish ceremony. Martha, who is three years old, always makes a beeline for Anna, who is in her 90s. Today the two are chatting about an upcoming visit to the hairdresser. 'My hair is getting longer,' says Martha. 'You have lovely hair,' says Anna, stroking her messy blonde locks, and adding, as if to herself: 'You wouldn't imagine there are 90 years between us.'

Anna then asks Martha about the green paint on her jeans. 'We were making pictures this morning,' she says. 'But it's not green, it's blue.' Anna laughs. 'Oh, that's my eyesight again.' Martha gives her a sweet, understanding look, and then turns to me to explain. 'Sometimes people don't see well when they're older,' she says, laying a hand on Anna's.

Judith Ish-Horowicz runs the intergenerational sessions and is amazed by how swiftly even the youngest children pick up on the residents' limitations. They remember whose hands or feet hurt, who has trouble hearing or standing up, who sometimes dozes off in the middle of a game. Instead of ridiculing or recoiling, they make allowances and offer help – the perfect two-step antidote to ageism. 'They learn they are not the centre of the world and that people are different at every age,' says Ish-Horowicz. 'Being here gives them a vision of the future, a sense that ageing is a natural part of life's journey, and they respond with so much empathy and intuition.'

Time for a word of caution. Studies show that ageism breaks down more quickly when we meet one-to-one across the generations. It takes longer in groups. That means you cannot just throw people of different ages together and hope for the best: you need to supervise, guide and set ground rules – otherwise even the best-laid schemes can go awry.

The Babayagas House in Montreuil, on the eastern side of Paris, offers a cautionary tale. Set up as a home for ethically minded women over the age of 60, it burst onto the scene in a blizzard of lofty rhetoric, promising to redefine communal living and ageing itself. As at Humanitas, several units were set aside for younger people. But two decades later the dream is in tatters. When I drop by to witness the local mayor renewing the lease, the atmosphere is edgy, and a little sour. Few residents have turned up for the celebratory lunch and everyone is grumbling about the lack of communal spirit. A recurring gripe is that the young residents, who live in a separate wing on the ground floor, keep entirely to themselves. 'We may as well be living on different planets,' says one of the older women. Humanitas dodges that bullet by doing two things Babayagas did not: it spreads its students around the building and obliges them to spend time interacting with the elderly residents. As Gea Sijpkes, the nursing home's director, puts it: 'We break down the groups so individuals can meet.'

Does that same principle hold in the workplace, too? You betcha.

~

Study after study suggests that breaking down age silos is good for the bottom line. Researchers at Lancaster University Management School in the UK found that McDonald's branches with a blend of younger and older workers score 20 per cent higher on customer satisfaction. Other surveys have shown that co-operation is at its highest in teams with a range of ages. Older employees play their part in that by being more socially agile and better at bringing out the best in others. As Haig Nalbantian, a senior partner at Mercer consultancy, puts it: 'It seems the contribution of older workers materialises in the increased productivity of those around them.'

Deutsche Bank finds that mixing up the generations evens out the strengths and weaknesses of each. 'In operational work older employees can be slower but they make up for that with greater experience and by making fewer mistakes, so in total they are not less productive,' says Gernot Sendowski, the bank's head of diversity. 'If we had teams with only older people, they'd be too slow; if we had teams with only young people, there'd be too many mistakes and not enough experience. The best teams have a mix of ages.'

In any business, the experience, patience and big-picture thinking of older employees can dovetail with the restless energy of younger ones. In other words, the longevity revolution can deliver precisely what the global economy needs: a blend of those who move fast and break things and those who move more slowly and question how, or even whether, things need to be broken in the first place.

You can see that yin and yang in action at Humanitas, where Stoffer is working with two residents to build up his urban farm business. Ans, who is in her 80s, chips in with design suggestions. Ter Braak helped plant the hydroponic garden and now lends a hand with sales. 'Patrick has limited experience in business so I help him plan and make the deals,' he says. 'At meetings I talk and open the negotiations and then give the floor to Patrick.' All three appeared together on that TEDx stage.

∼

As the longevity revolution marches on, passing know-how down the generations will become essential in every workplace. Yet mentoring is not always easy to arrange in large, complex organisations. Everything from work schedules to office politics to red tape can stop employees striking up the kind of relationship that exists between Stoffer and Ter Braak. One solution: formal mentorship programmes.

Schemes where the old coach the young are springing up in companies of every stripe, including Boeing, Time Warner, Caterpillar, Intel, KPMG and Dow Chemicals. Many of the insurance agents at Work At Home Vintage Experts (WAHVE) mentor their younger colleagues, and Scripps Health has gone one step further by creating an entirely new job: clinical nurse mentor. Daimler, a German car manufacturer, brings back its retirees to show young managers the ropes and John Deere does the same to help current employees develop software for its agriculture machinery.

Handing down experience is not the only benefit of formal mentorship. A few years ago, Skanska, a global construction company, decided that knowledge transfer across the five generations on its payroll was too patchy. Today, hundreds of its employees are enrolled in a mentorship programme that has galvanised its working culture. Not only is knowledge now being shared around more than ever, but collaboration, innovation and risk analysis have all improved. Mentors are helping to identify employees worthy of fast-track promotion and both morale and retention are up across the company. 'People feel more valued now,' says Israil Bryan, Skanska's head of diversity. 'They have an additional sense of purpose because it's no longer just about the project you're working on but about developing the next generation.' Spending an afternoon at the company headquarters outside London, chatting with participants in the mentorship programme, gives me a serious case of mentor envy. I come away wishing I'd been paired up with a seasoned journalist earlier in my career.

Of course, older workers can also learn from younger ones. Pioneered by General Electric in the 1990s, 'reverse mentoring' is now being embraced by companies ranging from Target and Microsoft to Cisco and Ernst & Young. The BBC recently launched a scheme for twenty-something staffers to help senior managers understand how younger audiences think and feel. But the truth is that the most fertile mentorships are always two-way streets. Skanska refers to its mentors and mentees as 'buddies' to encourage learning in both directions, and both the United States Military Academy and the US Marines mix up ages during training so that young and old can learn from each other.

Mixed-aged mentorship can also help ease generational friction in the workplace. Older employees can feel awkward answering to a younger boss, while younger ones can feel threatened by underlings with more experience. A study of 61 German firms found that for every two years that a supervisor is younger than his or her subordinates overall performance dips by 5 per cent.

That sounds alarming, yet there are reasons to think the problem will fade away. One is that younger and older workers increasingly yearn for the same things: flexible hours, wellness, enough leisure time, meaningful work and continued learning. The AARP's annual award for Best Employer for Over-50s often goes to a company that creates a congenial environment for workers of all ages.

There is also an historical precedent. The arrival of women en masse in the workplace in the 1970s sparked apocalyptic warnings about the breakdown in the chain of command. 'Will I be able to answer to a female boss?' many men wondered. Today, most of us no longer think twice about the gender of the person telling us what to do at work. By the same token, as we get used to working with, mentoring and being mentored by people of different ages, chronological age will come to matter less.

What about generational friction beyond the workplace? Is that a bomb waiting to explode as lifespans lengthen? You might think so if you consider the rich history of intergenerational discord. In the past, younger men often chafed against their fathers for hoarding the family wealth or competing with them for young wives. Cicero tells of how, in Ancient Greece, the sons of Sophocles decided he was neglecting his property by spending so much time writing for the theatre in his old age. To wrest away control of the family estate, they took him to court on the grounds that he had lost his marbles. Sophocles won the case by reading aloud from his latest play, *Oedipus at Colonus*, and asking the jury: 'Does that poem seem to you to be the work of an imbecile?' More than a millennium and a half later, in medieval France, people routinely and openly moaned about '*le père que vit trop*' (the father who lives too long). And don't forget the rich and universal tradition of mocking elders in plays and poems. In the other direction, older people in every era have dismissed the young as immoral, lazy, disrespectful, entitled, weak and inarticulate. 'They think they know everything,' thundered Aristotle in the fourth century BC. Chaucer put it mildly when he said, in the 14th century: 'Youth and age are often in debate.'

Even so, the sabre-rattling has never escalated into intergenerational warfare. Occasionally it threatens to do so, such as after the youthquake in the 1960s or the Brexit vote in 2016, but the rhetoric always cools down before full-blown hostilities erupt. Why? Because no generation is completely homogeneous. People of the same age have a range of views, values and economic interests. Not every sixty-something is a conservative homeowner, nor is every twenty-something an impecunious liberal – and that will be the case more and more as chronological age comes to mean less and less.

~

To make the most of our longer lives, we need to build trust, understanding and respect across generations – and the only way to do that is for people of different ages to rub shoulders more often. That will mean making the places where we live, work and play more age-diverse. And yet our ultimate aim should not be to make every single moment multigenerational. The mantra 'age is just a number' is stirring but also misleading. Even as chronological age comes to matter less, it will always matter. No one is the same at 80 as at 60, 40 or 20. Growing older changes us and each stage of life has its own unique ledger of pros and cons. As Muhammad Ali put it: 'The man who views the world at 50 the same as he did at 20 has wasted 30 years of his life.'

That means age separation will always have its place. Some forms of competition, such as sports and beauty pageants, make more sense grouped by birthdate. The other day I played in a hockey tournament for over-35s and quite enjoyed not lining up against 20-year-olds who can run like the wind. Let's be honest: sometimes there is comfort in being surrounded by your own age group, by those who understand your cultural references from childhood and are at the same point in the cycle of life. Generational mixing will never be the answer to every problem.

~

Back at the urban farm at Humanitas, Stoffer is tending to his crops. He tops up the nutrients in the plastic containers, checks the temperature gauges and twiddles a few knobs and dials. Chemical and vegetable aromas mingle pleasingly in the air.

Although he knows generational mixing has its limits, Stoffer plans to carry on doing it when he leaves Humanitas. And that includes staying in touch with Ter Braak. When I ask what is the most valuable lesson he will take away from living among much older people, he answers in a flash. 'I've learned that you do all these things in life and then at the end you discover that it's the simple things that matter,' he says. 'You spend all this time searching for happiness and then find it's right here in front of you whatever age you are.'

CONCLUSION
THE TIME IS RIPE

*Ageing is not lost youth, but a new
stage of opportunity and strength.*

—BETTY FRIEDAN

Ellen Langer had a hunch. The Harvard psychologist sus-
pected that thinking you are old makes your mind and
body decline, while thinking you are young has the opposite
effect. In 1981, she set out to test her theory by carrying out
a study whose methodology was so unorthodox and whose
results so startling that it was never submitted to a medical
journal for publication.

Her plan was to persuade eight men in their 70s that they
were actually 22 years younger – and then measure the
effects on their health. To do so, she and her team rented
a converted monastery in a quiet corner of rural New
Hampshire. They did up the interior like a time capsule,
with every detail chosen to evoke life in 1959. Magazines and

bestselling books from that year were placed on the shelves or left lying around. *The Ed Sullivan Show* played on a vintage black-and-white television set and an old radio crackled out tunes by Perry Como. Movies such as *Anatomy of a Murder* with Jimmy Stewart screened in the evenings. Anything, from mirrors to modern clothing, that might remind the men of their current age was removed. Only photographs of them in their youth were on display.

The men were told to imagine they were actually inhabiting their former selves rather than just reminiscing about the past. In that spirit, Langer and her team treated them as though they were much younger – leaving them to haul their luggage up the stairs without help from a porter, for instance. Each day, the men chatted about the black-and-white movies they had watched or 'current' sports stars like Wilt Chamberlain or 'news' events such as Fidel Castro's seizing of power in Cuba. Every 1950s-based conversation was conducted in the present tense.

The men spent a week in the monastery – and when they came out the results were so striking that Langer later invoked Lourdes. On almost every measure their health had improved markedly. They were more supple and had less arthritic pain. They had better grip strength and posture. Their memory, hearing and sight had improved and they performed better on cognitive tests. According to independent observers, they also looked much younger. On the final day of the experiment, in a scene worthy of the movie *Cocoon*, an impromptu game of touch football broke out as the men waited for their ride back home.

Langer's 'counter-clockwise' study has never been peer-reviewed. The same experiment – with varying results – has been carried out on television in Britain, South Korea and the Netherlands but never in an academic setting. Still, Langer helped pave the way for many other studies that all point to the same conclusion: how we feel about ageing affects how we age.

This would be wonderful news if our view of ageing were favourable. But it's not. As we saw at that pitching event in Shoreditch, it is yoked to the worst-case scenario, with longer living often portrayed as more burden than breakthrough. Langer's monastery experiment worked because the men held such a bleak view of being older.

What can we do about this? We could go the counter-clockwise route by denying our age and trying to trick ourselves into thinking we are younger than we are. Or we could do the sensible thing: tackle the root of the problem by adopting a more favourable view of ageing itself.

That will not be easy. No matter how many goji berries we guzzle or how many burpees we do before breakfast, ageing changes our bodies and brains in unwelcome ways. It diminishes our reproductive cachet, offends our instinct to stay alive and does cruel and ghastly things to some of us. The final stage before death is seldom a barrel of laughs for anyone. To add insult to injury, almost everything in the modern world flatters and caters to youth: language, design, advertising, technology, the arts, work, education, entertainment, media, sports, fashion, medicine. Bottom line: ageing is hard to sell.

But not impossible. And now we know there are reasons for optimism.

First, ageing is not nearly as bad as we fear. It is not a Rothian massacre. Even if we get worse at some things, we get better at others. Life can become richer, deeper, happier, often confounding our own worst expectations. Take Victor Hugo, author of *Les Misérables* and titan of the French literary pantheon. 'My body wanes,' he wrote in a letter in 1869, at the age of 67. Was he soon dozing and dribbling over his copy of *Le Monde*? The hell he was. Not only did Hugo continue to thrive as a man of letters, but he went on to be elected a deputy for Paris and then to the French senate at the age of 75. A year later, Flaubert, a friend and fellow literary giant, noted: 'The old fellow is younger and more delightful than ever.' Towards the end of his life, Hugo sounded like a drink-the-Kool-Aid advocate for ageing. 'When grace is joined with wrinkles, it is adorable,' he said. 'There is an unspeakable dawn in happy old age.'

Another reason for optimism is that we now have a pretty clear recipe for ageing better: Exercise the body and brain. Cultivate an upbeat attitude and a sense of humour. Socialise lots. Avoid excessive stress. Eat a healthy diet, consume alcohol in moderation and don't smoke. By following this formula, more of us are living longer, healthier lives than ever before.

The final – and perhaps most compelling – reason for optimism is that the world is changing in ways that herald a golden age of ageing. Every day, medics are getting better at managing the diseases and decline that come in later life. New techniques for restoring hearing and sight are coming on stream and neuroscientists are figuring out how to harness the brain to move prosthetic limbs and operate computers. Designers are racing to build wearable gadgets that will give older bodies a functional boost and technology is opening up new ways to take part in the world until the very end of life. Companies are making the workplace more congenial for older people and retailers are scrambling to do the same for stores, packaging, advertising and products. The world today is a much better place for an over-50 than it was 20 years ago. If we play our cards right, it will be even better 20 years from now.

Demographics are also shifting in favour of ageing. Every year there are more older people on the planet – and there is strength in numbers. It is harder to dismiss or denigrate a growing chunk of the population, especially when so many of them are taking life by the scruff of the neck. We now have a wider range of role models for ageing boldly than ever before. While some are going the super-geezer route by cycling up mountains in their 80s or kite-surfing in their 90s, many more are giving later life a better name simply by using it to socialise, travel, work, help others, fall in love, make art, start companies or families, dance, exercise, play sports or have sex. Put all this together and you reach the same conclusion as Pat Thane, the historian of ageing we met at the start of the book: 'This is the best time in history to be old, and there is no reason that shouldn't continue.'

But let's not get carried away. Our aim should not be to replace the cult of youth with the cult of the codger. No one age should be venerated or vilified because each comes with its own sorrows and comforts. To put it bluntly, there is no 'wrong' side of 30 or 40 or 50. Every age can be worth living. And every age should be celebrated – something that no longer looks like pie in the sky.

Half a century after the term was coined, ageism is coming under fire like never before. Older faces are proliferating in movies, television and advertising, and the media is starting to portray later life more as a rich smorgasbord of possibility than a wasteland of decline and despair. Celebrities are fighting back against ageist trolls more than ever. In 2018, Pink, a pop singer, won plaudits for unloading on someone who chided her on Twitter for looking older at 38 than she did in her 20s. 'I am of the mindset that it's a blessing to grow old,' she tweeted back. 'That if your face has lines around your eyes and mouth it means you've laughed a lot. I pray I look older in 10 years, cause that will mean I'm alive.' The very same week, public pressure forced Postmates, a food-delivery service in New York, to pull a flagrantly ageist advertisement. It read: 'When you want a whole cake to yourself because you're turning 30, which is basically 50, which is basically dead.' Ageism is jumping the shark.

Campaigns against it are gaining ground everywhere from Australia (EveryAGE Counts) to America (The Radical Age Movement), and growing numbers of students are signing up for university degrees in Age Studies. In an echo of the early years of the women's movement, people are joining consciousness-raising groups that show ageism to be a collective problem that must be solved by acting together. Jo Ann Jenkins, CEO of AARP (American Association of Retired

Persons), thinks we have already passed peak ageism and are starting to come out the other side. 'Ten years ago we had to practically beg celebrities to appear on the cover of our magazine,' she says. 'Now we are approached constantly by stars who want to be on the cover.'

Two things promise to supercharge this shift. One is that the battle against ageism can surf the wider push for diversity that has already revolutionised views on gender, race and sexuality. The other is that ageism also affects rich, white men, a demographic group with the clout to fight back.

The idea that too much longer living will bankrupt us all is also coming under review like never before, with some of the biggest voices in economics warming to the longevity revolution. The World Bank recently concluded that '. . . ageing does not necessarily imply substantial increases in dependency ratios, declines in productivity, or stark choices between unsustainable fiscal positions and widespread poverty among the elderly'. Strip away the dry, technocratic language and the message is clear: we can afford to live longer. The World Economic Forum goes further by touting the benefits that will flow from increased longevity: '. . . societies top heavy with experienced citizens will have a resource never before available to our ancestors: large numbers of people with considerable knowledge, emotional evenness, practical talents, creative problem-solving ability, commitment to future generations, and the motivation to use their abilities can improve societies in ways never before possible'. All of a sudden, the Zuckerberg Doctrine seems downright silly and ageing a whole lot more appealing.

The longevity revolution is a tectonic shift that will drive change in every walk of life, leaving us with two options. We can either squander the gift of the new demographics by clinging to the ageism of yesteryear, or we can embrace longer living and use it as a spur to make the world a better place for everyone to age in. Let's go for Option 2.

There is still a long way to go. A very long way. Making the most of the longevity revolution will mean rewriting the rules of pretty much everything: work, medicine, finance, education, consumption, housing, design, business and social care. We need to make the places we live cleaner, safer, more walkable and more socially connected. We need financial products that allow us to save and spend more flexibly throughout life, as well as a pension system that supports a wider range of working patterns and allows everyone to arrive at the end of their earning days with enough to live on. We must find ways to pay for the costs that come with caring for an ageing population and forge a model for dying that is more humane and less terrifying than the hypermedicalised status quo. As machines gobble up jobs, we must boost productivity at all ages and spread labour and its fruits more evenly. The time has also come to replace the current three-stage road map of life – learning, working, resting – with something more fluid. It is hard to say what that will look like but the starting point is clear: giving everyone the freedom to choose the mix of work, rest, caring, volunteering, learning and leisure that suits them best at whatever age.

To make any of this happen, however, will require a tidal shift in thinking. We must learn to measure personal worth in ways that go beyond economic output, embrace the benefits of slowing down and accept that depending on others is a part of life. If we get all of this right, the upshot will be a world where everyone can live longer and better.

This is ambitious but not utopian, and each of us can play a part in making it happen. How? By changing how we speak, think and behave. Start by carrying out small acts of defiance and rebellion: Be honest about your age online. Do an activity where everyone is older or younger than you. Experiment with letting your hair go grey. Post un-airbrushed photos of yourself on social media. Never stop exploring. Use each birthday as a moment to make peace with what you've lost, celebrate what you've gained and look forward to what the future holds. Carry on learning new skills that push you out of your comfort zone. Like Mary Ho with her guitar, Craig Ritchie, the dementia expert, plans to take up the piano when he reaches the age of 65. 'You are never too old to set a new goal, or to dream a new dream,' said C. S. Lewis, who published *The Chronicles of Narnia* and found the love of his life in his 50s.

Together, we need to change the way we talk about ageing. Language shapes views and behaviour, which is why debate rages over what words to use when discussing race, gender and sexuality. The same must now happen with age. As long as words like 'old', 'older', 'ageing' and 'elderly' remain freighted with dread and disdain, we should try to find more upbeat replacements. I like the way the Abkhazian people of northwestern Georgia refer to their elders as 'long living'. Gina Pell, an internet entrepreneur, coined the term 'perennial' to describe those who refuse to be defined or confined by their age. 'Perennials are ever-blooming, relevant people of all ages who know what's happening in the world, stay current with technology and have friends of all ages,' she says. 'We get involved, stay curious, mentor others, and are passionate, compassionate, creative, confident, collaborative, global-minded risk-takers.'

Even as we recruit new words and phrases to the cause, the way we use others needs rethinking. Let's start with grandmother and grandfather. Many find having grandchildren bittersweet because the change in status sounds ageing in an unflattering way. Martin Amis once likened reaching grandparenthood to 'getting a letter from the mortuary', and my own first thought upon discovering I was the oldest player at that hockey tournament was to write myself off as the resident grandad. So on the one hand it is a welcome corrective to see Grandma Mary ripping up the stage with her electric guitar, the 'kick-ass grandmas' of WOOLN making waves in high-end knitwear, Deshun Wang being touted as a hot grandpa on the catwalk and groups like Grandmother Power doing good works around the world. On the other hand, automatically reaching for the grandparent label when discussing someone in later life can be patronising. It's like saying all gay men understand fashion or all black people have rhythm. Many older people are not, nor ever will be, grandparents. And even those who are do not always want that status to be their defining characteristic.

We will know we have defeated ageism when WOOLN knitters are referred to simply as kick-ass women rather than grandmas, when seventy-somethings carve out music careers without christening themselves Grandma This or Grandpa That, when a comic talent like Jaco can joke about more than just her advanced age.

Some words and phrases are ripe for full retirement. 'Senior moment', 'for your age' and 'anti-ageing' are a good place to start. I am now careful to eschew the word 'still' when referring to anyone doing anything in later life. To me, people are playing hockey in their 50s, having sex in their 60s and running a business in their 80s; they are not 'still' doing any of those things. David Evans, the Grey Fox, avoids the phrase 'young at heart'. 'It's absolutely meaningless,' he says. 'You are the age you are, your attitudes are coloured by the age you are, and age brings advantages.'

The same treatment should be meted out to the cliché of 50 being the new 30 or 60 being the new 40. They are no such thing. Fifty and 60 are still 50 and 60 – and always will be. What has changed is that we now have it within our power to make every age a lot better than it was. Celebrating that breakthrough by pretending to be decades younger than we are does not erode ageism; it bolsters it.

When it comes to age, honesty is the best policy. Denying how old you are, even in jest, denies who you are, what you have lived and where you are going. It gives the number a power it does not deserve. Owning your age can wipe away the shame and self-loathing so often attached to ageing. If done with a dose of defiance, it can also help challenge ageism more broadly. One trick when asked how old you are is to answer truthfully but then follow up by asking why the other person wants to know. That way you shine a light on – and maybe start to undercut – the assumptions and biases linked to the number.

You can do something similar when someone says you look good for your age. My first reaction on hearing this is to feel flattered – hurray, I look better than my contemporaries! But then I feel queasy because it's a back-handed compliment. The underlying message it carries, whatever the speaker's intention, is: 'You look crap because you're older but at least you don't look as crap as everyone else your age.' Ashton Applewhite recommends responding with a little verbal jujitsu. 'If someone says: "You look great for your age", you can say: "You look great for your age too",' she says. 'Then let the awkward silence sit there for a bit, so the person reflects on why something they intended as a compliment doesn't feel like a compliment. It's easier to acknowledge a prejudice against yourself than one against someone else. It's also deeply liberating – especially once you start understanding that ageism is not a personal problem or failing but a shared social problem that requires collective action. Life is better on the other side of it, that's for sure.'

It's also better when we think more about our own future selves. What role will work, caregiving, service, childrearing, romance, creativity, sex, learning, leisure and travel play in my life? How much will I need to earn and save? How will I cope with bereavement? Who will help me when I can no longer look after myself? What kind of death would I like? In that spirit, Tom Kamber, the founder of Senior Planet, is compiling a tongue-in-cheek List Of Things You Only Do Well When

You're Old. So far it includes: Sitting around reading for 12 days without feeling guilty. Having the courage and honesty to speak your mind, which includes writing cantankerous letters to newspapers. Building deeper relationships. Becoming a collector of something. Having sex with more connection and confidence. 'That last one was a bit of a surprise to me,' he says. 'But sex comes up a lot with older people.'

My teenaged daughter plays a game with her friends where they imagine what kind of old ladies they will be. One wants to travel like Ms Q and dress like Helen Ruth Van Winkle. My daughter's dream is more traditional: she plans to wear cardigans, knit, bake and play board games with her grandchildren. Why don't we take a leaf from their book and encourage children at school to think about all the stages of life they will pass through and how they can prepare for each? Later we could offer everyone an Age MOT at the start of each new decade that would test our health and explain how the next 10 years are likely to affect our minds and bodies and how best to navigate those changes.

Firming up our plans for later life can also help take some of the fear out of ageing. Jacques Durand, a forty-something schoolteacher in Rennes, France, belongs to a group of 10 friends who have agreed to spend their retirement living together in a large farmhouse in Brittany. They will care for each other and pool their skills, from finance and plumbing to nursing and farming. 'Now that I can picture where I will end up when I am old, getting older itself no longer seems so scary,' says Durand. 'Instead, it seems like an exciting project – and I am almost looking forward to it.'

Almost is the key word there. Ageing is hard to love unconditionally because it takes things away from us, especially towards the end of life. Yet I no longer recoil from ageing, my own or other people's. I now feel happy to be the age I am because it means I have half a century of good living under my belt. Like anyone else, I still worry about what the passage of time will do to my health, my finances, my looks, my loved ones. Nor do I want my life to end. But such worries feel less daunting now because I know that, with a little luck and the right attitude, lots of good stuff awaits me in the coming years. I am looking forward to becoming the person I always should have been.

Given how this journey started, the most welcome side effect is that I no longer feel ashamed or constrained by the numbers on my birth certificate. To me, the choices I make about how to live my life trump my chronological age every day of the week. I realise this shift has occurred when I return to that same hockey tournament in Gateshead two years later.

A glance round the sports centre confirms that I am still the closest thing to a grandad, yet that no longer rankles. Bantering with other players about being an old fart makes me laugh rather than cringe. What matters to me now is not how old I am but playing well and having fun. My team rents a house near the centre and we stay up late drinking, playing cards and teasing each other in the way that friends of all ages do. Though I fail to score from a face-off this year, I do make a few plays that later bring a smile to my face. Instead of crashing out in the semis we go all the way to the final, narrowly missing out on winning the trophy.

Will I still be playing in that tournament a decade from now? I hope so, but who can say? What I do know is that I am already looking forward to returning next year – and maybe finally lifting that trophy.

ACKNOWLEDGEMENTS

Though mine is the only name on the front cover, many people had a hand in the making of this book.

My agent, Patrick Walsh, landed the publishing deals that made it all possible. Craig Pyette at Random House Canada and Ian Marshall at Simon & Schuster UK were patient, perspicacious and punctilious – just what you want in an editorial tag team. Miranda France and Pamela Honoré worked their usual magic on the manuscript and Cordelia Newlin de Rojas chipped in with valuable research.

My books are built on reportage, which means leaning heavily on others for logistical help. I am grateful to the interpreters who made interviewing possible in Thailand, Lebanon, Germany and South Korea: Ittiyada Chareonsiri, Samar Shahine, Hannah Weber, Kim Seo-Yun and Park Yeon-Han. Others who helped beyond the call of duty include Carmela Manzillo, Scott Ellard, Ashton Applewhite, Debora Price, Esme Fuller-Thomson, Eric Kaufmann, Hiba Farhat, May Nassour, Paulina Braun, Laila Zahed, Damian Hanoman-Cornil, Kathy Katerina, James Kimsey, Kat Ray and Marina Rozenman.

Finally, I am deeply grateful to the many people around the world who took time to speak to me about ageing. Without their knowledge, stories and insights, there would be no book.

Notes

Introduction: Birthday Blues

Dame Judi Dench has banned the word 'old'
Scott Feinberg, 'Judi Dench on Beating Failing Eyesight, Bad Knees and Retirement', *Hollywood Reporter*, 21 February 2014.

Samuel Johnson detected a familiar bias against ageing brains
James Boswell, *The Life and Times of Samuel Johnson* (London: Wordsworth Editions, 1999), 849.

We now drop US$250 billion on anti-ageing goods every year
Market Data Forecast, 'Anti-Ageing Market by Demographics, by Products, by Services, by Devices, and by Region-Global Industry Analysis, Size, Share, Growth, Trends, and Forecasts (2016–2021)'.

Yale study of ageism on Facebook
Becca R. Levy, Pil H. Chung, Talya Bedord, Kristina Navrazhina, 'Facebook as a Site for Negative Age Stereotypes', *The Gerontologist*, 54, 2, 1 (2014): 172–6.

Exposure to downbeat ideas about ageing causes older people to perform worse in tests

Lena Marshal, 'Thinking Differently About Ageing', *The Gerontologist*, 55. 4 (2015): 519–25.

Deirdre A. Robertson, George M. Savvy, Bellinda L. King-Kallimanis, Rose Anne Kenny, 'Negative Perceptions of Ageing and Decline in Walking Speed: A Self-Fulfilling Prophecy', *PLOS One*, 10, 4 (2015).

Suzete Chiviacowskya, Priscila Lopes Cardozoa, Aïna Chalabaev, 'Age stereotypes' effects on motor learning in older adults', *Psychology of Sport and Exercise*, 36, (2018): 209–12.

amateurs aged 40–49 running London marathon faster than twenty-somethings

'London Marathon: middle-aged runners faster than their younger counterparts', *Daily Telegraph*, 20 April 2015.

Nick Bostrom on chronological age having had its day

Catherine Mayer, 'Amortality', *TIME*, 12 March 2009.

1. How Ageing Got Old

rarely is there nothing more doctors can do

Atul Gawande, *Being Mortal* (London: Profile Books, 2015), 73.

People did not believe in progress before 16th century

Yohan Noah Harari, *Sapiens: A Brief History of Mankind* (London: Vintage), 294.

NOTES

Yasuhiro Nakasone penned haiku
  David Pilling, 'How Japan Stood up to Old Age', *Financial Times*, 17 January 2014.

2. Move: *In Corpore Sano*

diabetes, leukaemia, breast cancer punch harder in later life
  Robert N. Butler, *Why Survive: Being Old in America* (Baltimore: Johns Hopkins University Press, 2002), 18.

man can add 14 years to life by becoming a eunuch
  Tad Friend, 'Silicon Valley's Quest to Live Forever', *New Yorker*, 3 April 2017.

study of amateur cyclists between 55 and 79
  Ross D. Pollock, 'Properties of the Vastus Lateralis Muscle in Relation to Age and Physiological Function in Master Cyclists Aged 55–79 Years', *Ageing Cell*, 17, 2 (2018).

Norwegian study on benefits for men starting to get fit in 40s and 50s
  Erik Prestgaard, 'Impact of Excercise Blood Pressure on Stroke in Physically Fit and Unfit Men. Results From 35 Years Follow-Up of Healthy Middle-Aged Men', *Journal of Hypertension*, 36, 3, (2018).

healthy life expectancy rising in much of the EU
  'Getting to Grips with Longevity', *The Economist*, 6 July 2017.

a British boy born in 2015 can look forward to
 Institute for Health Metrics and Evaluation (IHME).
 GBD Compare. Seattle, WA: IHME, University of
 Washington, 2017. Available from http://vizhub.
 healthdata.org/gbd-compare.

similar healthy life expectancy trend in the United States
 E. M. Crimsons, Y. Zhang, Y. Saito, 'Trends Over Four
 Decades in Disability-Free Life Expectancy in the
 United States', *American Journal of Public Health*, 106, 7
 (2016): 1287–93.

3. Create: Old Dogs, New Tricks

we start using more of brain when tackling hard problems
 Barbara Stauch, *The Secret Life of the Grown-Up Brain: The
 Surprising Talents of the Middle-Aged Mind* (London:
 Viking, 2010), 92–8.

distractible mind picks up irrelevant information
 M. Karl Healey, 'Cognitive Ageing and Increased
 Distractibility: Costs and Potential Benefits', *Progress in
 Brain Research*, 169 (2008): 362.

middle-aged cling to status quo
 A. Eaton, 'Social Power and Attitude over the Life
 Course', *Personality and Social Psychology Bulletin*, 35, 12
 (2009): 1646–60.

inventors peak in late 40s
> 2016 study by Information Technology and Innovation
> Foundation

average age for filing a patent application is 47, most
lucrative over 55
> John P. Walsh, 'Who Invents?: Evidence from the Japan–
> US Inventor Survey', (2009).

Conceptuals, experimentalists, Welles, Hitchcock, Frost
> Adam Grant, *Originals: How Non-Conformists Move the World*
> (New York: Penguin Random House USA, 2016), 109–12.

John Goodenough is role model
> Pagan Kennedy, 'To Be a Genius, Think Like a 94-Year-
> Old', *New York Times Sunday Review*, 7 April 2017.

fMRI scans used to monitor brains of people studying for
the Knowledge
> Katherine Woollett, 'Acquiring "the Knowledge" of
> London's Layout Drives Structural Brain Changes',
> *Current Biology*, 21 (2011): 2109–14.

over-60s learning digital photography from scratch
> Denise C. Park, 'The Impact of Sustained Engagement
> on Cognitive Function in Older Adults: The Synapse
> Project', *Psychological Science*, 25, 1 (2013): 103–12.

Two-thirds of employers say older workers learn better
> Peter Capelli, *Managing the Older Worker: How to Prepare
> for the New Organisational Order* (Brighton: Harvard
> Business Review, 2010), 82.

aerobic exercise keeps us cognitively fit
Kan Ding, 'Cardiorespiratory Fitness and White Matter Neuronal Fiber Integrity in Mild Cognitive Impairment', *Journal of Alzheimer's Disease*, 61, 2 (2018): 729–39.

statistics on dementia
Taken from Alzheimer's Disease International: https://www.alz.co.uk/research/statistics

pianist Vladimir Horowitz found a way to play
Jeffrey Kluger, Alexandra Sifferlin, 'The Surprising Secrets to Living Longer – And Better', *Time*, 15 February 2018.

4. Work: Old Hands on Deck

US commentator detected rampant ageism in 1913
Pat Thane, Lynn Botelho, *The Long History of Old Age* (London: Thames and Hudson, 2005), 229.

60 per cent of US companies banned hiring over-45s
Capelli, 48.
'The Older American Worker, Age Discrimination in Employment', Report of the Secretary of Labor to the Congress (Washington, DC, 1965).

study with 40,000 fake CVs
David Neumark, 'Age Discrimination and Hiring of Older Workers', Federal Reserve Bank of San Francisco *Economic Letters*, 27 February 2017.

each year of age cuts chances of landing job interview by 4 to 7 per cent
  Capelli, 91.

using Facebook and Google to target younger job candidates
  Julia Angwin, 'Dozens of Companies Are Using Facebook to Exclude Older Workers From Job Ads', ProPublica report, 20 December 2017.

European study found older employees isolated
  'Working Conditions of an Ageing Workforce', EurWORK, 21 September 2008.

career progression in the UK
  Ros Altmann, 'A New Vision for Older Workers: Retain, Retrain, Recruit', report to government (March 2015), 31.

older workers better at suggestions boxes
  Brigit Verwarn, 'Does Age Have an Impact on Having Ideas? An Analysis of the Quantity and Quality of Ideas Submitted to a Suggestion System', *Creativity and Innovation Management*, 18 (2009): 326–34.

four key skills ripen around 50
  Joshua K. Harshorne, 'When Does Cognitive Functioning Peak?', *Psychological Science*, 26, 4 (2015): 433–43.

ageing tends to enhance our emotional intelligence
  Ashton Applewhite, *This Chair Rocks: A Manifesto Against Ageism* (Networked Books, 2016), 79.

pick up more information on first meeting
Barbara Staunch, *The Secret of the Grown-Up Brain: The Surprising Talents of the Middle-Aged Men* (London: Viking, 2010), 89

empathy, finding compromises, resolving conflicts
Igor Grossman, 'Reasoning about Social Conflicts Improves into Old Age', *Proceedings of the National Academy of Sciences of the United States of America*, 107, 16 (2010): 7246–50.

letters sent to professional agony aunts
Grossman.

ageing makes sense of humour more agreeable
Jennifer Stanley, 'Age-related Differences in Judgments of Inappropriate Behavior are Related to Humor Style Preferences', *Psychology and Ageing*, 29, 3 (2014): 528–41.

less prone to wild swings of emotion
Applewhite, 79.

under-25s twice as likely to kill pedestrian
Louise Butcher, 'Older Drivers', briefing paper, United Kingdom House of Commons, SN409 (2017), 5.

productivity improves with age in work that relies on social skills
'Retirement is out, new portfolio careers are in', *The Economist*, 6 July 2017.

staff performance at Days Inn call centre
William McNaught, 'Are Older Workers "Good Buys"?
A Case Study of Days Inns of America', *Management
Review*, 33, 3 (1992): 53–63.

social skills generated more jobs and higher wages
David J. Deming, 'The Growing Importance of
Social Skills in the Labor Market', National Bureau
of Economic Research working paper 21473
(August 2015).

motivation in survey of 35,000 employees
Roselyn Feinted, 'The Business Case for Workers Age
50+: Planning for Tomorrow's Talent Needs in Today's
Competitive Environment', report for AARP prepared
by Towers Perrin (December 2005), 22.

L. L. Bean relies on older workers
Capelli, 82.

older people show strong initiative when work has meaning
John R. Beard, 'Global Population Ageing: Peril or
Promise', World Economic Forum (Geneva, 2011), 40.

air-traffic commands in a laboratory setting
Capelli, 31.

Performance of 3,800 workers at Mercedes-Benz
Alex Börsch-Supan, 'Productivity and Age: Evidence
from Work Teams at the Assembly Line', Mannheim
Research Institute for the Economics of Ageing
discussion paper, 148 (2007): 1–30.

survey of typists aged 19–72
Timothy A. Malthouse, 'Effects of Age and Skill in Typing', *Journal of Experimental Psychology: General*, 113, 3 (1984): 345–71.

Judith Kerr quick on her cognitive feet
Judith Kerr, 'My Writing Day', *Guardian*, 25 November 2017.

ageing does not make us more risk-averse
Gary Charness, 'Cooperation and Competition in Intergenerational Experiments in the Field and the Laboratory', *American Economic Review*, 99, 3 (2009): 956–78.

surveys on risk tolerance conducted in 104 countries
Thomas Schott, 'Special Topic Report 2016–2017: Senior Entrepreneurship', Global Entrepreneurship Monitor, fig. 2.2, 21.

risk tolerance remains constant as we age
University of Basel, 'Willingness to Take Risks – a Personality Trait', 30 October 2017.

When GEM polled 18–29-year-olds
Schott.

study of all 2.7 million new businesses launched in the United States
Benjamin F. Jones, 'Age and High-Growth Entrepreneurship', National Bureau of Economic Research working paper 24489 (2018).

NOTES

Australian older founders earn double the profits
> Alex Maritz, 'Senior Entrepreneurship in Australia: Active Ageing and Extending Working Lives', Swinburne University of Technology (2015), 3.

nearly 70 per cent do not consider rising longevity in sales and marketing
> 'A Silver Opportunity? Rising Longevity and its Implications for Business', *The Economist* (2011), 3.

more older workers leads to more young workers
> Emma Jacobs, 'Working Older', *Financial Times Magazine*, 3 July 2015.

one in four Americans 'sharing economy' aged over 55
> 'The Sharing Economy', *Consumer Intelligence Series* (2015), 10.

BMW is stand-out example
> Christopher Loch, 'The Globe: How BMW is Defusing the Demographic Time Bomb', *Harvard Business Review* (March 2010).

automation could take a third of all work by 2030
> 'Jobs Lost, Jobs Gained: Workforce Transitions in a Time of Automation', McKinsey Global Institute (December 2017).

losing job at 58 can knock three years off life expectancy
> Lawrence H. Leith, 'What happens when older workers experience unemployment?', *Monthly Labor Review* (October 2014).

Freud put work up there with love as pillar of mental health
  Laura Carstensen, *A Long Bright Future: Happiness, Health
  and Financial Security in an Age of Increased Longevity*
  (New York: PublicAffairs, 2011), 275.

5. Image: Ageing Gets a Makeover

Juliet Stevenson sees road ahead narrowing
  Ceridwen Dovey, 'What Old Age Is Really Like', *New
  Yorker*, 1 October 2015.

assume memory worse than it is
  Dana R. Touron, 'Memory Avoidance by Older Adults:
  When "Old Dogs" Won't Perform Their "New
  Tricks', *Current Directions in Psychological Science*, 24, 3
  (2015): 170–76.

placebo sleep
  Christina Draganich, 'Placebo Sleep Affects Cognitive
  Functioning', *Journal of Experimental Psychology:
  Learning, Memory, and Cognition*, 40, 3 (2014): 857–64.

live an average of seven and a half years longer
  Mecca R. Levy, 'Longevity Increased by Positive Self-
  Perceptions of Ageing', *Journal of Personality and Social
  Psychology*, 83, 2 (2002): 261.

upbeat view of ageing blocked gene variant linked to dementia
  Becca R. Levy, 'Positive Age Beliefs Protect Against
  Dementia even among Elders with High-risk Gene',
  PLOS One, 13, 2 (2018).

UK over-50s hold 80 per cent of wealth
> Based on research carried about for SunLife's Welcome to Life After 50 campaign (2017).

Over-60s spending $15 trillions worldwide
> 'The Global Later Lifers Market: How the Over 60s are Coming into their Own', *Euromonitor* (May 2014).

fewer than 15 per cent have business strategy for over-60s
> Schumpeter, 'The Grey Market: Older Consumer will Reshape the Business Landscape', *The Economist*, 7 April 2016.

Crest's toothpaste for over-50s flopped
> Schumpeter.

Bridgestone golf clubs aimed at pensioners
> Schumpeter.

laughing boosts immune system
> 'Stress Management', Mayo Clinic staff: https://www.mayoclinic.org/healthy-lifestyle/stress-management/in-depth/art-20044456

doyen of this trend is Yoshihiro Kariya
> Martin Fackler, 'With a Poison Tongue, Putting a Smile on a Nation's Ageing Faces', *New York Times*, 23 March 2012.

people with good sense of humour live eight years longer
> Mark A. Yoder, 'Sense of Humor and Longevity: Older Adults' Self-Ratings Compared with Ratings for Deceased Siblings', *Psychological Reports*, 76, 3 (1995): 945–46.

6. Technology: iAge

proportion of American over-65s on social media has more than tripled.
Smart Insight, 'Global Social Media Research –
Summary 2018': https://wearesocial.com/uk/
blog/2018/01/global-digital-report-2018

89 per cent of 18–24s said Internet indispensable
'Age Does Not Define Us', Age of No Retirement (2017), 3.

Dropbox survey of 4,000 IT professionals.
Rob Baesman, 'What it Takes to be Happy and Creative
at Work', *Dropbox Business*, 8 June 2016.

programmers enhance knowledge and skills over time
Patrick Morrison, 'Is Programming Knowledge Related
To Age?: An Exploration of Stack Overflow': https://
people.engr.ncsu.edu/ermurph3/papers/msr13.pdf

older workers mastered new technology just as quickly
Jean Pralong, 'L'Image du Travail Selon la Génération
Y: Une Comparaison Intergénérationelle Conduite
sur 400 Sujets Grâce à la Technique des Cartes
Cognitives', *Revue Internationale de Psychosociologie*, 16,
39 (2010): 109–34.

tech helps narrow 'fundamental emotional disconnect'
Hal Hershfield, 'You Make Better Decisions If You "See"
Your Senior Self', *Harvard Business Review*, June 2013.

7. Happiness: Minding Less, Enjoying More

more accepting of slings and arrows
Lynn Segal, *Out of Time: The Pleasures and the Perils of Ageing* (London: Verso Books, 2013), 185.

AARP survey on being depressed in later life
Patty David, 'Happiness Grows with Age', *AARP Research* (August 2017).

anxiety, depression and perceived stress go down
Beard, 40.

fear of death diminishes as we age
Jeffrey Kluger, 'Why Are Old People Less Scared of Dying?', *Time*, 11 February 2016.

blog posts written by terminally ill
Amelia Grandson, 'Dying is Unexpectedly Positive', *Psychological Science*, 28, 7 (2017): 988–99.

odds of being 'very happy' rise 5 per cent every 10 years
Brooke E. O'Neill, 'Happiness on the horizon', *University of Chicago Magazine*, November–December 2009.

British adults happiest after 60
Based on research done by the UK Office of National Statistics. See fig. 1: https://www.ons.gov.uk/peoplepopulationandcommunity/wellbeing/articles/measuringnationalwellbeing/atwhatageispersonalwellbeingthehighest

happiness follows a U-shaped curve
Andrew J. Oswald, 'Do Humans Suffer a Psychological Low in Midlife? Two Approaches (With and Without Controls) in Seven Data Sets', National Bureau of Economic Research working paper w23724 (2017).

stop medical treatment to endure less suffering
Gawande, 178.

from 50 we narrow the lens
Laura L. Carstensen, 'Socioemotional Selectivity Theory and the Regulation of Emotion in the Second Half of Life', *Motivation and Emotion*, 27, 2 (2003): 103–23.

two-fifths tell researchers television is main form of company
Based on figures from Age UK and the Campaign to End Loneliness: https://www.campaigntoendloneliness. org/loneliness-research/

loneliness twice as common among Americans aged 45–49
AARP survey: https://www.aarp.org/research/topics/ life/info-2014/loneliness_2010.html

loneliness takes same toll as obesity or smoking
Tim Adams, 'Interview with (neuroscientist) John Cacioppo', *The Guardian*, 28 February 2016.

18–22-year-olds are loneliest in the United States
Based on research by Cigna, a global health services company: https://www.multivu.com/players/ English/8294451-cigna-us-loneliness-survey/

memory takes on rosier tint
Laura L. Carstensen, 'Ageing and Emotional Memory:
The Forgettable Nature of Negative Images for Older
Adults', *Journal of Experimental Psychology: General*, 132,
2 (2003): 310–24.

oldest Katrina survivors coping better
Vincanne Adams, 'Ageing Disaster: Mortality,
Vulnerability, and Long-Term Recovery Among Katrina
Survivors', *Medical Anthropology*, 30, 3 (2011): 247–70.

Bowie on becoming the person you always should have been
Aaron Hicklin, 'David Bowie: An Obituary', *Out*, 11
January 2016.

8. Attract: Swiping Right

Nambikwara people of Brazil have one word
George Minois, *History of Old Age* (Cambridge: Polity
Press, 1989), 10.

Racine mocked an older character
Thane, 134.

French print from 1800
Thane, 21.

men and women take human growth hormone
See the Mayo Clinic's healthy ageing webpage:
https://www.mayoclinic.org/healthy-lifestyle/healthy-
ageing/in-depth/growth-hormone/art-20045735

Simone de Beauvoir on fecundity
Minois, 303.

uncanny ability to guess a person's age
Susanna Mitro, 'The Smell of Age: Perception and
Discrimination of Body Odors of Different Ages',
PLOS One, 7, 5 (2012):

record number of older models on global catwalks
Based on figures from Fashion Spot.

'age-appropriate' clothing to work
Laura M. Hsu, 'The Influence of Age-Related Cues on
Health and Longevity', *Perspectives on Psychological
Science*, 5, 6 (2010): 635.

9. Romance: The Heart Has No Wrinkles

words of Horace widely quoted in early Europe
Thane, 134.

forty-something protagonist of Houellebecq's novel
Michel Houellebecq, *The Possibility of an Island* (London:
Phoenix, 2005), 182.

divorce rate for over-60s doubled in US
'Pensioners are an Underrated and Underserved Market',
The Economist, 8 July 2017.

53–72-year-olds are fastest-growing group on match.com
'Pensioners are an Underrated and Underserved Market',
The Economist, 8 July 2017.

sexual desire carries on throughout life
Segal, 89.

sexually active people between 50 and 90 satisfied with sex lives
David Lee, 'Sexual Health and Wellbeing Among Older
Men and Women in England: Findings from the
English Longitudinal Study of Ageing', *Archives of
Sexual Behavior*, 45, 1 (2015): table 5.

women find it easier to reach orgasm in their 40s
Based on research by OkCupid:
http://www.businessinsider.
com/10-surprising-charts-about-sex-2012-3?IR=T

erectile dysfunction more prevalent after 40
Boston University School of Medicine: http://www.
bumc.bu.edu/sexualmedicine/physicianinformation/
epidemiology-of-ed/

sexually active Britons over 80 report more closeness
David Lee, 'How Long Will I Love You? Sex and
Intimacy in Later Life' (2017): https://www.
researchgate.net/publication/315165295_How_long_
will_I_love_you_Sex_and_intimacy_in_later_life

best sex happens between partners after 15 years
Michael E. Metz, *Enduring Desire* (Abingdon:
Rutledge, 2010).

10. Care: We, Not Me

impulse to put purpose before personal gain in later life as strong regardless of income, education or health
> Encore.org, 'Purpose in the Encore Years: Shaping Lives of Meaning and Contribution' (2018), 10.

US retirees defined success as 'being generous'
> Merrill Lynch, 'Giving in Retirement: America's Longevity Bonus' (2015), 14.

helping others boosts the immune system
> Baris K. Yörük, 'Does Living to Charity Lead to Better Health? Evidence from Tax Subsidies for Charitable Giving', *Journal of Economic Psychology*, 45 (2014): 71–83.

giving stimulates same regions of brain as food and sex
> Jenny Santi, 'The Secret to Happiness is Helping Others', *Time*, 4 August 2017.

charitable giving delivers bigger emotional kick in later life
> Pär Bjälkebring, 'Greater Emotional Gain from Giving in Older Adults: Age-Related Positivity Bias in Charitable Giving', *Frontiers in Psychology*, 7 (2016): 846.

US retirees expected to donate $8 trillion
> Merrill Lynch, 'Giving in Retirement: America's Longevity Bonus' (2015), 3.

when old and young work together on a life problem altruism rubs off
> Kessler, 698.

11. Mingle: All Together Now

mingling with young boosts health, happiness and self-esteem of older people

Eva-Marie Kessler, 'Intergenerational Potential: Effects of Social Interaction Between Older Adults and Adolescents', *Psychology and Ageing*, 22, 4 (2007): 691.

less ageist towards those we know personally

Anne Karpf, *How to Age* (London: Macmillan, 2014), 92.

more contact with older people gives younger ones better attitude to ageing

Benevolent Society, 'The Drivers of Ageism' (2017), 26.

mixed-aged McDonald's teams score higher on customer satisfaction

Lancaster University, 'Research Shows McDonald's Customers Prefer Older Workers', 9 January 2009.

cooperation highest in teams with a range of ages

Charness.

study of 61 German firms

'Elders not Better: In Germany Mature Workers are Answering to Young Supervisors', *The Economist*, 15 December 2016.

Conclusion: The Time is Ripe

For more on Ellen Langer's counter-clockwise study

Bruce Grierson, 'What if Age is Nothing but a Mind-Set?', *New York Times Magazine*, 22 October 2014.

Further Reading

Ashton Applewhite, *This Chair Rocks: A Manifesto Against Ageism* (Networked Books, 2016).

Marina Benjamin, *The Middlepause: On Life After Youth* (London: Scribe UK, 2017).

Dan Buettner, *The Blue Zones (2nd Edition): 9 Lessons for Living Longer From the People Who've Lived the Longest* (Washington, DC: National Geographic, 2012).

Robert N. Butler, *Why Survive: Being Old in America* (Baltimore: Johns Hopkins University Press, 2002).

Peter Capelli, *Managing the Older Worker: How to Prepare for the New Organisational Order* (Brighton: Harvard Business Review, 2010).

Laura Carstensen, *A Long Bright Future: Happiness, Health and Financial Security in an Age of Increased Longevity* (New York: PublicAffairs, 2011).

Gene D. Cohen, *The Mature Mind: The Positive Power of the Aging Brain* (New York: Basic Books, 2006).

Marc Freedman, *The Big Shift: Navigating the New Stage Beyond Midlife* (New York: Public Affairs, 2012).

Atul Gawande, *Being Mortal* (London: Profile Books, 2015).

Christopher Gilleard, *Cultures of Ageing: Self, Citizen and the Body* (London: Rutledge, 2000).

Adam Grant, *Originals: How Non-Conformists Move the World* (New York: Penguin Random House USA, 2016).

Lynn Gratton, Andrew Scott, *The 100-Year Life: Living and Working in an Age of Longevity* (London: Bloomsbury Business, 2017).

Bruce Grierson, *What Makes Olga Run? The Mystery of the 90-Something Track Star and What She Can Teach Us About Living Longer, Happier Lives* (Toronto: Vintage, 2014).

Margaret Morganroth Gullette, Agewise: *Fighting the New Ageism in America* (Chicago: University of Chicago Press, 2011).

Anne Karpf, *How to Age* (London: Macmillan, 2014).

Anne Kreamer, *Going Grey: How to Embrace your Authentic Self with Grace and Style* (London: Little Brown, 2009).

George Magnus, *The Age of Ageing: How Demographics are Changing the Global Economy and Our World* (Hoboken: John Wiley & Sons, 2008).

Catherine Mayer, *Amortality: The Pleasures and Perils of Living Agelessly* (London: Vermillion, 2011).

George Minois, *History of Old Age: From Antiquity to the Renaissance* (Cambidge: Polity Press, 1989).

Joan Price, *Naked at Our Age: Talking Out Loud About Senior Sex* (Berkeley: Sea Press, 2011).

Lynne Segal, *Out of Time: The Pleasures and the Perils of Ageing* (New York: Verso Books, 2013).

Gordon F. Shea, Adolf Haasen, *The Older Worker Advantage: Making the Most of Our Aging Workforce* (Westport: Praeger, 2005).

Barbara Starch, *The Secret Life of the Grown-Up Brain: The Surprising Talents of the Middle-Aged Mind* (London: Viking Books, 2010).

Pat Thane, Lynn Botelho, *The Long History of Old Age* (London: Thames and Hudson, 2005).

Bill Thomas, *Second Wind: Navigating the Passage to a Slower, Deeper and More Connected Life* (London: Simon & Schuster, 2015).